Making Sense of Madness

'Jim Geekie and John Read have written a fascinating book about what psychiatrists call "schizophrenia". They address the usually ignored issue of how people who experience hallucinations and delusions make sense of those experiences themselves. They also tackle why it is that experts continue to disagree about what "schizophrenia" is and, indeed, whether it exists at all. This is a "must read" for all mental health professionals and everyone else interested in madness.' **Professor Paul J Fink, Past President American Psychiatric Association, Temple University School of Medicine, USA**.

'One can only hope that every new trainee in mental health will first read this book before exposing him - or herself to the confusing amount of theories and categorizations that have become accepted as "knowledge" of madness. Developing an attitude of continuously contesting and questioning accepted knowledge will help close the current gap between subjective experience and professional reductionism.' **Prof. dr J. van Os, Dept. Psychiatry and Neuropsychology, Maastricht University, The Netherlands**.

'At long last, a book that eloquently demonstrates the necessity to listen to subjective experiences of madness in order to gain real insight into sanity, madness and the human condition. Humane, accessible and illuminating.' **Jacqui Dillon, Chair of the National Hearing Voices Network, England**.

The experience of madness – which might also be referred to more formally as 'schizophrenia' or 'psychosis' – consists of a complex, confusing and often distressing collection of experiences, such as hearing voices or developing unusual, seemingly unfounded beliefs. Madness, in its various forms and guises, seems to be a ubiquitous feature of being human, yet our ability to make sense of madness, and our knowledge of how to help those who are so troubled, is limited.

Making Sense of Madness explores the subjective experiences of madness. Using clients' stories and verbatim descriptions, it argues that the experience of 'madness' is an integral part of what it is to be human, and that greater focus on subjective experiences can contribute to professional understandings and ways of helping those who might be troubled by these experiences.

Areas of discussion include:

- how people who experience psychosis make sense of it themselves
- scientific/professional understandings of 'madness'
- what the public thinks about 'schizophrenia'

Making Sense of Madness will be essential reading for all mental health professionals as well as being of great interest to people who experience psychosis and their families and friends.

Jim Geekie is a clinical psychologist who has been working for Auckland District Health Board in New Zealand since 1995, mostly in the area of early intervention for psychosis. Before moving to New Zealand, he worked in Scotland and England as a psychologist, and before that he spent a few years living in East Africa, where he was employed as a teacher of psychology and philosophy.

John Read is an Associate Professor in Clinical Psychology at the University of Auckland, New Zealand. Before that he worked for twenty years as a clinical psychologist and manager of mental health services – predominantly in services for people diagnosed psychotic in the USA and New Zealand. He is the coordinating editor of *Models of Madness: Psychological, Social and Biological Approaches to Schizophrenia* (Routledge 2004) and editor of the journal *Psychosis: Psychological, Social and Integrative Approaches*.

The International Society for the Psychological Treatments of Schizophrenias and other Psychoses book series

Series editor: Brian Martindale

The ISPS (the International Society for the Psychological Treatments of the Schizophrenias and other Psychoses) has a history stretching back more than fifty years during which it has witnessed the relentless pursuit of biological explanations for psychosis. The tide is now turning again. There is a welcome international resurgence of interest in a range of psychological factors in psychosis that have considerable explanatory power and also distinct therapeutic possibilities. Governments, professional groups, users and carers are increasingly expecting interventions that involve more talking and listening. Many now regard skilled practitioners in the main psychotherapeutic modalities as important components of the care of the seriously mentally ill.

The ISPS is a global society. It is composed of an increasing number of groups of professionals, family members, those with vulnerability to psychosis and others, who are organised at national, regional and more local levels around the world. Such persons recognise the potential humanitarian and therapeutic potential of skilled psychological understanding and therapy in the field of psychosis. Our members cover a wide spectrum of approaches from psychodynamic, systemic, cognitive, and arts therapies to the need-adaptive approaches, group therapies and therapeutic institutions. We are most interested in establishing meaningful dialogue with those practitioners and researchers who are more familiar with biological based approaches. Our activities include regular international and national conferences, newsletters and email discussion groups in many countries across the world.

One of our activities is in the field of publication. Routledge have recognised the importance of our field, publishing the ISPS journal *Psychosis: Psychological, Social and Integrative Approaches* www.isps.org/journal.shtml. The journal complements Routledge's publishing of the ISPS book series which started in 2004. The books aim to cover many topics within the spectrum of the psychological therapies of psychosis and their application in a variety of settings. The series is intended to inform and further educate a wide range of mental health professionals as well as those developing and implementing policy.

Some of the books will also promote the ideas of clinicians and researchers well known in some countries but not familiar to others. Our overall intention is to encourage the dissemination of existing knowledge and ideas, promote healthy debate, and encourage more research in a most important field whose secrets almost certainly do not all reside in the neurosciences.

For more information about the ISPS, email @isps.org or visit our website www.isps.org

Other titles in the series

Models of Madness: Psychological, Social and Biological Approaches to Schizophrenia
Edited by John Read, Loren R. Mosher and Richard P. Bentall

Psychoses: An Integrative Perspective
Johan Cullberg

Evolving Psychosis: Different Stages, Different Treatments
Edited by Jan Olav Johanessen, Brian V. Martindale and Johan Cullberg

Family and Multi-Family work with Psychosis
Gerd-Ragna Bloch Thorsen, Trond Gronnestad and Anne Lise Oxenvad

Experiences of Mental Health In-Patient Care: Narratives from Service Users, Carers and Professionals
Edited by Mark Hardcastle, David Kennard, Sheila Grandison and Leonard Fagin

Psychotherapies for Psychoses: Theoretical, Cultural, and Clinical Integration
Edited by John Gleeson, Eión Killackey and Helen Krstev

Therapeutic Communities for Psychosis: Philosophy, History and Clinical Practice
Edited by John Gale, Alba Realpe and Enrico Pedriali

Beyond Medication: Therapeutic Engagement and the Recovery from Psychosis
Edited by Davis Garfield and Daniel Mackler

Making Sense of Madness

Contesting the Meaning of Schizophrenia

Jim Geekie and John Read

Routledge
Taylor & Francis Group

LONDON AND NEW YORK

First published 2009
by Routledge
27 Church Road, Hove, East Sussex BN3 2FA

Simultaneously published in the USA and Canada
by Routledge
270 Madison Ave, New York, NY 10016

*Routledge is an imprint of the Taylor & Francis Group, an Informa
business*

© 2009 Jim Geekie and John Read

Typeset in Times by
RefineCatch Limited, Bungay, Suffolk
Printed and bound in Great Britain by
TJ International Ltd, Padstow, Cornwall
Paperback cover design by Hybert Design

This publication has been produced with paper manufactured to
strict environmental standards and with pulp derived from
sustainable forests.

British Library Cataloguing in Publication Data
A catalogue record for this book is available
from the British Library

Library of Congress Cataloging in Publication Data
Geekie, Jim, 1961–
  Making sense of madness : contesting the meaning of
schizophrenia / Jim Geekie & John Read.
    p. cm.
  1. Schizophrenia.   2. Psychoses.   I. Read, John, Dr.   II. Title.
  RC514.G434 2009
362.2′6–dc22

                                                2008046664

ISBN: 978–0–415–46195–5 (hbk)
ISBN: 978–0–415–46196–2 (pbk)

To my son, Jerome, just for being Jerome, and my mother, Janet, for being willing to share her story
Jim G

To Jim, for letting me be part of this fascinating journey and for helping a rather stubborn older man open his mind to new perspectives
John R

Contents

Figures and tables

Figures

Table

Acknowledgements

We would like to express our deepest thanks to the many clients who, over the years, have shared their stories of the experience of psychosis with us. We extend particular thanks to those clients who agreed to participate in Jim Geekie's research into subjective experience (described in detail in Chapter 3): we appreciate your generosity in sharing such precious stories.

Jim Geekie would also like to thank his employer – Auckland District Health Board – for its support of his research. Special mention needs to be made of Dr Nick Argyle, Clinical Director, who acted as co-supervisor of Jim's research. Particular thanks are also due to Jim's colleagues at St Luke's CMHC and his immediate workmates in the 'first episode psychosis' (FEP) team, all of whom contributed to making working in mental health such a pleasure.

Abbreviations

APA	American Psychiatric Association
DSM	*Diagnostic and Statistical Manual of Mental Disorders*
FEP	first episode psychosis
ISPS	International Society for the Psychological Treatments of Schizophrenias and other Psychoses

Chapter 1

Introduction

As this is, in many ways, a book about stories, we have decided that we should begin this book with a story. A true story.

A young mother sits at home every night thinking about her predicament. Her two boys, aged 2 and 5, are asleep, and her husband is out working night shift in a coal mine. He won't be back until early the next morning. She's preoccupied with how her life has been going recently, and finds she thinks about nothing else once the kids are in bed. Night after night after night, she returns to the same old issues, the same old questions, and finds she reaches the same old dead-ends in looking for answers.

As the weeks pass, the content of her thoughts remains much the same, but the way in which she thinks about her situation starts to change. It moves from being an internal monologue to being an external dialogue. She finds that instead of having her thoughts running around in endless circles in her mind, she is now having a discussion with her own head, which has somehow, miraculously she thinks, started to appear in the top corner of the bedroom, looking down on her, talking to her and contributing ideas and suggestions about ways of dealing with her current circumstances. Her head appears pretty much every night, and she finds that the discussions she has with her head are more fruitful than just having the thoughts running around in her mind.

After some months of these nocturnal discussions, the young mother and her disembodied head together find a solution. It's simple: she just has to kill herself. That now seems fairly straightforward to her. However, this in itself creates another problem: what to do with the children? It would be cruel to leave them behind. Indeed, she would find it impossible to do so given the circumstances. The solution to this dilemma also develops out of the dialogue the young woman has with her head. Again, it's a simple and obvious solution. She will kill her two children first, then she'll kill herself, thus ensuring that they all escape and that the kids are not left behind to face the situation on their own.

It seems so clear and simple, yet something about it does not sit easily with the young woman. Somehow it just doesn't feel right. She decides to go to see her family doctor, hoping there's something he might be able to do that will prevent her ending her own and her children's lives. She decides not to start off by telling him about the discussions she's been having with her head. Instead, she begins by talking about another problem she's been having. She believes she's been walking in a strange way, with her body leaning over to one side. She told her family, but they dismissed her concerns, saying she walks just fine. She believes they are lying, for some reason deliberately hiding something from her. She tells the doctor about her walk and he responds, not surprisingly, by asking her to walk around the surgery. The doctor sees nothing remarkable about her way of walking and tells her so. She believes the doctor is in cahoots with her family. The doctor senses the young woman is troubled, and, this being the early 1960s, he gives her a pre-scription of phenobarbitone, which she never actually uses. She's seek-ing help, but she's been distrustful of medicine ever since she was offered, and refused, thalidomide while pregnant with her second child. The doctor, clearly of the opinion that the young woman is mentally unwell, then tells her that if she doesn't stop thinking this way, he'll have to send her off to the mental hospital to see a psychiatrist. The woman experiences this as a veiled threat, becomes more frightened, and decides – wisely, we might think – to say no more about her difficul-ties. The doctor hears nothing about her conversations with her head.

The young woman doesn't kill herself, nor does she kill her children. Instead, she decides to leave her husband, a task which proves far from easy as she has few other supports. After leaving her husband, she finds that, in time, the discussions with her head cease, and she no longer feels that she's leaning over to one side when walking.

The above story is one which confronts us with a number of important ques-tions and many of the issues which we hope to explore in this book. What are we to make of this woman's experience? Is she mad? Does she have a mental illness? Does she need help? What kind of help? We might also ask about her children. Are they safe? Is she safe? We might also wonder what she herself makes of her difficulties seeing as she is clearly troubled by them. Some of these questions are rather academic at this point in time, given that the events took place in the 1960s, and the woman and her now grown-up children are safe and well. She no longer has experiences of such intensity, which would cause us to have concerns about her, or anybody else's safety. She has never received any input from mental health services. However, although these events happened quite some time in the past, we can still fruitfully consider the question of what we are to make of this woman's story. While her story is, of course, unique in its details, it also has elements which it shares with other people's experiences and, as such, the question of what we make of these stories has ongoing relevance.

First, let's consider the woman's relationship with her family doctor. She feared that if she had told him her whole story, he would have viewed her as insane, and treated her accordingly, most likely by sending her off to the 'mental hospital'. In this respect, she is almost certainly correct. Her story can be construed from a clinical perspective, where we find a vast literature aimed at investigating, making sense of, and 'treating' experiences of this nature. From this position, which, for our purposes, we are assuming her doctor would have upheld, her experiences are indeed seen as indicative of a mental illness. Using medical terminology, we would say she was experiencing psychosis: hallucinations of a visual and auditory nature along with delusional ideas about her way of walking and her family conspiring to hide things from her. Both at that time in the 1960s and in the present day, she would, in all likelihood, receive a diagnosis of schizophrenia were she to share her experiences with her doctor. Given the apparent risk issues, where her own and her children's safety seemed of concern, she would, as she feared, have been hospitalized and, both then and now, medication would have been the mainstay of the treatment she received.

However, the clinical perspective, as would have been embodied and enforced by her doctor, is not the only perspective that could have been brought to bear on this woman's experience. She could also have solicited the opinions of family and friends. She did speak to them about her concerns about walking to the side, but, as with her doctor, she kept from them the parts of her experience that she considered most likely to cause them alarm. She felt 'shunned' by her family when she mentioned any of her troubles, and she suspected that if they knew more of the story they too would have seen her experiences as indicating that she had something seriously wrong with her mind. She believed they would have seen her as mad, and most probably would have wanted her to be hospitalized and treated with medication. She assumed they would have felt that her experiences lay outside their realm of expertise and they would have seen medical professionals as the most appropriate people to address these experiences.

Because of her fears about the ways in which the medical profession and her family and friends would have construed and responded to the most unusual aspects of her experiences, the young woman chose to keep these experiences to herself. In some ways this compounded her distress, making her feel all the more alone with what was going on and uncertain about what to make of it. Of course, we might add that by not sharing her story with these significant others, the woman thereby excluded herself from any assistance that she might have been offered by her family or by the medical profession. We should also recognize that the woman did not, in fact, solicit opinions from her family about her talking to her head, but rather she surmised what they were likely to think, based on her knowledge of them and on how they had responded to her other difficulties. It is possible that she may have been mistaken in this regard. However, whether or not she was correct in her assumptions about what others would have thought (and we suspect she was not mistaken), her story nonetheless illustrates that different perspectives can be brought to bear on such experiences.

In asking the question of what we are to make of this woman's story, the professional, clinical opinion of her doctor and the lay perspectives of family and friends are, of course, both important. They tell us a lot about how such experiences are construed from these perspectives and provide us with some ideas about how we might respond to the person who is having these experiences. It so happened in this situation that there was considerable overlap between the medical and family perspectives, something which, as we shall see later in this book (Chapter 4), is not always the case. Further, it is important to recognize that the perspectives expressed in this story are specific instances of both clinical and lay understandings of such experiences. Each of these broad frameworks – the professional and the lay – encompasses a wide range of ways of making sense of the kind of madness experienced by this young woman. Later in this book we will explore in more depth the range and variety of ways of understanding madness that we find in both the professional literature (Chapter 5) and in research that investigates family members' and other lay understandings of psychosis (Chapter 4).

Illuminating though the professional and the lay perspectives are, they are clearly not exhaustive in terms of the positions from which such experiences can be understood. Another important perspective, often overlooked in research into schizophrenia and psychosis, is that of the very person who has the experiences, in this case the young woman. Might it be that she herself could shed some light on these unusual and distressing experiences? Perhaps we should consider the advice of the great American psychologist, George Kelly (1955: 322) who suggested, somewhat ironically, 'If you don't know what's wrong with a person, ask him: he may tell you'. Kelly is here pointing out the folly of assuming that only the 'experts' can make insightful observations about clients' subjective experiences; a folly sadly found still in much of today's research literature on mental health difficulties and clinical approaches to offering help to those who have such experiences.

So, let us return to our young woman's story, to see if she, with her unique perspective based on lived experience, is able to help us make some sense of what might have been going on when she started speaking with her own head, and developing her plan to kill her children and herself. Looking back on this time, the woman, now in her sixties, comments:

My life was in very real danger. My husband was beating me severely more or less every day when he came home from work. The beatings were so bad that I believe that if I hadn't got out of that situation, he really would have killed me. I felt ashamed about the beatings, as if they were my fault, and I had no-one I could turn to. Friends and family shunned me and either didn't notice, or pretended not to notice my bruises from the beatings. I felt stuck in the situation, and could see no way out. Talking to my head at least provided me with an outlet for some of my distress, and let me consider my options from different points of view. Killing myself and my children was preferable to being killed by him. It took me a while to see that there were other options, and that even if it would be difficult, I could leave him, as I did, and continue living with my bairns. It was the 1960s, so there weren't many supports for battered women at that time. As for why I thought I was walking to the side ... Well, that's a bit of a strange one, eh?

Here then, we see another way of making sense of the woman's unusual experiences. We can see these experiences, or some of them at least, as being related in important ways to her lived experience. In particular, she suggests that her madness can be made sense of in the context of her life circumstances at the time. Though the comment above was given retrospectively, the woman was clear that even at the time of her psychotic episode, she saw these experiences as closely connected to the abusive nature of her marriage, and her limited options for escaping this. The fact that her experience of talking to her head as well as her thoughts about killing herself and her children stopped after she had left her husband, shows that her understanding of the situation was a useful one which led to a successful resolution of her difficulties. We might ponder what the outcome might have been if she had followed the path of telling her family doctor, and then being admitted to the mental hospital. One of the points we wish to make in reference to this story is the seemingly simple claim that the person who experiences such distressing and confusing experiences is, just as George Kelly suggested, able to make an important contribution to how it is that we might understand such experiences. Surely, not a contentious position to take, one might think, although in fact (as we shall see in Chapter 2) people who experience madness have, by and large, been excluded from discussions about how to understand the experience and how to help those troubled by such experiences.

Our story above illustrates many of the themes that we will be exploring in this book. First, the story serves to illustrate the kind of unusual, even bizarre, and often distressing experiences that this book focuses on. Having a discussion with one's disembodied head about killing one's own children is not, we assume, a commonplace experience. Similarly, believing that your family is conspiring against you to cover up your unconventional way of walking seems like an unusual belief to have, particularly in the absence of any convincing evidence to support it. In the psychiatric literature these experiences would be referred to as hallucinations and delusions and would most likely lead to the individual being given a diagnosis of schizophrenia.

Second, the story illustrates the variety of ways in which these experiences can be understood. The woman herself was troubled by her experience, and perplexed by aspects of it. However, and this is a crucial point, she did not see her experiences as lacking meaning. She identified a connection between what was going on in her life at that time and the seemingly bizarre experiences, thus rendering them less bizarre to her. There were aspects of her experience (such as the feeling of walking to the side), that did not make much sense to her, and we might hypothesize that were she able to discuss these experiences in some detail with someone else, this might have helped her develop an understanding of these experiences too. However, although she was aware that others would construe her experiences differently, she did not feel that she was able to do this with those around her. She believed that her doctor, as well as her family and friends, would pathologize her experience, consider her dangerous and so take what they consider to be appropriate steps to contain this danger. Of course, the fact that the young woman did not tell others about her story means we cannot be absolutely sure that those around her would have seen her experience in this way. Nonetheless, her assumption about how others would see her experience does illustrate a common way of making sense of her experience, namely, as signs of a mental illness, or in lay parlance a 'mental breakdown' or 'madness'. The focus of this book will be on the various ways we can understand experiences like those in the woman's story.

We believe that the experience of 'madness' is a quintessentially human experience, found in all human societies, and as far as we know, across all times. The propensity for the mind to deviate from what is considered 'normal' and acceptable in any given society, and for other members of this society to construe these deviations as signs of madness seem to us to be central aspects of what it is to be human. The kinds of deviations from 'normality' that we are talking about here are generally those where some of the fundamental assumptions about the world, or how we perceive the world, are called into question. This might include, for example, perceiving something that others cannot perceive (such as a voice), or developing a firmly held belief that is not shared by others, nor based on what might be considered sound reasoning (and so might be referred to as a delusion). Experiences such as these, which can be intense in nature, inevitably generate a range of questions: questions for the individual concerned, for others around him or her, and more generally, questions for all of us engaged in and concerned with the human enterprise. These questions might include, for example, how these experiences come about, how they can be responded to and how we might make sense of them. In this book we want to explore some of these questions, which emerge from a consideration of the experience of madness.

Our main focus here will not be on how it is that madness manifests itself in its various forms (such as hallucinations, delusions or thought disorders), interesting though this is. Rather, our primary concern we will be the various ways in which we can, and do, make sense of the experience of madness. It is our contention that madness is, somehow, a fundamental aspect of what it is to be human, and that the ways in which we identify and explain madness, at any given time and place, says much about the particular notions of what it is to be human which are operating, usually tacitly, in a particular culture at a given time. Similarly, how a given society responds to such experiences also, we believe, expresses something important about the nature of that society.

Before we move on to discuss the topic of madness in detail, there are a few matters we feel require some clarification. To this end, there are three main issues we will address in the remainder of this chapter: first, we will discuss in some detail the notion of 'storytelling' which, we believe, provides us with a useful framework for thinking about the various ways in which we can make sense of madness (indeed, for many aspects of human experience that we aim to understand). We will then look at the contentious and problematic issue of terminology in this area. By this we mean specifically the language used to refer to the experience of madness. This is a topic which has given rise to considerable, sometimes heated, discussion. Our purpose here will be primarily to state our own position and to clarify our own use of this terminology in this book. Finally, we will provide a brief introduction to the positions and experience of the authors in relation to madness, in both their personal and professional lives.

Storytelling

> Those whom the gods wish to destroy, they first make mad
> Euripedes (Greek playwright; 480–406 BC)

We see from the quote above, usually attributed to Euripedes, that in ancient Greek society, one of the ways in which madness was construed was for it to be understood as resulting from the machinations of the Gods, and their endeavours to drive some poor soul mad. Further, we might see this explanation of madness as expressing at least something of how, at the time, humans were viewed, suggesting the fragile nature of the human psyche in relation to the sometimes pernicious influences of the Gods. The point we wish to stress here is, simply, that the ancient Greeks had their own particular ways of making sense of madness: ways of thinking about the experience that helped them understand and relate to it within the context of their culture. Now, this particular way of viewing madness may seem somewhat alien to us in modern Western culture, where our views of humans as well as our notions of the Gods are quite different to those of the ancient Greeks. But this example does serve the purpose of drawing our attention to some of the variation that exists in how madness is understood at different times, in different places and by different individuals within the same place and time. This is one of the central points that we will be making in this book: that wherever we look, we find a multiplicity of ways of making sense of madness. We will explore this multiplicity of understandings throughout the book, but, before doing so, it will be helpful to consider a general framework that will help us to navigate our way through the myriad understandings we will encounter. To this end we find the notion of 'storying' or 'storytelling' a fitting framework that can assist us in acknowledging and evaluating this diversity of understandings.

> We live in stories the way fish live in water, breathing them in and out, buoyed up by them, taking from them our sustenance, but rarely conscious of this element in which we exist.
>
> (Taylor 1996: 5–6)

The way in which we are using 'story' here is related to but not identical to its common everyday usage. In the quote above, Taylor gives us a powerful metaphor which portrays stories as things which sustain us, while remaining largely invisible to us, in the same way that water is, we presume, invisible yet essential to fish. That is, stories here are viewed as the largely invisible, yet essential, foundations which shape or determine how we understand the world about us. As part of our exploration of madness, we think the metaphor of 'storytelling' is a helpful overarching framework that allows us to consider the various explanations for madness that will be discussed throughout this book.

The role of stories in shaping how we view ourselves and how we see and navigate the world around us is conveyed nicely by Taylor's quote. Now, of course, what Taylor gives us is just a metaphor, but it is nonetheless a powerful one, which draws our attention to and invites us to consider how it is that stories function in our lives and in our ways of making sense of the world. This invitation to consider the role of stories is one we would like to accept in this book, and to extend by looking at the ways in which we make sense of, or 'story', one particular aspect of what it is to be human: the experience of madness. Throughout remaining chapters of this book, we could say that we will be looking at the various ways in which the experience of madness has been 'storied' (or made sense of) by various contributors to discussions about this topic. Our hope is that we can shed some light upon this, thereby enhancing our understandings of the sometimes painful, sometimes bizarre, and often confusing experience of madness.

It is important to note that 'storytelling', as we are using it here, is not intended to imply a form of fiction. We are using it in a much broader sense to cover the ways in which we choose to make sense of a particular aspect of the world: how it is that we 'story' aspects of the world, by putting them within a narrative framework that renders our experiences meaningful. Thus, whereas the ancient Greeks seemed to see madness as manifesting the whims of the Gods, others (such as the young woman in our story above) might be more inclined to locate madness within a perspective which sees it as being related to one's immediate personal life experiences and circumstances. Yet others might construe madness as being the product of, say, faulty brain chemistry. Indeed, these are all positions from which madness has been viewed. Within the storytelling framework, we might say these are all different ways of 'storying' the experience of madness. This 'storytelling' notion therefore is a kind of 'meta-framework' which encompasses a wide array of ways of making sense of madness and views each as one of many possible ways of making sense of experience. Those who believe that one of the stories (invariably their own, of course) is the ultimate 'truth' or 'reality' of the matter, may struggle with this way of thinking. Our invitation at this point is to put any reservations aside for a moment, and see where our notion of multiple stories takes us in our endeavour to understand madness.

So, from this perspective, ways of storying the experience of madness would include scientific attempts at making sense of the experience, as well as, at the other end of the continuum, unique personal narratives based on lived experience. While we will explore these, and other, ways of storying madness, it is not our intention here to claim that all stories are equal. On the contrary. The point we wish to make is that all stories (or all ways of making sense of a particular set of experiences) are different, and that they differ along a number of dimensions. For example, some stories, such as scientific stories, may have a stronger 'evidence base', whereas others may have more personal meaning and relevance for an individual, despite a lack of 'scientific evidence'. Different cultures will develop different ways of making sense of madness, and within any one culture, there may be competing explanations from different groups or individuals within that culture. Explanations will also differ in the implications they have and they may have quite different implications for different parties. Some explanations may be more attractive to the individuals who experience madness, while being less appealing to the individual's family, or more broadly to members of the subculture to which the individual belongs. Some ways of storying madness may serve the interests of particular groups by, for example, indicating that they are the experts on providing professional assistance to those who are troubled by madness. The storytelling framework then is, we believe, helpful in drawing our attention to some of the implications which emerge from the various ways of making sense of madness and it is, therefore, a useful framework which fits well with our intention here to look at ways of making sense of the experience of madness. In considering the different explanations of madness that we encounter, we think it is helpful to keep in mind a range of questions. In addition to the usual questions such as 'Does this make sense?' and 'Does it correspond to any evidence?' it is also, we believe, crucial to consider other questions such as 'Is it helpful?

And if so, to whom?', and, more generally, 'Who's interests are best served by this particular explanation?'

Now, of course, this notion of storytelling as a way of conceptualizing how we make sense of and relate to experience is not an invention of ours, but is something we are borrowing from a much broader intellectual tradition, which, like so many great ideas, has its roots in philosophic thinking, and which has come to have some impact on the sciences, particularly the social sciences. Some have argued that the storytelling framework is part of a major 'paradigm shift' within social science, which brings with it quite different assumptions about how we think about such fundamental matters as what it is to be human and how we should conduct scientific investigations in this area (for example, see Harré 1998; Rabinow and Sullivan 1987). This new approach to the understanding and study of human beings has been referred to as, among other things, 'the interpretative turn' (Rabinow and Sullivan 1987), 'discursive investigations' (Harré 1994), 'social constructivism' (Gergen 1977), 'deconstructionism' (White 1991) and 'folk psychology' (Bruner 1990). The common thread to approaches subsumed by these terms is that meaning-making is a central feature of what it is to be human, and that meaning is something that we individually and collectively actively construct in our engagement with the world.

Historically, we can trace the roots of this perspective to the interest in rhetoric found in the classical writings of the likes of Aristotle and Cicero and their interest in how it is that meaning is conveyed through persuasive argument (Sloane 2001). While rhetoric went somewhat out of fashion with the birth of the scientific era, there was something of a resurgence of interest in the role of meaning-making in the twentieth century. This resurgence of interest in meaning-making has been attributed, at least partly, to the 'linguistic philosophy' movement, especially the works of the influential Austrian philosopher, Ludwig Wittgenstein. Wittgenstein was particularly interested in the way in which language constructs and conveys meaning and his views on the relationship between language and meaning have had a significant impact on science in general, and the social sciences in particular (Wittgenstein 1922, 1953). This emphasis on the importance of meaning-making, and the role that language has within this, has extended beyond philosophy and has spawned considerable amounts of research in the social sciences.

As already noted, one of the basic principles of the storytelling approach is the notion that we human beings are, first and foremost, meaning-makers, actively involved in interpreting the world around us, rather than being passively subject to and influenced by our experience. One of the fundamental ways in which we make meaning, and convey this meaning to others, is through weaving a narrative (or a 'story') which renders our experiences meaningful. So, in this context then, a 'story' is a way of making sense of experience in a narrative framework, which reflects our active, constructive engagement with the world. One assumption of the storytelling approach is that the stories we construct are not merely *descriptive* of experiences, but are seen as *constitutive*. That is, stories do not merely describe an independent objective reality. Stories are seen as constituting the very fabric which makes life meaningful. In this vein, the late Australian therapist and writer Michael White (1991) commented:

> The narrative metaphor proposes that persons live their lives by stories, and that these stories are shaping of life, and that they have real, not imagined, effects.
>
> (White 1991: 28)

Within psychology, meaning-making and storytelling are most readily subsumed within what are referred to as 'constructivist' approaches. It is in the work of American psychologist George Kelly (1955) that we can trace the first comprehensive expression of the constructivist framework within psychology, although the focus on meaning does, of course, have a longer tradition within psychology, being found to varying degrees in the works of some of the founding fathers of psychology such as Wundt (1897), James (1890) and Freud (1904). George Kelly argued that it is through the application of our own 'personal construct' system that we navigate reality. Kelly's position has been developed by Mair (1977, 1988) and Bruner (1990), who have proposed that a natural elaboration of Kelly's constructivist framework and a fruitful model for investigating how meaning is constructed is that of 'storytelling'. This approach has proven particularly fertile within the area of clinical psychology, where a therapeutic model, narrative therapy, based on this premise has been developed (Mair 1988; White and Epston 1990). It is important to note that this storytelling approach, and the constructivist framework from which it derives, is more than simply a way of looking at how experience is made meaningful. There is a well-established constructivist literature which discusses broader philosophical implications of constructivism, such as ontological (relating to 'being') and epistemological (relating to knowledge) matters (Bakhtin 1986; Mancuso 1996; Rorty 1980). While this is a complex literature, outlining the constructivist view of what it is to be human, this complexity is captured nicely by Gilbert (2002), who contrasts this perspective with that of conventional quantitative scientific approaches when she says that as humans 'we live in stories, not statistics'.

Interesting implications which emerge from the storytelling epistemology include the notions that the boundary between 'fact' and 'fiction' is blurred, and the idea of there being a single 'truth' is called into question. Instead, we are faced with an epistemology (or theory of knowledge) which allows for, even encourages, multiple stories, and a multiplicity of 'truths', each reflecting one particular way of storying the experience being considered. Claims to have access to an undisputed or objective 'truth' are viewed with some suspicion. Roberts (1999a: 5) suggests that 'it may be only the deluded and the fundamentalist who *know* the truth'. From this position, claims to some form of objectivity are viewed with considerable scepticism and seen primarily as a rhetorical device, aimed at persuading others of the superiority of one interpretation over all others. We can see that this perspective is congruent with the critical position of the French philosopher Michel Foucault, who used historical analyses of social phenomena to show that knowledge, power and social practice are closely interrelated. Foucault (1980) argued that those with power in society will use this power to legitimize their own knowledge claims, while endeavouring to disqualify, or discredit, competing knowledges (or 'discourses'). For Foucault there is no knowledge or truth outside of networks of power relations.

The extension of the interest in meaning-making and storytelling from the confines of philosophy to the world of empirical investigations has brought with it the need for the development of methods of doing research that are congruent with this approach. While conventional science has traditionally used statistical methods as the basis of scientific investigations, many (for example, Geertz 1983; Heron 1981; Shotter 1993) argue that quantitative methods are ill suited to the study of meaning-making, and other related topics such as interpretation and culture: issues which are of central concern to this new breed of social scientists. Incorporating these philosophical notions within science required the development of new ways of conducting research: 'qualitative methods' which are more suited to the study of meaning and meaning-making (Denzin and Lincoln 2000). A detailed exposition of the various qualitative methods is beyond the scope of this book. However, it is possible to identify some general characteristics of qualitative research, in terms of strategies and aims, which are common to the different qualitative methods. Morse (1992) suggests that among the common characteristics of qualitative research is a focus on the participants' subjective understanding of experience. Qualitative methods commonly aim to provide a framework for developing a deeper understanding of the experience being studied and to do so from the perspective of participants. The central feature of qualitative methods is that they place emphasis on meaning over measurement. A substantial portion of this book (Chapter 3) will focus on one particular qualitative study, carried out by the authors, investigating the subjective experience of madness as expressed by clients diagnosed as being 'psychotic' or 'schizophrenic'.

Terminology

This brings us now to the important but rather difficult matter of terminology. The particular aspect of human experience that we are concerned with in this book is what might be variously referred to as 'madness', 'schizophrenia', 'psychosis' or more generally perhaps as a 'nervous breakdown'. This book is an exploration into the stories we tell when the mind (or, some might argue, the brain) goes astray, when the person starts to have unusual perceptions, ideas or experiences which tend to be neither shared nor endorsed by others and which may result in out of character behaviour. We have already noted that these experiences might include phenomena such as hearing things (for example, voices) that others cannot hear, or holding beliefs that just do not seem to make much sense to others and which appear not to be based on sound evidence or reasoning. One of the common threads to these experiences is that they seem to conflict with our more general stories of how reality is, or perhaps ought to be, experienced. In our own explorations of madness in this book, we ourselves will, of course, inevitably be weaving our own narrative about how we might construe such experiences. Our own position will be stated explicitly in Chapter 6, though we suspect it will be implicit in different ways throughout the book.

We have, perhaps somewhat confusingly, already used a number of different terms – madness, psychosis, schizophrenia – to refer to the subject matter of this book. So, before we manage to make things even more confusing, it will be helpful at this point to try to clarify these terms and, in particular, how we will be using them in this book. One of the issues which we face in considering terminology is that currently there is no term that is 'neutral', simply descriptive of the experience and quite free of any theoretical assumptions and connotations. Indeed, perhaps it is impossible for there ever to be such a neutral term, as whatever language we use will, in however subtle a manner, betray something of our position, or way of thinking about these unusual experiences. Each term brings with it its own baggage and has its own connotations that take it beyond the merely descriptive. The three terms that we will consider here are 'schizophrenia', 'psychosis' and 'madness'.

We will begin this discussion with a consideration of terms used in the professional clinical framework. We do this not because we want to suggest that this framework is the only or even the most appropriate way of making sense of these experiences, but because as clinical psychologists working clinically and researching in the area of mental health, it is this terminology with which we are most familiar. Also, it would be fair to say that it is in this domain that the terminology has been most thoroughly developed and most clearly articulated and defined, with the twin concepts of 'schizophrenia' and 'psychosis' both being firmly rooted in the medical tradition. As such, these terms carry with them clear medical overtones, suggesting as they do that the experiences they refer to are appropriately seen as 'symptoms' of a 'mental illness', a perspective that, as we shall see, not everyone endorses. While there are a range of terms used within the clinical framework (others include, for example, schizoaffective disorder, bipolar disorder and schizophreniform disorder) each with subtle, but important differences, here our focus is on the two terms most closely related to our main concerns: schizophrenia and psychosis. They are the two terms most commonly used in clinical practice and in the research in this area.

Schizophrenia is the more clearly defined term, having been coined approximately 100 years ago by the Swiss psychiatrist Eugene Bleuler (1911), being a development which eventually replaced the earlier notion of 'dementia praecox' proposed by nineteenth-century German psychiatrist Emil Kraepelin (1919). Despite the fact that there have been continual modifications to the definition of schizophrenia, and an even wider variety of developments in attempts to explain and treat schizophrenia, the basic notion of schizophrenia has remained largely intact, though certainly not unchallenged, since the times of Kraepelin and Bleuler.

The current operational definition of schizophrenia which is most commonly used in clinical settings and in research is to be found in the American Psychiatric Association's (APA) *Diagnostic and Statistical Manual of Mental Disorders*, DSM IV-R (APA 2000). This manual uses what has been referred to as a 'Chinese menu' approach to diagnosis, where a specified number of symptoms from a set list are required for a diagnosis to be made (Bentall 2003: 60). In the DSM IV-R, schizophrenia is defined as the presence of any two from a list of five 'characteristic symptoms': delusions, hallucinations, disorganized speech, grossly disorganized or catatonic behaviour, and negative symptoms (such as affective flattening, or avolition). Only one of these five symptoms is required if the delusions are considered 'bizarre' or if the hallucinations are of a particular type (that is, voices providing a running commentary on the person's behaviour or voices conversing with one another). In addition, importance is given to the duration of the symptoms and any loss of function; some disturbance must be apparent for six months (including at least one month duration of the symptoms listed above) before a diagnosis can be made. The diagnostic manual also lists a range of subtypes of schizophrenia, such as paranoid, disorganized and simple.

The term 'psychosis' has generally been less clearly defined than schizophrenia. Like schizophrenia, how the term has been used has varied over time. In the 1970s, 'psychosis' meant 'out of touch with reality' or 'understandable', and was used in contrast with 'neurosis', which implied understandable, and recognized by the individual as a problem. This psychosis–neurosis distinction was once the bedrock of the diagnostic framework but has since been removed from the diagnostic manual (Bentall 2003: 38). Nowadays the DSM IV-R uses the term 'psychosis' to refer to a range of symptoms which vary across diagnostic categories. Somewhat oddly, and rather confusingly, the term has slightly different meanings depending on which particular diagnosis it is being used with. For example, in schizophrenia (and other closely related diagnoses), 'psychosis' refers to hallucinations, disorganized speech or behaviour, whereas in delusional disorder, 'psychosis' is (tautologically) equivalent to 'delusional'. Not surprisingly, given its lack of a clear operational definition, the term psychosis is much less commonly used in research than are diagnostic terms such as 'schizophrenia'.

Despite (or perhaps because) of the relative looseness with which the term psychosis has been used, it does seem to have found favour among certain clinicians and researchers, many of whom are critical of the diagnostic approach favoured by the American Psychiatric Association. For example, an influential report by the British Psychological Society (2000) recommends the use of the term psychosis, rather than schizophrenia, arguing that psychosis can be used to cover a whole range of unusual perceptions and beliefs and that it is a less pejorative and stigmatizing term than schizophrenia. Further, a significant development in clinical services, particularly in the developed world, is for the term psychosis to be preferred over schizophrenia, particularly when people are presenting for the first time to mental health services. Since the late 1990s there has been a proliferation of the establishment of 'early psychosis' services in many different parts of the world, including New Zealand, Australia, Scandinavia and the UK.

A recent development in the use of language in this area is a campaign to abolish the label 'schizophrenia' which has been gathering some momentum in the UK and elsewhere (www.asylumonline.net). Supporters of this campaign argue that the concept of schizophrenia is unscientific, lacking sufficient reliability or validity to be a helpful scientific concept (Bentall 2003; Boyle 1990) and, further, that the term is stigmatizing and as such damaging to those to whom it is applied and that therefore, it should be abolished. Some family-based organizations have already dropped the term. For example, the Schizophrenia Fellowship in England now calls itself 'Rethink'.

In contrast to these medically oriented terms, we have the lay notion of 'madness'. This term, like most lay language, has been much less clearly defined and operationalized. The *American Heritage Dictionary of the English Language* (2006) defines madness as 'The quality or condition of being insane'. The *Oxford English Dictionary* adds to this the notion of having a 'disordered or dysfunctional mind'. The quality of losing one's sanity or one's mind is a common thread that runs through the various dictionary definitions of madness. While the term 'madness' has, like schizophrenia, also often been used in a pejorative, stigmatizing way, recent years have witnessed attempts to 'reclaim madness' from within the psychiatric consumers' movement, in the same way that gays and lesbians have reclaimed 'queer'. This has seen those who have personal experience of 'madness' and who may have been diagnosed as having, for example, schizophrenia or psychosis, adopt the term 'madness' in their personal accounts of the experience (for example, Russo 2001). This term has also been adopted by groups such as the international Mad Pride movement (www.mindfreedom.org), where the term is used as a way of reappropriating the experience through the use of a lay term rather than a medical term. British service users Dillon and May (2002) argue that traditional clinical language is used to 'colonize' people's subjective experience. They propose that the use of lay terms, such as madness, can help overcome this by acknowledging and valuing the client's perspective. Some, no doubt, continue to use the term 'madness' as derogatory and many certainly use the term as a put down.

Our position is that these terms – schizophrenia, psychosis and madness – refer essentially to the same kinds of experiences, but that they do so from different positions. Or, we could say, they 'story' the experience differently. The first two terms locate these experiences within a clinical, predominantly psychiatric, framework which brings with it the assumption that expertise on these experiences lies with clinicians. When we use the term 'madness' to refer to the same sets of experiences, this gives less emphasis to the clinical perspective as it locates the experience more within the realm of ordinary everyday language, and thus, ordinary (or extra-ordinary) everyday human experience, so making it a topic that all of us, including those who have such experiences, are able to contribute to meaningfully. By using the term 'madness' the experience is wrested from the grip of a select few experts on 'schizophrenia' and 'psychosis', and portrayed not as a medical condition with an obscure Greek or Latin derived title, but rather as an aspect of the human condition, about which we all can have our say.

In this book, our preference is for the use of the term 'madness', reflecting our sympathy for the arguments outlined above. Our intention is to give greater emphasis to subjective experience and to the endeavours of a wide range of people, including, but not limited to, clinicians and scientists in this area, to make sense of these experiences. However, we will at times be obliged to use the clinical terms, when, for example, referring to research carried out by others who have used these clinical terms in their reports. It is not our intention to devalue the clinical perspective. As clinicians and researchers ourselves we obviously have some knowledge of, attachment to, and indeed respect for the clinical perspective. Despite this, we believe that clinical terms can unnecessarily and unhelpfully limit participation in discussions about experiences such as madness, which, we want to argue, are, first and foremost, aspects of the human condition about which we all have a vested interest, and which none of us, least of all those directly affected by these experiences, should be alienated from.

Whatever terms we may use, and whatever reservations and criticisms may be levied at those terms, it is important that we do not lose sight of the fact that 'madness' is a significant and often highly distressing experience for the individual and for his or her family and loved ones. We certainly do not want to downplay this aspect of madness, but we do want to stress that the medical perspective does not have a monopoly on acknowledging the suffering that commonly (although not universally) accompanies madness. In fact, we might argue that any language which functions to alienate the person from the experience, or to 'colonize' this experience, is only likely to compound whatever suffering the experience itself entails for the individual.

This book then is an attempt to look at how we can go about making sense of madness, whether we choose to refer to this experience as 'schizophrenia', 'psychosis' or 'madness', terms which we take to be largely synonymous. Our exploration of these topics will include a substantial discussion of the subjective experience of madness, as expressed by those who have first-hand lived experience and who have been generous enough to share this experience and their personal understandings of it with us.

Where are we coming from?

Given that this book is an exploration of the various ways in which we can make sense of madness, and that our starting point is that madness can be viewed differently from different positions, none of which can have a genuine claim to objectivity, we feel that it is appropriate that we declare relevant aspects of our personal and professional backgrounds, so allowing readers to recognize the contribution these may make to our analyses of the various topics explored in this text. We do this not because we believe there is any-thing especially unique either about us, or about the topic of madness. We believe that it is disingenuous to approach the study of any aspect of what it is to be human without recognizing that those who conduct such research are themselves part of the human enterprise and aspects of their personal experi-ence will inevitably influence the positions and approaches they adopt in addressing the particular aspect of the human world under investigation. To this end, we now provide a brief summary of our own experience, in order to make more transparent the positions we adopt, which influence how we construe and relate to the experience of madness.

Jim Geekie

Jim grew up in a working-class Scottish home, as part of a tight-knit and generally loving extended family. His first exposure to the world of madness came as a young child when his mother had a 'breakdown'. Jim's mother's story is in fact the story we used to begin this chapter. This story is, of course, shared with permission of Jim's mother, who requested the story be given in the third person. As the younger child in this story, aged only 2 at the time, he has no personal recollection of the events related above, though this is not to claim that they had no impact on him.

In terms of personal experiences that might be construed as 'psychotic', Jim has had the very occasional experience of hearing a hallucinatory voice, an experience which he finds neither distressing nor confusing, although the first such experience did come as something of a surprise. In his professional life, Jim spent a few years living and teaching in East Africa, before returning to the UK, where he completed his training as a clinical psychologist in 1992. He has a long-standing interest in psychosis, and has worked in the area of first episode psychosis (FEP) since 1996. He has a particular interest in how the individual who experiences psychosis makes sense of this experience him or herself.

Jim's interest in madness is part clinical (how can we best help those who are troubled by these experiences?) and part philosophical (what does it tell us about the nature of the human mind that it can have experiences of this sort?). His personal position is that there is no one thing that 'is' madness (or schizophrenia, or psychosis) and that the complexity of the experiences which come under these terms means that no one approach, be it philosophical, biological, psychological, sociological or whatever, can possibly fully explain these experiences. He believes that understanding the experience of madness, and responding to those troubled by such experiences, requires a flexible approach, informed by multiple perspectives and a recognition that whatever understandings we bring should be seen as tentative in nature and be evaluated, ultimately, by the extent to which they help us successfully navigate a given situation (such as, in the clinical domain, helping an individual lessen the distress associated with an experience). Any attempts to reduce madness to a simple explanation with a simple remedy diminishes not only the experience of madness, but, by extension, the richness of what it is to be human, and so to be prone to such experiences.

John Read

John suspects that for everyone who spends a significant part of their life experiencing or responding to madness, there is a life history, often intergenerational, that partially explains this. His paternal grandfather was a London cobbler who expected his two sons to call him 'sir' and refused to answer their questions about why he had only one leg. His maternal grandfather grew up in a Birmingham orphanage and threatened to sentence his little girl to the same fate whenever she was naughty. His maternal grandmother was pleased to marry this man, any man, to escape the sexual abuse she was experiencing from her father. She did not have to spend too much time with her husband because she sewed seventy hours a week in a Birmingham sweat shop. One of the two sons of the one-legged London cobbler met this little girl years later, just after being demobbed from the Royal Air Force at the end of the Second World War. He had joined up when life expectancy for a fighter pilot was just seven weeks. He flew for four years, repeatedly getting very close to fellow pilots only to see them blown out of the sky. When John was 22 his Dad told him this story for the first time, to explain why he had never been able to feel closeness or show feelings since then. John's Mum added, 'I never knew that'.

John had grown up in a safe but, like many at that time and place, emotionally restricted home. 'Anger is what causes wars', his Dad had helpfully explained to him. He had been happy enough and just loved his soccer. (He would have played for England but his parents moved the family from London to Hereford when he was 9 and the scouts never visited this sleepy rural outpost.) His parents were thrilled when, at the age of 11, John won the only scholarship to a local posh school. Within two years John came bottom of his class. He now proudly shows off a report card stating 'This year John has tried very hard to be good and once he almost succeeded', without mentioning that part of the reason is that he had spent several sessions on the lap of the headmaster with the old man's hands down his trousers.

No wonder he chose psychology at university. However, he found it very dry until he discovered Ronnie Laing (Laing 1960, 1967; Laing and Esteron 1970). He knew then where he was headed. His first job was in a psychiatric hospital in New York. At the time he thought he just wanted to help people but now he understands that he was there partly because he found it reassuring that there were people in the world even more screwed up than he was. When the psychiatrists praised him for being able to make contact with even the most psychotic patients, he was so paranoid he thought they were mocking him. John found that Laing was right; even the weirdest thoughts and behaviours often make sense when you know the person's life story. The only experience of madness that John is willing to share publicly occurred when his best friend visited him the day after he had been killed in a car crash.

After training as a clinical psychologist and many years working as such, and as a manager of mental health services, in the USA, the UK and New Zealand, John accepted a position in the Psychology Department of the University of Auckland in 1994. His research into the social causes of madness seems to confirm what his clients had always told him. His understanding of loss and trauma has been deepened by being a lifelong supporter of Tottenham Hotspurs football club.

Concluding comments

The central argument of this book will be that those who have first-hand lived experience of madness are able to comment on this experience in unique ways and that they can make an important contribution to our understandings of these experiences. In Chapter 2, we will discuss why we believe that subjective experience is so important in this area, and consider some of the implications of this having been so neglected in research into madness, then go on to suggest how this may be redressed. In Chapter 3, our focus will again be on the subjective experience of psychosis, but with greater attention to research in the area. A substantial portion of this chapter will be devoted to Jim's research looking at the subjective experience of madness. This chapter will also include a discussion of first-person accounts as well as other research into the subjective experience of madness. In the subsequent two chapters, we will extend our discussion beyond subjective understandings of madness, and look at how others have made sense of madness. Chapter 4 will examine lay understandings of madness, looking at research that investigates how members of the general public as well as family members of those who have experienced madness understand these experiences. Following this, in Chapter 5, we will look at scientific and clinical ways of making sense of madness. These three chapters will show us that there is a dizzying array of understandings of madness, from the subjective, lay and scientific/clinical perspectives. In Chapter 6, we will outline our response to the various understandings of madness that one encounters in this field. We will propose a novel way of thinking about the disagreements regarding what madness is, by suggesting that disagreeing about what madness really is, is integral and essential to the very meaning of madness. In our final chapter, we will explore some of the implications – for theory, research and clinical practice – which emerge from this position, which we are advocating is one way of making sense of madness.

Chapter 2

The subjective experience of madness

One of the central points we want to make in this book is that consideration of the subjective experience of madness has much to contribute to our under-standings of madness. Indeed, we would go further than this: our position is that any understanding of madness which overlooks subjective experience will inevitably provide an incomplete and, ultimately, inadequate conceptual-ization of the experience. This is, we believe, true of much human experience, but particularly true of madness given that it is the individual's subjective experience (such as hearing a voice, or having a 'delusional' belief) that is at the heart of how we define madness when we use terms such as psychosis and schizophrenia. To try to understand madness without recognizing, acknowledging and incorporating the subjective aspects of the experience into our understandings is an impossible task, doomed to failure.

Despite this, it seems to us that much of the scientific literature and research in this area has tried to develop theories of madness that pay little heed to subjective experience. The voice of lived experience has been all but extinguished, and, as a consequence, the theories we encounter are deprived of the human aspects, and the humanity, of the experience, managing to make those who have such experiences sound barely human, as if they were part of 'a logically distinct species' (Bannister 1968). We should keep in mind that theories of madness are not mere academic theories, with little impact on practical matters. On the contrary, how we understand madness informs and shapes the kinds of clinical approaches offered to those who may find their experiences troubling. Understandings of madness also influence how lay people respond to these experiences (see Chapter 4). If, as we contend, these understandings are impoverished or inaccurate as a result of neglecting the subjective experience, then we should expect that our clinical approaches will be similarly impoverished and less helpful than they could be.

Another consequence of the exclusion of subjective experience is that those who have first-hand acquaintance with the experience are deemed unable to contribute to our understandings of such experiences. They are effectively silenced, excluded from discussions about what the experience is, about what the experience means and about how to offer help to those who find the experiences troubling. This seems patently bizarre to us: as if only those who had never tasted chocolate were really able to explain what it was like, or as if being, say, a Scot, excluded one from the discussion of what it means to be Scottish. Surely, such a scenario would seem absurd, unhelpful and unacceptable in almost any other domain of human existence and experience. Yet, this is exactly the scenario we find in the all too human experience of madness: those who are most intimately acquainted with the experience have been sidelined in our efforts to understand and work with the experience, although there are signs that this might be changing, as consumers of mental health services come to have greater input into how such services are organized and delivered (Deegan 1996; O'Hagan 2001).

In this chapter we will put forward our case explaining why we believe subjective experience is crucially important, despite having been largely neglected. We want to challenge the notion that madness can be made sense of by bypassing the subjective aspects of the experience. To do this we will show, first, that this is indeed a neglected area of study, before going on to look at the research that has been done in this area, the findings of which clearly demonstrate the importance of such research. In subsequent chapters, we will look in more detail at other aspects of the subjective experience of psychosis.

To begin this discussion it is worth briefly considering how it might have come to pass that subjective experience came to be excluded from scientific investigations into human experiences such as madness. From its origins the scientific method has valued investigations which emphasize objective observation and measurement over subjective experience. So long as the focus of scientific investigations is inanimate objects and matter, one might have few objections to this approach, given that, we assume, inanimate aspects of the material world, such as sub-atomic particles, gravitational forces, and electrical currents have no subjective experience of their own being. However, in the nineteenth century, these same scientific methods, which were proving so successful in the study of the material world, were adopted by health researchers and social scientists, whose focus was not on inanimate objects bereft of subjectivity, but was, rather, on a quite different animal, characterized, one might argue, by its capacity for reflecting on its own experience: the human being.

The person most commonly identified as responsible for importing this perspective from the natural sciences into the social sciences is the nineteenth-century French thinker, Auguste Comte. Comte developed his influential philosophical doctrine of 'positivism', at the core of which are two principles, namely, that general 'facts' about human beings can be developed and that these facts must be based on scientific (or 'objective') observations. This position tended to downplay, or even exclude completely, the role of subjective experience as part of the scientific enterprise. As noted in Chapter 1, the twentieth century witnessed challenges to the 'positivist' perspective, particularly from those who embraced the notions that meaning and interpretation are central to the study of human beings, within what has been called the 'interpretive turn' within the social sciences (Rabinow and Sullivan 1987). While it is not our intention to discuss these theoretical issues in detail here, we mention it now to acknowledge the broader context within which the question of the significance or otherwise of subjective experience is located. Our position, which we hope is clear by now, is that if we truly want to understand such a complex human experience as schizophrenia, we need to embrace both conventional 'objective' scientific research and research which is sensitive to subjective aspects of the experience, such as what it means to the individual concerned.

The status of research into the subjective experience of madness

So, let us now look at the position of research into subjective experience in the area of schizophrenia. We have already argued that this occupies a marginalized role, with there being relatively very few investigations into subjective experience. We now want to substantiate this claim, one which we are not the first to make. In a review of research in this area, Lally (1989) pointed out that within mental health there is a general lack of research into patients' perspectives. More specifically, in the area of psychotic experiences this lack of research is even more pronounced. Molvaer et al. (1992: 210) examined the research in this area and concluded that 'research dealing with patients' own attributions for their illness has been virtually non-existent', a conclusion very similar to the one reached more recently by Drayton et al. (1998: 270), who complain: 'There is a paucity of research concerned with the individual's psychological adaptation to psychosis.'

This neglect of research into clients' understandings of and relationships with their experience is somewhat curious, when we remind ourselves that in the area of mental health diagnoses depend almost entirely on the clients' own description of their experience (as opposed to being derived from diagnostic biochemical tests such as are used in other areas of medicine: see Newnes, (2002) for a discussion of this matter). It seems almost as if the client can be (indeed *must* be) relied upon to provide a history and description of his or her experience, on which the diagnosis will rest, but, once the client has provided this information, he or she is then viewed as having little to contribute towards understandings of these experiences. The paradox here is that while diagnosis depends upon seeing the client as a valuable, indeed necessary contributor to the process, once the client has been diagnosed with a psychotic illness, this *ipso facto* seems to render him or her unable to contribute to the discussion regarding what this condition means.

Though there is a general lack of research in this area, a few notable and influential writers have made a strong case that this is an important clinical and research consideration that ought not to be overlooked. In his classical text Jaspers (1963) dedicated an entire chapter to the patient's attitude to illness and made some effort towards developing a classification of the individual's ways of understanding and responding to psychotic experiences. Jaspers (1963: 417, original italics) argued that 'Much can be learned from *patients' own interpretations*, when they are *trying to understand themselves*.'

Another early text which drew attention to the importance of clients' understandings was by Mayer-Gross (1920, quoted in Dittman and Schuttler 1990). Mayer-Gross considers the opinions of people diagnosed with schizophrenia and suggests a classification for how the individual responds to their experience. Mayer-Gross (1920) proposes five ways in which the client may respond to the experience: 'despair', 'renewal of life' (seeing the experience as offering this), 'shutting out' (as if nothing happened), 'conversion' (where the psychosis is viewed as a revelation) and 'integration' (of the experience into the notion of self). These terms have not been adopted within clinical practice or research. More recently, in other important psychiatric texts, Sims (1988, 1994) argues that a full and proper assessment of the client's difficulties must involve a detailed phenomenological exploration of the client's subjective experience, and an empathic appreciation of the same. Sims (1994: 445) makes the point that within clinical practice 'There is a great need to acknowledge, have respect for, and use in treatment, the patient's *own* experience'. Promisingly, this call is echoed in an editorial in the *American Journal of Psychiatry*, where the writers suggest that those responsible for updating the diagnostic manual should give serious consideration to incorporating subjective aspects of experience within DSM-V (Flanagan et al. 2007).

Sadly, these calls to value the client's own experience have not been much heeded in either research or in clinical practice. One of the ways in which the neglect of the client's experience is manifest is in the lack of an accepted well-developed language to refer to, describe, or categorize clients' understandings of and responses to their own experience. This leaves us in the kind of predicament described by the philosopher Ludwig Wittgenstein (1922) where our lack of language limits what we can say. This point is identified as an obstacle to research in this area by American psychiatrist and professor of medical anthropology and cross-cultural psychiatry Arthur Kleinman (1988), who notes:

> Clinical and behavioral science research also possess no category to describe human suffering, no routine way of recording this most thickly human dimension of patients' and families' stories of experiencing illness.
> (Kleinman 1988: 28)

One rather simple way to investigate the question of whether or not subjective experience is given adequate attention is to look at research into schizophrenia, and see what proportion of this focuses on subjective aspects of the experience. This is possible through the use of electronic databases such as MEDLINE and PsycINFO, which collate research into a wide range of health and psychological issues and are generally accepted as providing comprehensive access to the scientific literature in the field. We used both these databases to consider the status of research into the subjective experience of schizophrenia. We searched these databases, using the search terms 'schizophrenia' (which is the term most commonly used in scientific studies) and 'subjective experience' (which yielded more hits than similar terms such as 'subjectivity' and 'first-person accounts'). We present our findings from these searches in Table 2.1.

What we can see clearly in Table 2.1 is that subjective experience is very much on the periphery of scientific investigations into schizophrenia. In MEDLINE (covering the period 1966 to 21 June 2008), only 0.17 per cent of the total schizophrenia literature is related to subjective experience. Using PsycINFO (covering 1806 to June 2008), we find this figure is a little higher, at 0.33 per cent. This increased figure in PsycINFO is probably attributable to the fact that the database covers social sciences, whereas MEDLINE has a more medical orientation. Clearly, both figures indicate that research into subjectivity occupies but a very small proportion of the literature on schizophrenia, so demonstrating the marginal nature of this research. However, this table also shows that when we limit our results to specific time periods we find that there has been a growth of research in this area, both in terms of absolute numbers, and as a per cent of total schizophrenia research. In MEDLINE we find the proportion of schizophrenia research involving subjective experience has more than doubled each decade, from 0.01 per cent (1 article) in 1965–1975, growing to 0.3 per cent (69 articles) in 1995–2005. A similar pattern is found using PsycINFO, with the figures growing from 0.07 per cent (4 articles) for the decade to 1975, to 0.53 per cent (119 articles) in the decade ending 2005. There is a clear trend of increased interest in this area, though we should not lose sight of the fact that these figures are very small, in both percentage figures and in absolute terms.

It seems reasonable to ponder why it might be that we find this neglect of the client's understanding within mental health research and practice. One explanation is proposed by Mechanic (1972), who suggests that in mental

Table 2.1 Showing % of schizophrenia research which investigates subjective experience (numbers of articles in parenthesis)

	MEDLINE	PsycINFO
Totals	0.17% (109)	0.33% (184)
1965–1975	0.01% (1)	0.07% (4)
1975–1985	0.05% (5)	0.13% (11)
1985–1995	0.12% (18)	0.24% (36)
1995–2005	0.30% (69)	0.53% (119)

health care it is more difficult to separate the attribution from the entity about which the attribution is made. That is, the client's understanding of the experience, and the experience itself, given that they are both essentially psychological processes, are difficult to disentangle, and, perhaps as a consequence of this, the client's understanding of the experience tends to be overlooked by clinicians and researchers.

Kleinman (1988) offers a different and, to us, more persuasive argument, when he locates the problem more squarely within the realm of modern medicine and medical training (rather than being somehow inherent in the experience, as Mechanic (1972) seems to suggest). Kleinman argues that the biological focus within medicine and the kinds of practice that this engenders precludes inquiry into the meaning of the experience. Kleinman (1988: 17) suggests that the tendency to overlook the patient's perspective is developed in medical training where clinicians 'have been taught to regard with suspicion patients' illness narratives and causal beliefs'. A similar position is taken by Jennings (1986: 866), who argues that 'The emergence of biomedicine's remarkable effectiveness in curing disease has apparently been accompanied by a relative neglect of patients' experience of disease.'

Equally critical of the neglect of the client's perspective, though proffering another take on why this might be so, is the late Loren Mosher, who ran the successful Soteria House project in San Francisco from 1971 to 1983, which showed that non-medically driven treatment, from non-professionally trained staff who show respect and tolerance for psychotic experience, is effective (Mosher 2001; Mosher et al. 2005). Mosher suggests that traditional, narrowly biological medical approaches to people who are psychotic may have been developed to allow clinicians to keep the troubled person at a distance arguing that: 'When looked at contextually, these interventions seem to be designed to allow the rest of us to avoid having to deal with these persons' humanity – that is, their subjective experience of psychosis and its effect on us' (Mosher 2001: 389).

Mosher's position is that ways of understanding madness which emphasize diagnoses, by using terms such as schizophrenia, reflect an understandable human tendency to want to distance oneself from the confusing and painful experiences of others, but this also has the dehumanizing effect of negating the value of the person's subjective experience. He advocated that staff working with psychotic clients should above all aim to understand the client's experience and respect the client's understanding of the experience. Sadly, despite research showing that Soteria was effective, it was closed down due to lack of funding in 1983. Although currently there are a few Soteria-like facilities in Europe (Sweden, Switzerland, Germany and others) which operate with a similar philosophy, such facilities remain very much on the periphery of mental health services for those who experience psychosis, which are dominated by medically oriented services, which operate within the diagnostic framework, with its tendency to emphasize categorization of clients' experiences and which, as we have seen, pays little serious attention to the client's subjective experience.

What can be done?

How then might we overcome this tendency to neglect the subjective experience of the individual who experiences psychosis? However we might go about this, we need to heed Mosher's (2001) point that approaching the subjective experience of a troubled soul may, in itself, be distressing to some and therefore appropriate training and support will be necessary. It seems to us that addressing this neglect will involve adopting an attitude to psychosis/madness which recognizes it as an essentially human experience and similarly acknowledges that those who experience psychosis are 'experience-based experts' who have valuable contributions to make. Fully acknowledging these points will entail embracing methods of conducting research and clinical practice which are congruent with these principles. These issues will be further explored when we discuss research into subjective experience (Chapter 3) and when we outline one way of conceptualizing psychosis which explicitly values various forms of expertise, including experience-based (Chapter 6).

Why is subjective experience important?

We will now move on to consider some of the reasons why we believe subjective experience of psychosis is important, beginning with an ethical argument, before moving on to consider empirical findings which illustrate quite convincingly that to understand and work with psychosis we need to take subjectivity into account.

Ethical arguments

A general ethical position arguing for the importance of attending to subjective experience is stated forcibly by Fulford and Hope (1993: 691) who argue that 'understanding the patient's actual experience is the basis of sound medical ethics': attending to the patient's understanding is a *sine qua non* for ethical medical practice. In a more general sense, the phenomenological philosophical position, as espoused by the likes of Husserl (1962), operates from the starting point that immediate experience is necessarily unique and that to be human is to interpret or 'thematize' one's experience: to be human is to make one's unique sense of one's own unique lived experience. Failure to treat another individual as having this capacity is to fail to treat that person as fully human; surely not a basis upon which an ethical medical practice could be based. Though Husserl's concern was more with the human condition in general rather than the more specific domain of medicine, his perspective has been adopted within medical research by the likes of Kirmayer who summarizes this argument nicely:

> Caring begins with accepting the phenomenal reality of the patient's suffering, including its moral significance to the patient and others. Accepting the patient as person leads to a willingness to explore the personal meanings of distress beyond the theories of biomedicine.
>
> (Kirmayer 1988: 82)

Another concept relevant here is Shotter's (1981) notion of 'authoring'. Shotter argues that whether or not one is allowed to be the author of one's own experience is more than just a psychological or sociological issue. He argues that 'authoring' should be thought of as a moral right, proposing that 'In a moral world, no one but the person in question has the status, the authority, under normal conditions, to decide what his experience means to him' (Shotter 1981: 278).

Shotter goes on to suggest that this right is a central part of autonomy and that 'authoring' extends not only to establishing for oneself what one's experience means but also being able to share this understanding with others: 'To be autonomous . . . is to be accorded the right of expressing one's self, of telling others one's thoughts, feelings, and intentions, and the right to be accorded their author' (Shotter 1981: 279). This theme is echoed by Lakoff (1995), who looks more at the impact on the person, arguing that being denied the ability to define one's own experience 'is to be deprived of self-knowledge, and of full consciousness' (Lakoff 1995: 33). Another consequence of not being able to define and describe one's own experience is what Roberts (1999b) refers to as the 'silencing' of the individual's story. These issues relating to 'authoring' are of considerable importance in our own research into the client's experience of psychosis and will be discussed further later (Chapter 3).

In short, we believe there is an overwhelming ethical argument for acknowledging the importance of the client's understanding of his or her experience of psychosis, and that to fail to do so would be to fail to meet one of the first requirements of an ethically sound clinical practice. Even if one were to accept that there are aspects of the experience of psychosis which are difficult, even impossible, to articulate and further that those who experience psychosis may be compromised in their capacity to express this experience clearly and fully, this does not, in itself, render this ethical argument invalid. The ethical importance of being author of one's story, and of having that story heard by others, remains true even if one accepts these limitations. However, lest this ethical argument on its own is not convincing, let us now consider some of the empirical findings from research into subjective experience which further underlines its importance.

Empirical arguments

In this section, we will provide an overview of research which demonstrates relationships between important clinical variables and the subjective experience of psychosis. While there are many aspects of subjective experience that one can study, areas which are commonly investigated include the individual's understanding (or 'explanatory model': how the individual explains the experience), the individual's attitude to and relationship with the experience, and the individual's phenomenological descriptions of the experience. As we will see research in each of these areas provides us with important insights into the nature of psychosis, and gives us significant pointers regarding how to work clinically with those who are troubled by psychosis.

Explanatory models: how the individual understands the experience

The concept of 'explanatory model' comes from the work of Arthur Kleinman, who has written extensively about explanatory models, particularly in relation to chronic physical illness (for example, Kleinman 1986, 1988, 1993). Kleinman defines explanatory models as 'the notions about an episode of sickness and its treatment that are employed by all those engaged in the clinical process' (Kleinman 1988: 121). In the same book, Kleinman proposes that illness experiences must be rendered meaningful by the individual and that developing meaning for an illness experience helps turn a 'wild, disorganized natural occurrence into mythologized, controlled, cultural experience' (Kleinman 1988: 55). Explanatory models are not simply beliefs that one has about an experience of illness, but are broader than this, being frames, usually provided by one's culture, that render such experiences meaningful (Good 1986). Explanatory models can be thought of as a story that the patient and significant others construct and tell to give coherence to the events and course of suffering. These stories tend to be derived from a particular cultural context, are often tacit rather than explicit, and may at times be contradictory and may shift in content.

Perhaps the first question one might ask regarding clients' explanatory models for psychosis is whether or not individuals do in fact develop understandings, or models, of their experience. Research findings are consistent in this regard: the vast majority of clients of mental health services (whether new presenters or longer standing clients) do indeed have explanatory models for their experiences. For example, Angermeyer and Klusmann (1988) carried out survey and interview research in Germany, asking approximately 200 patients with a diagnosis of schizophrenia if and how they made sense of their experience. They found that the majority of clients had some notion of likely causes of their experience: 74 per cent expressed their explanation in interview, whereas 93 per cent of their sample were able to identify their own particular understanding of their experience from a checklist of possible causes. Similarly, Bannister (1985) studied explanatory models of 60 patients newly admitted to a British psychiatric hospital and found that patients had already developed fairly sophisticated understandings of their experience within the first three days of admission, with only 18 per cent saying it was a 'total mystery'. Further, Dittmann and Schuttler (1990) report that among patients with a diagnosis of schizophrenia in Germany, when asked about causes of their experience, only 12 per cent were unable to offer an explanation. It is clear then, that those who have psychotic experiences do indeed strive to make sense of and build explanatory models for their experience.

An important point to make here is that explanatory models, just like stories, are not merely explanations which have no impact on the experience itself. Explanatory models are best thought of as 'constitutive' in that they are an important dynamic component of the whole experience. An individual's understanding not only reflects or describes illness experience but also contributes to the experience of symptoms and suffering. Kleinman (1988: 9) explains this by suggesting that 'The meanings communicated by illness can amplify or dampen symptoms, exaggerate or lessen disability, impede or facilitate treatment.' One study which illustrates the dynamic relationship between the person's understanding of experience and how this experience develops was carried out by Escher et al. (2002) in the Netherlands. In this study, the researchers looked at children who had heard voices. At the beginning of the study these children were not considered to need input from mental health services, as the experiences were not of such a magnitude to indicate this. Over the next three years these children were followed up to see which, if any, might go on to meet 'caseness' (defined in their study as needing the care of mental health services). They found that the progression from hearing voices to needing mental health care input was associated with the child's and parents' appraisals of the voices rather than the voices themselves. That is, children or families who at the initial assessment had a more negative explanatory model for the voices, seeing them as more problematic and indicative of pathology, were, over the course of the next three years, much more likely to require input from mental health services. This study suggests that the understanding one adopts for an unusual experience (such as hearing a voice) may play a role in how this experience develops over time, and whether or not it progresses such that it causes levels of distress which indicate that mental health service input is required.

The degree to which psychotic experiences are distressing to the individual is an important though, at times, overlooked variable. This may reflect the assumption that psychotic experiences are inherently and inevitably distressing. However, research such as that by Romme and Escher (1989) in the Netherlands, demonstrates that this is not always the case. They found that significant numbers of voice-hearers have a neutral or even positive relationship with their voices and that the degree of distress associated with voices is related to the understanding that the person has of the experience, as opposed to being attributable only to factors inherent in the voice-hearing experience itself (such as the content of the voices). Those who understood their voices in a 'benevolent' framework (for example, seeing the voices as being a part of the self, or a guiding spirit) were less likely to report distress than those whose explanatory models were more 'malevolent' (for example, seeing the voices as being from a powerful negative source, such as the Devil). Research into voice-hearing in New Zealand found that those who understand their voices in a spiritual framework tend to be less distressed by the voices, and have less contact with mental health services than those who understand their voices in either biological or psychological terms (Beavan 2007).

Given that one of the primary goals of mental health services is to alleviate distress, it is clear that to achieve this goal clinicians must attend to the client's understandings of the experience. A common assumption held by mental health services is that the primary focus of treatment should be reducing symptoms. However, recent research has shown that the client's subjective appraisal of improvement (that is, feeling better) does not correlate with measures of symptoms, casting doubt upon the assumption that symptom relief is the main consideration for clients (Kupper and Tschacher 2008).

There is also research showing that one of the reasons that childhood trauma increases the risk of psychosis is that the previously traumatized group make negative attributions about and are therefore more distressed by their first experiences of hearing voices (Morrison et al. 2003). Other research which demonstrates the way in which one's explanatory model influences the actual experience include Birchwood et al.'s (1993) study which showed that those who view their experience of psychosis as an 'illness' (that is, those who accept the medical diagnosis) have higher rates of depression, and Fisher and Farina's (1979) research which found that people who view their psychotic experience in medical terms are less likely to develop and apply their own recovery strategies.

When considering the client's understanding of his or her experience, it is important to note that this does not exist in a vacuum; clinicians too have explanatory models for the client's difficulties. Client and clinician may, to varying degrees, have understandings which are congruent with each other, or which may be in conflict. For example, a New Zealand study of service users, most of whom received a diagnosis of psychosis, found that 69 per cent of those who had a history of being abused believed this was a causal factor in their mental health problems, but only 17 per cent thought their clinician believed this was the case (Lothian and Read 2002).

What are the clinical implications of the congruence, or lack thereof, between client and clinician explanatory models? Bannister (1985) investigated this very issue in relation to the psychotic experiences of patients in a British hospital. He found that congruence between the client and clinical staff on notions of the causes of psychotic breakdowns was associated with good outcomes for the client. He also found, however, that clinician–client agreement on what constitutes appropriate treatment bore no relation to the outcome. Based on these findings, Bannister (1985) warns of the risks of clinicians adopting a narrow biomedical perspective which may make it difficult for them to understand or appreciate the client's perspective and may blind the clinician to the personal significance of the experience and the client's wish or need to reflect on this experience. Some support for Bannister's argument can be found in the already mentioned Soteria House project, where good outcomes were found for clients who had had psychotic experiences (Mosher 2001). Staff exploration and validation of the clients' understandings were central to these successful outcomes. Within the recent British cognitive-behavioural approaches to psychosis, great emphasis is placed on clinician and client endeavouring to reach a joint understanding of the client's experience, which is seen as an important step in developing a helpful therapeutic relationship (see Bentall 2003; British Psychological Society 2000).

The research outlined above demonstrates that how one comes to think about and understand an experience has a significant role to play in a range of important variables, including the impact of the experience, how the experience develops over time, and how the individual responds to the experience as well as how the client and clinician relate in terms of looking at ways of dealing with the experience. Important considerations in the client–clinician relationship include how the client responds to advice from the clinician. This advice may include, for example, suggestions about medication and/or other ways of coping with psychosis. Medication is generally considered an important component of clinical treatment of psychosis, although there are well-documented reports that a significant proportion of clients do not follow medical advice regarding the use of anti-psychotic medications (Nosé et al. 2003). Budd et al. (1996) found that clients' beliefs are a good predictor of whether or not the client will comply with taking anti-psychotic medication. Of course, this is not at all surprising, as Helman (1981: 550) remarks 'Only if the prescribed treatments make sense to the patient will they be taken as directed.' This is consistent with advice given by Leventhal et al. (1992), who suggest that exploring the client's theory of illness can help shed light upon the reasons for non-compliance with medication, and as such, rather than being something which should be subject to further 'treatment' through 'adherence therapy' (Kemp et al. 1996) as is sometime suggested, non-compliance can be explored in an open and respectful way by clinicians, to help minimize potential conflict between the client and the clinical service. An interesting twist on the non-compliance literature is provided by Van Putten et al. (1976), who found that for a portion of in-patients who are non-compliant with anti-psychotic medications, this may reflect a conscious, deliberate choice showing a preference for the psychotic state over the 'treated' state. Here again we see potential for misunderstanding or even conflict between clinician and client if there is a failure to explore subjective aspects of the experience for the client, which may indicate that for some clients, at least some of the time, the psychotic state may actually be preferred to the medicated state.

Another important aspect of clinical work which has received considerable attention over recent years is in the use of coping strategies to deal with psychotic experiences (for example, Carr 1988; Falloon and Talbot 1981; Tarrier 2002). Research in this area shows, not at all surprisingly, that people who experience psychosis and find it troubling develop and utilize different ways of coping with the experience, with some coping strategies tending to be more effective than others. These findings have been adopted clinically, where clients are often instructed in the use of different coping strategies. However, such interventions commonly overlook an important finding from this research: clients do not develop or apply coping strategies randomly, but rather, the coping strategies they are willing to use are those which make sense *to the client* in terms of the client's own understanding of psychosis (Carr 1988; Falloon and Talbot 1981). Thus, clients' explanatory models have an important influence on which coping strategies will be applied, and clinical interventions aimed at teaching clients new coping strategies must also consider if and how such strategies fit within the clients' understandings. In the area of hearing voices, Romme and Escher (1993) note that if voices are seen by the individual as simply an 'illness', this tends to prevent any form of identification with the voices, which they see as a necessary condition for effective coping.

Attitude to and relationship with the psychotic experience

Closely related to, although not identical with, the way in which an individual understands his or her experience of madness, is the individual's attitude to, and relationship with the experience. This is an area of research which has made significant contributions to clinical practice in recent years. Central to this research are the twin concepts of 'sealing-over' and 'integration', which were first articulated by McGlashan et al. (1975). The recent revitalization of psychological approaches to psychosis has seen a resurgence of interest in these concepts. McGlashan and his co-workers use these terms to refer to the individual's attitude to and response to psychotic experiences. Those who 'seal over' tend to have fixed, usually negative views of their psychotic experiences, and may dismiss the experiences as having little or no personal significance; they put little effort into trying to develop a personal understanding of the experience, which is largely encapsulated and dismissed as irrelevant. By contrast, 'integrators' express interest and curiosity about the experience, which they see as having personal relevance, being somehow related to the ongoing patterns of their life and they look to learn about themselves from the experience of madness, seeing it as an opportunity to develop and grow. Integrators take a more open and flexible attitude to the experience, and are more likely to accept some personal responsibility, as well as seeing the experience as being linked to other life experiences such as stressful events, trauma, guilt etc., whereas 'sealers' do not see a relationship between the psychotic experiences and prior life problems, and may dismiss the whole experience as meaningless.

Though sealing-over and integration are sometimes discussed as if they were distinct ways of responding to psychosis, McGlashan et al. (1976) point out that they are best thought of as opposite ends of a continuum. McGlashan et al. (1976) show, through illustrative case studies, how the same individual can fluctuate between sealing-over and integrating. They suggest that factors influencing the stance an individual adopts include the response of significant others (including clinicians) and the use of medication, which may promote sealing-over. Larsen (2004) describes a small-scale study in Denmark looking at how clients relate to their experience and found that clients adopt both sealing-over and integration responses to their experience and which stance the individual adopts is related to the particular context within which he or she is discussing the experience: some ways of discussing the experience with the client are more likely to encourage an integrative response, whereas other ways of discussing the experience are more likely to engender a sealing-over response in the client.

Research into the relationship between client attitude to psychosis and outcome of the condition, though not conclusive, suggests that integrators fare better than those who seal over. McGlashan and Carpenter (1981) looked at in-patients with a diagnosis of schizophrenia and found some relationship between attitude to illness and outcome, with those who were less pessimistic about their experience tending to have better outcomes. Looking specifically at integration and sealing-over, McGlashan (1987) found that there was a tendency for integrators to have better outcomes. This finding was also evident, though less powerful, among those who had a diagnosis of schizophrenia. More recent research (Birchwood et al. 2000a, 2000b; Drayton et al. 1998) has found a clear relationship between attitude to psychosis and post-psychotic depression, with those who seal-over being far more at risk of depression in the post-psychotic period. Birchwood and his co-workers report that in their sample, all clients who became moderately to severely depressed following a psychotic episode had adopted a sealing-over response to their psychosis, with *none* of the integrators becoming depressed to this degree. This is quite persuasive evidence of the significance of client attitude to psychosis as being an important variable in course and outcome. Drayton et al. (1998) suggest that client attitude to psychosis and recovery styles may be related to early attachment experiences, such as trauma. This proposal found some support in another study which showed that 'sealer-overs' reported higher rates of childhood abuse from parents, suggesting that they may have lower psychological 'resilience' to deal with difficulties in later life, so leading them to seal over (Tait et al. 2004).

As McGlashan and others have pointed out, it is not only clients' attitudes to psychosis that can be conceptualized as reflecting a sealing-over versus an integrative approach: clinicians' understandings can also be considered along this continuum. Professional theories which emphasize biological factors would seem to fit more on the sealing-over end of this continuum, whereas those which locate the psychotic experience within the life experience of the client (such as psychodynamic, trauma-based and other psychological perspectives) are more integrative in their orientation. This may have some implications for the ways in which the client responds to the experience and also for how the client responds to treatment. One largely neglected study, with quite startling results, was reported by Whitehorn and Betz in 1960. They studied clinicians working in the USA with psychotic clients and found that the attitude held by the clinician towards the experience of psychosis was highly significant in influencing the outcome for the client. Clinicians who adopted a flexible, curious attitude to the client's inner world achieved positive outcomes for 75 per cent of their clients, which contrasted sharply with only 27 per cent positive outcomes being achieved where clinicians had dogmatic, inflexible, authoritarian approaches to the client's experience. The magnitude of this difference (75 per cent versus 27 per cent) is quite remarkable, comparing favourably with any difference found between interventions and control groups, including the use of anti-psychotic medications. Although this study is, inevitably, flawed in its methodology (with no clear control group, and measures of both clinician style and outcome in need of refinement), it is nonetheless disappointing that it has not led to further investigations to replicate or refute these findings. This research points to the role of the clinician's attitude to psychosis being a factor which may influence outcome for the client.

One model which may help us conceptualize the relationship between explanatory models and outcome for psychosis is proposed by Lafond (1998), who draws parallels between the normal process of grieving and response to mental illness. Lafond argues that it is crucial to consider how the person is responding to their experience, particularly for clients having their first psychotic episode, and that if the experience is properly processed by the individual (rather than being just dismissed), this may improve the outcome. Whether or not one accepts this particular model to conceptualize the research findings, it seems clear that client and clinician understandings of, and attitude to, psychotic experiences *do* have some impact on the course and outcome of the condition.

A persuasive personal perspective on this matter is provided by Rufus May (2002, 2003) who argues, from his own personal experience of psychosis and his clinical experience as a psychologist, that developing a personally meaningful explanatory model ('an enabling personal narrative') is a crucial part of recovery. He notes in passing that being diagnosed 'schizophrenic' was particularly unhelpful as it did not allow him to develop such a narrative. May is not alone in identifying the diagnosis of 'schizophrenia' as having a negative impact on the individual and being an obstacle to recovery over and above the experience itself. Reviewing studies of the disease model of mental illness, Mehta and Farina (1997) conclude that those adopting an illness model for mental distress report increased stigma from other people as well as increased self-stigma in the shape of a negative self-concept. Ritsher and Phelan's (2004) review of the literature in this area reaches a similar conclusion, noting that the process of internalizing negative stereotypes of mental illness is associated with demoralization, lowered self-esteem and unemployment. In their own study into psychotic patients, they found that internalized stigma is particularly common for this population, and that 'alienation' (the subjective experience of feeling not a full member of society, with 'spoiled identity') was a major component of this, and is associated with poorer outcomes and more depressive symptoms.

Warner (1994), reviewing empirical studies in this area, argues that those who accept a medical diagnosis of their condition may conform to the stereotype of incapacity and worthlessness, leading to poorer outcomes. Considering the now well-recognized, though poorly understood finding that in non-industrial societies those meeting criteria for a diagnosis of schizophrenia tend to have better outcomes than those who live in wealthier, more industrialized societies, Waxler (1979) proposes the possibility that this difference may relate to the different understandings of mental illness found in those societies.

May (2002) speaks about the importance of challenging the prevailing notion that mental health problems are to be seen only as 'disabilities'. He suggests that this can be done through seeing positives in the experience and recommends celebrating the uniqueness and resilience of those who have been through the mental health services. He refers to organizations in the UK, such as the Hearing Voices Network and Mad Pride, which are challenging cultural stereotypes by promoting a more positive perspective on the experience of mental health difficulties.

Most of the research into subjective aspects of psychosis that we have outlined so far has focused on how the individual understands and/or relates to the experience. These are, as we hope we have shown, important areas of research which can enhance our ways of making sense of madness. Another approach to investigating the subjective experience of psychosis is to consider how the individual describes the experience itself. Within mental health, and in particular within psychiatric diagnostic symptoms it is, as we shall see, common for assumptions to be made about the phenomenological nature of psychotic experience, and for these assumptions to be embodied in the names given to certain experiences (for example, 'thought disorder', which is, in fact, based on a description of disordered speech, and 'blunted affect', which is based on the individual *appearing* blunted). Now, the acid test of the accuracy of these assumptions and descriptions is, of course, the extent to which they correspond to the lived experience of the individual, given that it is this which they purport to describe. Research into subjective descriptions of the phenomenology of the experience by the individual can help draw attention to faulty assumptions about the nature of the experience and so can help us develop more accurate understandings and, potentially, more helpful treatments. We will illustrate this point by looking at research into negative symptoms of schizophrenia, although other features of psychosis (such as hearing voices, or delusional beliefs) can be, and indeed have been, subject to similar investigations which also shed further light on the nature of these experiences.

Phenomenological research – negative symptoms

The concept of 'negative symptoms' is a core component of current notions of schizophrenia, forming part of the DSM IV-R (American Psychiatric Association 2000) diagnostic criteria. Poverty of affect (or 'blunted affect') is a prime example of a negative symptom, considered a central feature of schizophrenia and, as the term implies, denotes a general lack of emotional responsiveness and emotional experience in the individual. This has now become a central tenet within the psychiatric literature, with countless research projects incorporating this concept. Our purpose here is not to provide an overview of this extensive research into negative symptoms, but to illustrate how research into the subjective experience of these negative symptoms can help us develop more accurate conceptualizations of what is actually going on.

When those who have been identified as suffering from 'blunted affect' are asked about what they are experiencing (Boker et al. 2000; Selton et al. 1998), we find that many report that they actually experience intense emotions (such as anxiety), despite appearing to others to be emotionally and cognitively dulled: that is, for some clients it may be that the paucity of emotion relates only to the expression of emotion, not to the actual emotional experience. As discussed more fully by Kring and Germans (2004), research of this sort shows that there can, at times, be a discrepancy between what observers may assume and what the individual is experiencing. This research draws our attention to an implicit, usually unstated assumption made within the psychiatric terminology, namely that expression of emotion (as noted by others) corresponds directly to the experience of emotion. This mistaken assumption reflects what Jenkins (2004) calls a 'failure of intersubjectivity': a failure to attend to the subjective experience of the other. There are clear clinical and research implications associated with this failure. Findings such as these point to the grave risks inherent in assuming that the internal state and experience of another can be gauged accurately and reliably by an outside observer without at least checking out these assumptions against the subjective reports of the individual. Here then, we have a prima facie case for the necessity of research into subjective experience if we hope to develop an adequate understanding of schizophrenia/madness, as well as helpful clinical services for those who have such experiences. In passing, it is worth noting that some (such as Healy 2002) have questioned whether or not the difficulties commonly considered to be negative symptoms of schizophrenia may, in fact, be attributable to side-effects of neuroleptic medications, being part of a 'neuroleptic-induced deficiency syndrome'.

Conclusions

Our intention in this chapter was to substantiate our claim that to develop an understanding of madness, we need to recognize, acknowledge and incorporate subjective aspects of the experience (which, by definition, are only accessible to those who have the experience) into our understandings. Unfortunately, as we have shown, this is a much neglected area as far as scientific research into madness is concerned, and an inevitable consequence of this neglect is that our conceptualizations as well as our clinical treatments are diminished. Remedying this situation will require a change of attitude, such that those who have experienced psychosis are recognized as experienced-based experts who can make valid and valuable contributions to our understandings of psychosis. Adopting such a position may require us to develop new ways of thinking about what we mean by madness/schizophrenia/psychosis. In Chapter 6 we outline our framework, which developed out of our own research in this area, and which we believe provides a way of thinking about madness which allows for, indeed assumes, that a multiplicity of perspectives be brought to bear on the complex set of experiences that we refer to as madness. In addition, new methods of doing research, which are more appropriate to investigating such elusive areas as phenomenology, personal understanding, and the meaning of experience and which compliment rather than replace traditional methods, will need to be developed and utilized in order for such research to be done. In Chapter 3, we will discuss our own research into the subjective experience of psychosis which illustrates one way in which such research might be carried out.

Chapter 3

Making sense of madness I

Subjective experience

We are now ready to embark on the journey that is at the core of this book: making sense of madness. Now, before this rather lofty-sounding, perhaps even grandiose title engenders a set of expectations that we would find impossible to satisfy, it might be appropriate at this point to make clear what our aims are here and exactly how we intend to go about the business of making sense of madness. First, we should declare that it is not our intention to endeavour to provide a full and definitive explanation of what madness 'really' is, were such a thing ever possible: our position, as will be stated in Chapter 6, is that, ultimately, it is not. Our ambitions are more humble than this, and hopefully, as a result, more achievable. What we hope to do over Chapters 3, 4 and 5 is to consider some of the ways in which madness can be, and indeed has been, made sense of from different perspectives or positions. Our aim here is to demonstrate the myriad ways in which madness is understood by different contributors to the question of what we are to make of this unusual human experience.

To this end we will, in this chapter, look at those ways of making sense of psychosis which give emphasis to those who have first-hand, lived experience of psychosis. In the two subsequent chapters, we will look at what we know about how ordinary everyday 'lay people' make sense of madness (Chapter 4), before looking at some of the ways in which professionals and researchers in the area of mental health construe the experience of madness (Chapter 5). We should acknowledge that in this overview, we look primarily at conceptualizations of madness found in the English-speaking, Western world. We recognize that this means that we have largely overlooked the vast literature on cross-cultural understandings of madness. We would not wish this exclusion to be seen in any way as a reflection of our position on the relative importance of perspectives from other cultures. As we hope will be clear in Chapter 6 when we put forward our own proposal on how we can respond to the diverse range of models of madness, we value highly the contributions that cross-cultural comparisons can make to our understandings of the experience of madness. Our reasons for not including this cross-cultural literature here are first, it is an area in which we can claim no expertise, and second, while we feel reasonably confident in arguing that our theory of 'essential contested-ness' (Chapter 6) is an appropriate and helpful way to think about madness as it is seen and experienced in the English-speaking world, we suspect that there are others far more qualified than we are who are better placed to consider if this argument might be applied in other cultural settings, where different understandings of madness prevail. Nevertheless, it can safely be argued that the fact that different cultures adopt a range of perspectives is consistent with our basic argument that multiplicities of views about madness exist.

We will now begin our exploration of ways of making sense of madness by considering approaches which focus on subjective aspects of the experience. Clearly, there are many ways in which one could go about covering this wide and diverse area. For example, there are vast numbers of personal accounts of psychosis available in the public domain (in books, journals and on the internet), and these would provide a sound basis for considering subjective aspects of the experience. There is also an increasing body of scientific research which looks into the individual's subjective experience, and this too would be a suitable starting point to this investigation. While we recognize the value of each of these possible approaches to this area, neither will be our main focus in this chapter, although we will provide a brief discussion of both areas towards the end of the chapter.

Our main focus in this chapter will be to present research that we ourselves have done into the subjective experience of psychosis. This research is, in essence, an in-depth analysis of some personal stories of psychosis which were shared in psychotherapy sessions with Jim Geekie: these stories, and our analysis of them, form the bulk of our exploration of the subjective experience of madness in this chapter. We will describe this research and our findings in some detail. In choosing to emphasize our own research, as we have done, we do not wish to imply that this reflects the significance or importance of our research vis-à-vis the vast body of literature expressing and investigating the subjective experience of psychosis. Choosing to focus on our own research here reflects a combination of our close familiarity with this material along with our desire to share our research findings which, we hope, provide a faithful and sensitive portrayal of the subjective experience. Following our explication of our research, we will look more broadly at literature which focuses on, or expresses, the subjective experience of psychosis, including personal accounts of the experience.

As clinical and research psychologists working in the area of psychosis, we have both had a long-standing curiosity about the nature and meaning of madness. This curiosity has, of course, been nurtured by the kind of work we do, where we have the great fortune and privilege to hear, as a regular part of our respective jobs, the stories of those who are experiencing, or have recently experienced, what might be – indeed is – referred to as psychosis. For both of us, our curiosity about madness predates our entry into the profession of clinical psychology, and, rather than being something which emerged out of our work, it is more the case that this curiosity was what guided us into this line of work in the first place. Perhaps as a result of our personal histories, as outlined in Chapter 1, or perhaps reflecting our temperaments and personalities, we found ourselves at relatively young ages wondering about this thing called madness (which, only later in our personal development did we come to appreciate could also be referred to by more technical-sounding terms such as 'psychosis' or 'schizophrenia'). This curiosity brought with it a whole range of questions. What is madness? Where does it come from? What does it mean? How come it happens to some people but not others? Does it have any intrinsic value or is it merely the random ravings of a cracked mind? What, if anything, does it tell us about what it is to be human, about the human condition? What do those who experience madness make of the experience? And, of course, how should we respond to it when it causes distress? How might those who are troubled by madness deal with it effectively? These are, we believe, questions that are, or at least should be, of some concern to anyone who has an interest in what it is to be human, given that madness is, we assert, a fundamental facet of what it is to be human.

So, it was this curiosity, manifested in questions such as the above, which fuelled our desire to work in the area of mental health. It was this very same curiosity, combined with a sense of dissatisfaction with the answers to such questions found in the standard mainstream scientific literature on psychosis (discussed in Chapter 5), which motivated us to carry out our own research investigating the subjective experience of madness. Central to this research is the assumption that those who have first-hand lived experience of psychosis can, if given the opportunity to do so, comment meaningfully on the experience, and can do so in unique ways. This assumption reflects our own clinical experience, where we have found, again and again, that those who experience psychosis have important insights about the experience which we, as mental health professionals, are keen to learn from. We designed our research with the explicit aim of more thoroughly and formally exploring the unique insights that can be found in expressions of the subjective experience of psychosis. One place, we thought, where the meaning of the experience to the individual may be developed and expressed, is in psychotherapy sessions, where these experiences, and their meanings, are explored in some detail. It is our hope that our research helps illuminate understandings of the experience of psychosis, while remaining faithful to the subjective experiences of those who generously agreed to participate in this research. In the following paragraphs we will describe some of the background details and methods we used in conducting this research. Those with little interest in this technical information could skip this section and go straight to the stories themselves (pp. 45–88).

Background to the research

Our research was carried out at an out-patient community mental health centre in Auckland, New Zealand, where one of the authors (Jim Geekie) is employed full-time as a clinical psychologist working with clients who have experienced psychosis. Jim conducted the research which we will describe below as part of his PhD research, under the supervision of the co-author of this book, John Read, from the University of Auckland. A full description of the research described here is available in Jim's thesis (Geekie 2007).

Jim works in a multidisciplinary 'first episode psychosis' (FEP) team, set up specifically to try to assist young people (between the ages of 18 and 35) who are having, or have recently had their first experience of psychosis. Other members of the team include an occupational therapist, a family worker, a psychiatrist and a nurse. This is a government-funded service, which is free to service users at the point of delivery. The FEP team adopts an explicit recovery-oriented philosophy (Deegan 1996; O'Hagan 2001) and endeavours to foster a sense of optimism and hope in clients and families, who are expected to play an active role in negotiating with the clinical team about how the team can best meet their clinical needs. An evaluation of the FEP team found this service is valued by clients and is effective at helping reduce the symptoms of psychosis (Theuma et al. 2007). As a routine part of care, almost all clients of the FEP service will be offered psychological input, though not all will accept this. Approximately 70 per cent of FEP clients will meet with the psychologist at least once and the vast majority of these (approximately 80 per cent) will engage in therapy.

In developing our ideas about this research, we carried out fairly wide-ranging consultation. This included, of course, gaining ethical approval for the research from the local health board ethics committee. In addition, we sought advice from other bodies, such as consumer organizations (Mind and Body, Auckland, New Zealand), cultural groups (in particular Māori and Pacific Island clinical services in Auckland), as well as a wide range of other clinicians (clinical psychologists, psychiatrists, psychiatric nurses, occupational therapists, family workers, social workers) and researchers working in the area of early intervention for psychosis. All those consulted expressed enthusiastic support for the project, stating that it was congruent with their own particular aims and understandings of mental health difficulties, including one consumer consultant expressing regret that she had not been given the opportunity to discuss her understandings of her experience of psychosis when she first became a consumer of mental health services.

Feedback from Māori and Pacific Island mental health services, while generally supportive of the research, included an important caveat: namely, that it was considered impossible and culturally inappropriate for a Pakeha (New Zealander of European descent) researcher to conduct research into Māori or Pacific Island culturally specific understandings of mental health difficulties. This led to fairly lengthy and productive discussions about whether or not Māori and Pacific Island clients should be included or excluded from the study. The advice received on this issue was that these clients should be included in the study, but that an in-depth exploration of cultural themes should not be subsumed within the remit of the research (this was, anyway, very unlikely to be the case, as clients who were eager to explore cultural understandings of their experience as part of their clinical care tended to do so with culturally appropriate clinicians and support workers from the aforementioned clinical services).

Research participants

With this consultation completed, and ethical approval gained, we were now ready to move on to recruiting participants for the research. Essentially, this consisted of Jim Geekie asking clients already engaged in psychological therapy with him if they would be willing to participate in a research project looking at the experience of psychosis. In practical terms, the only difference in agreeing to participate in the research entailed was that meetings between the client and Jim would be recorded using a small tape recorder. To avoid the possibility of actual or perceived coercion, clients who were under the Mental Health Act were not invited to participate in the research. (In fact, no clients were excluded based on this criterion as at the time of carrying out the research, there were no suitable candidates for the research who were under the Mental Health Act.) In total, Jim asked seventeen clients if they would be interested in participating, with fifteen of those agreeing to do so. The two who declined (one male, one female) explained that they would not feel comfortable with a tape recorder in the room as they thought this would make them self-conscious and thus less able to fully engage in psychotherapy. Those two clients did, of course, continue to see Jim for therapy, but this was not recorded for inclusion in the study.

So, fifteen clients in total participated in this research – eleven males and four females, with ages ranging from 20 to 37 years old, giving an average age of 26.8 years old. In terms of cultural orientation and ethnicity, ten participants identified themselves as Pakeha (of European descent), two as Māori, three as Pacific Islanders and two as Asian (some clients identified with more than one ethnicity). Primary diagnoses of participants, made by the psychiatrist working in the FEP team using DSM-IV criteria, were: schizophrenia (six), schizoaffective disorder (three), bipolar affective disorder (two), brief psychotic disorder (three) and schizoid personality disorder (one). All clients had had psychotic experiences as part of their initial presentation to mental health services. All names and other identifying characteristics have been changed to protect the anonymity of participants.

Data and data analysis

The 'data' which our research is based upon is quite different from the usual numerical data found in much scientific research, and as such, required quite different methods of analysis from the usual statistical procedures. Our focus is on the meaning of the experience for the individual, and therefore requires methods of gathering and analysing data which are sensitive to this. Our 'data' consists of recordings of individual psychotherapy sessions where clients shared and explored their stories of psychosis with Jim. These recordings – of which there were sixty-two in total – were transcribed by Jim, to maintain confidentiality. As you might imagine, this yielded a rich and vast data set, consisting of transcriptions of sessions where clients related their experience of psychosis, often in very moving ways and in considerable detail.

Analysis of such a rich data set inevitably presents researchers with the problem of how to go about the business of trying to make sense of such rich narratives. Thankfully, this is a problem that many researchers before us have confronted and have developed appropriate ways of dealing with. Our research is quite firmly rooted in the tradition of qualitative research, some general features of which we have already discussed in Chapter 1. While there are a number of different qualitative research methods, we decided that the approach most suitable for our research was grounded theory, which was developed specifically with a view to establishing a set of flexible procedures which help researchers analyse research participants' views of whatever experience is the focus of the study (Glaser and Strauss 1967). The primary aim of grounded theory is, as the name suggests, to help develop theory which is 'grounded' in the data (remembering that 'data' here is participants' own accounts of their experience). Looking at the role of grounded theory in psychological research, Pidgeon and Henwood (1997) comment that grounded theory can help stimulate conceptual development in the area investigated through identifying themes which permeate the interview material: 'Grounded Theory is most typically well suited to the analysis of the broad "themes" and content of participants' accounts' (Pidgeon and Henwood 1997: 260).

We do not intend to specify in detail the procedures we used for our data analysis, but we do want to point out a few general features of how we analysed the data. Essentially, our analysis involved multiple readings of each interview transcript, looking for and gathering together (or 'categorizing') comments which shared common threads, or themes. Our initial categorization was based purely on the explicit content of the comments and generally used the client's own words in developing categories. For example, the comment 'I feel sometimes that it may be a case of having too many thoughts' was categorized under 'too many thoughts'. This analysis yielded a large number of initial categories (164 at one point). Further refinement of these categories reduced this number to 103, through identifying overlaps and commonalities between various categories which were then subsumed within single categories. Simultaneous to this process of merging overlapping and highly similar categories, the next stage of analysis also developed. This involved looking for patterns and relationships within and between the categories already created. For example, 'too many thoughts' was subsumed with other comments which suggested that some kind of cognitive overload may have caused the experience of psychosis. Eventually, this process led to the development of a complex framework, or map, outlining the various categories and subcategories we developed in our analysis of our participants' narratives about the experience of psychosis (see Figure 3.1 for an illustration of this framework).

While this analysis does, of course, involve us imposing some kind of order on our data, it is, nonetheless largely descriptive in nature in that it involves describing rather than aiming to uncover underlying patterns which explain the data. Grounded theory predicts that through the researchers' immersion in the data, theoretical constructs will 'emerge' as a product of the researchers' deep immersion in and growing familiarity with the area being investigated (Glaser and Strauss 1967; Strauss and Corbin 1990). Though it was with some doubt and reservations regarding this 'emergence' that we entered into this study, we were, in fact, surprised to note that, as predicted, this is exactly what happened. Three theoretical constructs did 'emerge' from this analysis. Though these constructs were refined as the analysis developed, they nonetheless proved robust and enduring in terms of capturing the essence of the data. It is important to acknowledge that, despite our use above of passive-sounding language such as 'emerge', we fully recognize and acknowledge that this is *our* analysis, and that these theoretical constructs did not simply emerge *from* the data, but rather they emerged from *our* attempts to makes sense of the dizzyingly complex data set that we were faced with. They represent, therefore, *our* best efforts to grapple with the stories of psychosis of those who were generous enough to share them with us in this research project.

We will now present our research findings in two sections, beginning with what is essentially a detailed descriptive overview of how participants spoke about the experience of psychosis. Following this, we will present the three theoretical constructs which we developed and which, we hope, help convey something of the essence of the subjective experience of psychosis. Earlier publications (Geekie 2004; Geekie and Read 2008) have provided brief outlines of our research findings.

The experience of psychosis

A brief look at our overall map of the 'experience of psychosis' (Figure 3.1) illustrates the complexity and sophistication of how those involved in our research spoke about their experience and should answer any lingering doubts that one might have about whether or not those who have first-hand, lived experience of psychosis are able to comment insightfully about the nature of

Causes of psychosis

Storytelling and authoring	Psychological factors			Development and experience	Biological factors	Spiritual factors	Functions of psychosis
	Emotions	Self	Info processing				
• Attitude to storytelling	• Low mood	• Disintegration of self	• Imagining	• General experience and history	• Drugs	• Other beings	• Expressing or avoiding painful emotions
• Uncertainty and multiplicity	• Guilt	• Integrity of self, 'leaky mind'	• Interpretations	• Isolation	• Brain	• General spiritual matters	• Giving voice to suppressed thoughts
• De-authoring and invalidation	• Anxiety, fear and worry	• Self sabotage	• Cognitive overload	• Abuse	• Heredity		• Making sense of things
• Diagnoses	• Stress	• Interpersonal sensitivity	• Metacognition	• Interpersonal relationships	• Sub-vocalization		
• Impact of understanding	• Uncertainty	• Perceptual sensitivity	• Questioning fundamental beliefs	• Becoming independent			
	• Jealousy	• Self-esteem and confidence	• Having weird beliefs Internal dialogue				
	• Bottling things up	• Subconscious mind	• Extra-sensory perception				

Descriptions of the experience	Impact of the experience				Responses and coping	Spirituality	Māori issues
	Relationship to self & mind	*Relationships with others and world*	*Trauma of psychosis*	*Attitude to experience*			
• Metaphors	• Loss of faith in own judgements	• Changed relationship with world		• Positive	• Medication	• General spiritual matters	
• Analogous to dreaming				• Negative	• Distancing or detaching self		
• Normalizing	• Sense of discontinuity of self	• Feeling written off, avoided, rejected			• Reality checking	• Spiritual fragmentation	
• State of mind						• Good versus Evil	
• Psychosis reflects mood	• Increased understanding of self and world	• Feeling different from others			• Reframing experience		
• Control & power					• Normalizing by sharing	• Differentiating spirituality and psychosis	
• Explaining hallucinations	• Dampened enthusiasm				• Psychotherapy		
• Feeling connected/ disconnected	• Increased confidence					• Spiritual implications and consequences	
• Personal or 'different' reality	• Misc. changes in self						

Figure 3.1 All categories and subcategories within the experience of psychosis.

this experience. The participants in our research, who, we remind you, were clients of a mental health service receiving treatment for a first episode of psychosis, many still 'symptomatic' (that is, experiencing ongoing psychotic phenomena) spoke eloquently and thoughtfully about the nature of their experience. The analysis which follows provides, we believe, a prima facie case that those who experience psychosis are indeed able to speak meaningfully about their experiences and thus make important contributions to the business of making sense of madness. How great a contribution this can be depends on the willingness of those in positions of influence and power to listen to these voices.

Let us now have a look at what those who participated in our research had to say about their experiences. As can be seen in our overall map (Figure 3.1), we identified seven major categories, each of which subsumes several 'subcategories'. These major categories (which are shown separately in Figure 3.2) will now be discussed in turn. The order we have chosen to present these categories is based partly on the order that, in our experience, issues commonly arise within therapy. This does, of course, vary from client to client, but, as a general pattern, initial concerns often relate to what may have caused the experience, which develops into (and is informed by) a deeper discussion about what constitutes the experience, how it impacts on the person, and what the person is doing, or can do, to respond to the experience. Generally, it would be after these immediate concerns are addressed that more abstract issues relating to the nature of telling one's story and spiritual matters emerge. We have, as far as is possible, presented the data in this chapter to reflect this pattern. The exception to this is that we begin by discussing participants' comments on 'storytelling and authoring', because this provides a helpful context for much of what follows, in that it delineates participants' thoughts about the whole issue of telling one's story (see Figure 3.3). Throughout this chapter, we will, of course, provide examples of comments by participants which illustrate the category being discussed. However, the richness of data, combined with a limitation of space here means we will not be able to discuss each subcategory in detail. We will, instead, provide illustrative examples of selected subcategories which, we hope, will convey something of the richness and sophistication of our participants' accounts of their experiences of psychosis.

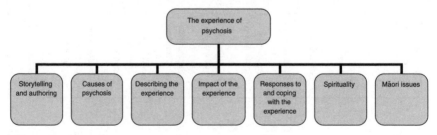

Figure 3.2 Major categories within the experience of psychosis.

Figure 3.3 Storytelling and authoring.

Making sense of madness: storytelling and authoring

Making sense of their experience, whether it was referred to as madness, psychosis, schizophrenia or some other term, was an issue of central importance to participants. The search for meaning was a prominent concern, as was the desire to share this meaning with others. Just how crucial an issue this could be is conveyed by Isa, a young articulate Pacific Island man who experienced what in conventional psychiatric nomenclature would be referred to as paranoid delusions:

> It is only through me understanding it that allows me to carry on living. Otherwise it would just be a void.

Here Isa is suggesting that without meaning in his experience, life itself would be intolerable. He was far from alone in his need to find meaning – and, importantly, personal meaning – in his experience. Others expressed similar sentiments. For example, Sara, an Asian woman whose strong Christian faith had helped her through a period of psychosis which followed the birth of her child:

> Um, just because I mean because I want to find out why it has happened and why it has happened to me.

Paul, a European migrant to New Zealand whose experiences had included hearing voices which both complimented and insulted him, politely and not without some humour explained, after reading an information pamphlet on psychosis:

> Well, yes, that's very interesting. But I need to make my own sense of it.

The desire to make sense of the experience should not be confused with a wish for simplistic explanations, nor for an inability to tolerate uncertainty. Exploring the meaning of the experience, and an openness to consider multiple, sometimes competing understandings characterized participants' attitudes to their own understandings. Moana, a Māori woman who had developed an ongoing complex persecutory delusional system that involved intense hallucinatory experiences, was explicit about her understandings of her experience:

> Yeah. I actually have variations, em, I've got a number of different ways of looking at it.

A corollary of developing a meaningful narrative was the importance of sharing this with others, and crucially, how others responded to this. As part of the process of telling one's story, many reported that they struggled with the feeling of being discounted, defined, or 'invalidated' by others. Participants complained that they often felt that their storytelling capacity (in relation to psychosis, and more generally) was being undermined, as if they were being denied the right to 'author' their own stories. Margaret, a Pakeha women in her thirties who had strong spiritual beliefs which influenced how she understood her voices ('auditory hallucinations'), expressed a sense that being invalidated by others extended beyond her psychotic experience, to feeling that she herself was being written off by friends:

> Well, mine [experiences] aren't being validated as real. All my close friends . . . one close friend from Wellington almost has written me off, doesn't even bother with me now. Because it's almost like 'Margaret is a lost cause to this. There's no way she's going to make it, she's cracked.'

Having one's experience explained in other frameworks, in particular the diagnostic framework, caused difficulties for some, who struggled with the idea that their experience could be explained in diagnostic terms, such as 'psychosis'. This, they felt, invalidated their own authorship, by denying them the right to determine the meaning of their own experience. This was a major issue for Isa, here referring to being diagnosed:

> I feel down when I think other people are judging me or categorizing me.
> I feel good when I feel validated.

Similarly, Raj, an Indian man in his twenties, found having his experience (aspects of which he felt very positive about) explained in terms of psychosis troubled him. While he did see parts of his experience in terms of psychosis, he felt convinced that other experiences he had (in particular, hearing the voice of a deceased loved one) were more spiritual in nature. He felt that the notion of psychosis undermined his belief that parts of his experience were spiritual in nature and this distressed him:

> Being told it's psychosis and then that makes my experience not real.

And it's . . . that's what's made me more confused. Telling me I've gone
through psychosis and all this. It's made me worse in the last two years.
I haven't done anything. It's got me so down and out.

Paul, who as part of his contact with mental health services had been told
by a staff member that his experiences were symptoms of schizophrenia,
challenged this diagnosis as inaccurate, and also unhelpful:

It [diagnosis of schizophrenia] definitely doesn't help you to get on with
your life.

Others, however, reported that they found some solace in being diagnosed,
as it conveyed to them that others had had this experience too. Leon, a
New Zealander of European descent in his early twenties, said:

Oh, I suppose it just lets you know that it's psychosis, that it's not just
you. You know, it's like, other people have had it.

As the comments above indicate, participants identified consequences for
them which were directly attributable to how they, or significant others, viewed
the experience. This was most apparent when the understanding changed
over time. Margaret initially saw her voices as spiritual, but later had come
to see them as a consequence of earlier abuse that she had experienced
and a manifestation of having a negative self concept. She found this latter
understanding reassuring and felt it offered her hope:

I know now, that the voices are just not sort of . . . that I'm not going
crazy, but it's something that I can change.

To sum up this section, we can conclude that the business of making sense,
personally meaningful sense, and having the opportunity to share this sense
with significant others is an important concern for those who experience
psychosis, and that both the sense that is made of the experience and the
response of others have implications for the impact that the experience has
on the individual.

Making sense of madness: causes of psychosis

All participants were interested in considering the possible causes of their
experience, which was commonly the first issue they wanted to address in
therapy. In our analysis, we distinguish between notions of 'causality' and
'descriptions' (the latter will be discussed in the next section). The essential
difference is that within 'causes of psychosis', we include comments about

why the experience occurred, whereas under 'descriptions' the focus is on what it was like to experience psychosis.

A quick look at our overall map of the experience of psychosis (Figure 3.1) will immediately convey to the reader the range and diversity of participants' views on possible causes of their experience. After refining our analysis we found that we were left with thirty-six distinct factors seen by participants as being implicated in the cause of their experience. We were able to impose some order on this diversity, by subsuming these thirty-six factors under five general headings, as shown in Figure 3.4.

Clearly, given the number of causal factors identified by participants, here we are unable to provide more than an overview, with some representative comments by way of illustration of selected notions of causality. What is important to note is that each participant expressed a variety of ways of understanding causes of the experience, rather than adopting a single unchanging perspective. In addition, even within a single understanding of the experience, participants commonly held multi-factorial accounts of causality, rather than attributing psychosis to a single variable. Further, we should hold in mind that participants tended to offer causal explanations for specific experiences (such as 'hearing a voice', or 'feeling confused') rather than operating with broader diagnostic terms, such as 'schizophrenia' or 'psychosis', which might encompass a number of experiences. That is, they operated predominantly within the 'individual symptoms' rather than a diagnostic, syndrome-level framework (see Persons (1986) or Costello (1992) for further discussion of this distinction). Thus, participants may have adopted, say, a psychological explanation for one symptom, a biological explanation for another and a spiritual account for yet another. These notions tended to be held flexibly, as possible explanations, rather than in a rigid fashion.

The five major subcategories of causality, shown in Figure 3.4, were not equally represented in terms of the numbers of specific causal factors mentioned by participants that each subsumes. In fact, there were many more 'psychological causes' (twenty-two in total), than any of the other subcategories. There are a number of possible explanations for this: perhaps as psychologists ourselves we are more able to identity and distinguish psychological causes in participants' comments; or perhaps psychologically minded clients were more likely to see the psychologist and therefore to participate in

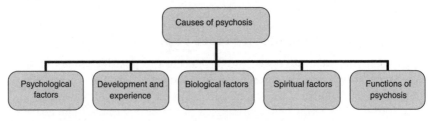

Figure 3.4 Subcategories within the causes of psychosis.

this research. Whatever the reason, we do not wish to dwell on this here as it is not a critical component of this analysis.

So, moving on from these general points, let's look at some specific examples of how participants understood their experiences to have been caused. We'll begin with psychological factors, under which we brought together comments that attributed the cause of psychotic experience to psychological factors typically within the individual. Further subdivisions here were 'emotions', 'the self' and 'information processing'.

Causes of psychosis: psychological

A wide range of emotions were identified as being possibly responsible for causing the experience of psychosis. For example, John, a Pakeha man who had been hospitalized when he became quite disorganized in this thinking and behaviour and was considered at risk of coming to some harm, noted that he had had a car accident a few months prior to becoming psychotic, and felt that guilt relating to this had a role in him developing paranoid thinking:

> I think I was just getting paranoid about the accident. Maybe feeling like, quite a lot of like blame and things on me, from myself.

Interestingly, Spencer, a young Māori man who had also spent some time in hospital during a manic episode with ideas of reference, also saw guilt as implicated in his tendency to experience ideas of reference (the tendency to interpret events as having a personal significance or reference to oneself):

> It's more of a guilt trip, and I suppose I look for signs of the people around me knowing I'm not doing the right thing.

Other participants identified anxiety, stress, and jealousy as being implicated in causing their experience. A couple of participants attributed the experience not to emotion directly, but to their way of dealing, or failing to deal, with strong emotion. Mark, a hard-working man in his mid-thirties, who had a strong sense of responsibility for harmony within his family, and an associated tendency to go to great lengths to keep the peace, had had a psychotic episode with elements of both grandiosity and persecution, and had ended up rather impulsively moving to another city, saw his way of hiding emotions as underpinning much of his experience:

> The manic phase of my experience was exactly what I would in my own term describe as bottling things up.

While the above refer to relatively fleeting emotional states as causing

psychosis, other, more enduring aspects of 'the self' were viewed by participants as having rendered them vulnerable to developing psychosis. One theme
which permeated the way in which many participants understood their
psychotic experiences was that of 'disintegration' of self. By this, we mean
a sense that the self is somehow experienced as not being as coherent as it
might be, with a sense of being 'out of balance' with one's self often being
conveyed. Michael was a young, friendly and amiable Pakeha man, a talented
musician, who prior to experiencing a wide range of psychotic phenomena,
including distressing visual hallucinations, had been outgoing and seemingly
confident. However, this did not correspond to how he experienced himself
while experiencing psychosis:

> Everyone's got a place, but I haven't got a personality or anything. I'm
> not in sync with my personality and my self or anything.

Moana, in her own insightful and philosophical way, often generalized
from her own experience and understanding to articulate a more general
explanation for people experiencing mental distress, expressing here her profound and moving notion of conflict within, brought on, as the context makes
clear, by a disintegration of the self as causing psychosis:

> Well, we're actually struggling with ourselves. If we're mentally ill,
> the characters that we make up in our sickness are just parts of our
> selves.

Other aspects of 'the self' identified by participants as causally related to their
experience of psychosis, but which, unfortunately, lack of space prohibits
us from discussing here included the notions of having a 'leaky mind', self-
sabotage, interpersonal and perceptual sensitivity, low self-esteem, and the
'sub-conscious mind'.

The final subcategory within psychological causes of experience is that of
'information processing'. Here we collated comments where participants
indicated that how they process information is causally implicated in the
origins of psychosis. Janet, a woman in her late twenties who had experienced
voices and other hallucinatory phenomenon on and off since her childhood,
saw these as being the result of how her imagination works:

> To me what I experience, like when I go into my little world is just
> imagination. I don't see it as part of the mental health.

Sometimes complex and sophisticated notions such as 'metacognition'
(thoughts about thoughts), which, by the way, psychologists have only in
recent years come to investigate in relation to psychosis, were identified

by participants as having caused their psychosis. Isa expressed his general understanding of mental illness, based on his own experience, succinctly:

> I constantly think that the notion of mental illness is a misconception. All it is, is failing to understand your own thoughts.

Other aspects of information processing seen as contributing to psychosis included developing unusual ways of interpreting information, feeling cognitively overloaded, and questioning one's fundamental beliefs and values.

Causes of psychosis: development and experience

While participants did seem to have a strong tendency to identify internal psychological factors as important in bringing on psychosis, this did not preclude attributions which saw life experience as also contributing. As noted already, participants had no difficulty with – indeed we could say they had a strong preference for – multi-factorial understandings of the causes of their experience. There were a number of comments that attributed psychosis to past experiences in a general sense, without singling out specific instances. For example, Margaret, reflecting on what might have caused her psychosis, commented:

> The past. Because I have had so much of it in my life that I perceive everybody as rejecting me when actually they're just being themselves in their own space.

An experience which was notable in participants' stories was having spent prolonged periods of time feeling, and being, socially isolated. This was the case for Kevin, a shy young man who had an almost painful sensitivity to how others were construing him and who was convinced that isolation was a factor in causing his psychosis, a theme echoed by many participants, and expressed with poignant simplicity by Leon:

> For me I think it was just like being left on my own too much.

The general notion here was that participants saw their loneliness as creating a vacuum which was filled by the psychosis.

Other factors identified as possible causes of psychosis included conflict in interpersonal relationships, difficulties associated with becoming independent, and abusive experiences (sexual abuse, bullying, and emotional abuse). Illustrative of the tendency for sophisticated explanations of the experience, which not only identified the cause, but also specified how this cause might operate, is Margaret's moving reflection on her abuse:

When you saw the way my father used to behave around me and that, I think well no bloody wonder you've got a mind like that, Margaret. When your father bloody [whispers] exposes himself in front of you and things like that. Unintentionally, you've got to sit there and look at it. No wonder you've got this shit [voices] going on inside you. No wonder you feel dirty and unworthy.

Causes of psychosis: biological

Many participants posited the notion that biological factors were also involved in the development of psychosis. Commonly, when biological factors were referred to, it was in a fairly broad general sense. Under this heading we find comments which see the brain, usually without further specification, as being implicated. The context makes clear that these participants were referring to the brain in organic terms, rather than using the term to refer to psychological processes within the brain. Here, Janet expresses this position clearly:

I always believed that it was to do with my brain.

This sometimes coincided, not surprisingly, with participants identifying, again in a fairly general sense, hereditary factors as being involved. Again, Janet expresses her thoughts on this succinctly:

I thought just that I'd been born with something not right.

A number of our participants had used recreational drugs (mostly cannabis and LSD), and some saw drug use as having contributed to their experience of psychosis. We included this under biological causes because, as the wider context makes clear, when they spoke about drugs, participants were generally referring to them in terms of their biological effects on the brain. While many participants spoke about drug use and psychosis, not all agreed on what kind of relationship, if any, existed here. In fact, a number of different relationships between drug use and psychosis were expressed, sometimes by the same individual. For example, in one session, Leon reported having a smoke of 'weed', after having none for a year or so, and felt this caused paranoia:

So, not very good. Cos I haven't had it for like more than a year. So, I did after that, got a bit paranoid.

Whereas later, he expressed a quite different position:

Nah, never. It's definitely not brought on by drugs, my psychosis.

Others, such as Isa, also expressed more positive thoughts about cannabis use, suggesting that it was either unrelated to psychosis, or that it helped open up new ways of thinking which he found helpful:

> I just find that for some strange reason it [cannabis] effects . . . I don't know . . . maybe the chemistry in my brain, on a level that I can't reach when I'm not using, but in a positive way.

Another biological theory for explaining psychotic experience (in this case auditory hallucinations and associated delusional beliefs) was developed by Tony, a Pakeha man in his mid-twenties whose rough and ready appearance and manner seemed incongruous with his great sensitivity and capacity to reflect on and express his own subjective experience. He reported that he had noticed that when he heard voices, he also felt an unusual sensation in his voice box:

> Just been wondering if my . . . like, if this chatter's turning into some-thing in my voice box and I'm speaking under my breath unconsciously.

Initially, Tony considered that this belief of his was probably delusional in nature:

> It's a feeling I have had for a while, that is in my throat and it's kind of like a delusional feeling that there's something going on there.

He was surprised, but reassured to hear that his ideas corresponded closely to a theory of auditory hallucinations ('sub-vocalization') that respected researchers had developed and found evidence to support (Gould 1949).

Causes of psychosis: spiritual

One of the most pervasive features of how participants spoke about their experience, and which marks a clear departure from how mental health researchers and clinicians tend to speak about psychosis, was their interest in spiritual aspects of the experience. As we will see throughout this chapter, spiritual matters were of great important to those who participated in our research (and, our experience tells us, to many clients of mental health ser-vices). At this point, we will concentrate only on those comments which suggested a causal role for spiritual elements.

Some expressed the view that spiritual matters of a fairly general nature had somehow contributed to the cause of their psychosis, often involving notions of 'good' and 'evil'. Moana:

I spent probably the last eight months thinking about the Devil and thinking that He's after me and thinking 'far out, what is this about, who's after me?' You know, someone out there's got a problem with me, and like, em, yeah, I think it's probably caught up on me now.

Leon also often mentioned spiritual themes when he spoke about how he felt his psychosis had come about:

Yeah, spiritual, like all your things that you've done bad, and you've done good, and it makes you laugh and it makes you depressed to the extremes, makes you like wear emotions to the extremes. It seems like something pre-planned but not really.

A couple of participants felt that some of their psychotic experiences may have been produced by spiritual beings, through some kind of influence or 'possession'. Generally these theories were associated with some distress for the individual as they felt themselves subject to some form of attack by a being beyond their control. Michael, demonstrating flexibility in how he thinks about his experience and a willingness to entertain competing explanations, nonetheless clearly considers external spiritual influence as one plausible explanation for his experience:

Yeah, but it's either coming from these beings, whatever they are, or it's coming from my head, from me.

Moana, who, as we have already seen, often drew upon her own experience, as well as the experiences of other clients (who she had met in hospital or in groups), was confident that those who experience psychosis often attribute their experience to spiritual interference:

I think a lot of us think that there are spirits that play around with us and that there is actually something out there that's shooting things into our head.

Causes of psychosis: functions

The final subcategory within understandings of possible causes of psychosis is somewhat different from the others in that here we find the idea that psychotic experiences perform a particular function for the individual, and this is seen as explaining why the psychosis occurred. These functional explanations tended to be psychological in nature. That is, the psychotic experiences were seen to have been caused by the need for the individual to address certain emotional or cognitive matters. There is considerable overlap between functions of psychosis and other notions of causality noted above. The essential difference here is that it is the function which the psychosis serves (for example, overcoming depression) which is seen as causing the experience, rather than the difficult feeling (for example, low mood) itself.

Some viewed their psychosis as reflecting, and having been caused by, their own way of expressing or avoiding painful emotions. Tim, a European man who had a fully blown manic episode, accompanied with strong, grandiose thoughts relating to his 'saving' the music industry by becoming a major rock star overnight, saw his manic episode as being his way of dealing with underlying feelings of inferiority:

> I suppose maybe that was my attempt to crush my inferior feelings. Maybe I just thought if I push myself to be just overly confident then I wouldn't get those em ... cos I was thinking that when I was in the manic state that I was about how I used to be, and I would laugh it off and think, I'll never be like that again.

Moana commented that psychosis had helped cure her from depression, a theme which she expanded on to suggest that the psychosis had in fact saved her from suicide:

> It was like a miracle cure for my depression or something, but I haven't experienced it since. Like, it's almost like I feel like I've been walking my whole life quite depressed and suffering from something, and all of a sudden it's cured.

A couple of participants (Moana and Paul) suggested that their psychotic experiences functioned to help them avoid addressing difficult emotional issues, by distracting them from the matter. The context of these comments indicates that both saw this as having a causal component to it. Paul notes that while in the midst of his psychotic experiences he was able to feel good about himself, as it allowed him to ignore major changes in his life which threatened his sense of well-being:

> See I was feeling good about myself and about life and about everything. So that I, for me to accept that, that something has changed, would be like everything around crashed on me. So this way, I felt so alive, I felt so good about everything.

Janet and Tony both felt that hearing voices was sometimes their way of giving voice to suppressed thoughts, which they felt unable to express, even to themselves, using more conventional means. Janet felt that her voices helped her express her true wishes:

> Em, part of me is thinking that it's like instead of being voices there in my thoughts, maybe that's what I'm wanting to do.

Whereas Tony felt that his voices expressed what he did not want to express:

> Yeah, it's like, kinda like . . . what do I want to say, like can't really find it, so what I don't want to say starts coming up.

Making sense of madness: describing the experience

We have seen above that participants came up with a wide range of different ways of thinking about what may have caused their experiences of psychosis. We will now move on to the next major subcategory of how participants related their experience of psychosis: 'Describing the experience'. In this section we have collated, and further categorized, the ways in which participants explained what it was like to experience psychosis. That is, this section relates to participants' efforts at conveying what they felt was happening when they had psychotic experiences, rather than attempting to identify the origins or causes of the experience. Subcategories that we identified within this section are shown in Figure 3.5. Again, due to lack of space we will be able to give only selected examples of the rich diversity of ways in which participants described their experience of psychosis.

While it has often been suggested that people who experience psychosis, or who have a diagnosis of schizophrenia, tend to be 'concrete' thinkers, with a limited ability for abstraction, we find that when participants described their experiences, metaphors were often invoked to convey a sense of what it felt like to be psychotic. These metaphors vividly capture important aspects of subjective experiences which often do not submit easily to description. These metaphors help convey a greater sense and understanding of the experience to the clinician and so can open up new ways of thinking about the experience and new avenues to be pursued in terms of therapy.

To express the richness of these metaphors we provide several examples here. Describing her distorted visual experiences (which were at least partly

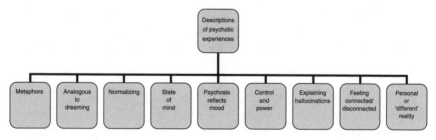

Figure 3.5 Ways of describing the experience of psychosis.

hallucinatory) and the associated sense of alienation, Janet used the metaphor of watching a sped-up movie:

> And it feels like things are happening so fast like you see on some pro-grammes how people just stand there and the world goes by. That's what it feels like. That I'm standing there and the world's rushing by and I'm just sort of standing there.

Leon used a metaphor from the world of computing (defragmenting a hard drive) to describe his sense of falling apart when psychotic. This metaphor provided him with a framework which not only described the experience, but also indicated steps to remedy this situation, which included his understanding of how medication worked for him:

> It's like defragmenting, you know, in a computer, and all the bits go back into the right places, or you've got to put them back, and that's what the medication helps do.

The struggle to contain the feelings of pressure associated with the voices in his head is captured by Tony's metaphorical image:

> Em [laughs], it's kind of like trying to hold a balloon under water. When I am feeling bad, the balloon keeps getting bigger and bigger and harder to hold under the water.

One specific analogy that featured in a number of accounts was that of liken-ing the experience of psychosis to the experience of dreaming. Moana:

> I thought it was similar to dreaming, because I couldn't figure out, I just could not figure out.

In describing their experiences many participants used a 'normalizing' framework, comparing the experience to normal processes. The psychotic experience was described as a process which most people experienced (possibly taken out of context as a result of increased scrutiny) or a normal response to a difficult situation. The common thread here is that psychotic experiences are considered a normal aspect of human experience, rather than being qualitatively different experiences. Tony saw aspects of his experience as an inevitable and normal response to having too much free time:

> Em, got a lot of time on my hands to think about things. Except even when I was working it still happens. Em, I don't know. I don't see myself as much different from other people.

Four participants referred to their moods when trying to describe their psychotic experiences, and commented that they felt that the psychosis was an expression or reflection of their underlying mood (though they did not imply, in these comments, that there was a causal relationship between mood and psychosis). Kevin notes that when he listens to his voices:

> It sounds like it's mirroring the way I am inside. I mean I notice the negative stuff in other people.

The issue of control over experience was something that some participants discussed. Some described their psychotic experiences as consisting of a sense of losing control of one's thinking or feeling. Janet reported that when she experienced a hallucination:

> It almost like feels like you're losing control of your mind.

Similarly, Michael, describing how he feels when he experiences ideas which he feels are not fully his own:

> It's like, this is me right, and I'm back here, I'm not up the front control-ling me, like feeling like I'm controlling me. I'm back here feeling like I'm out of control.

Participants who experienced auditory hallucinations were generally asked, as a routine part of therapy, how they discriminate the experience of a 'voice' from that of a 'thought'. This line of questioning led participants to describe in some detail the experience of hearing a voice, and to identify the properties of the experience of hallucinations that distinguish them from thoughts. The general notion within conventional psychiatric literature is that voices are distinguishable from ordinary thoughts because they have an audi-tory quality that thoughts lack. That is, the difference between thoughts and voices is seen as being phenomenological and perceptual in nature. This is consistent with how Tony described his auditory hallucinations, saying it was like:

> Having an audio thought without producing it myself.

This is a description which fits comfortably with the standard notion of auditory hallucinations found in psychiatric textbooks, with the emphasis on auditory aspects of the experience. However, others who heard voices described them quite differently, and differentiated them from thoughts on quite different grounds. Michael identifies voices as being different from thoughts based on voices being experiences which he has no notion of having produced intentionally:

> Yeah. It doesn't feel right, because like something will just pop out of my mouth and I'll be completely, like I wasn't even there when I said it sort of thing.

Whereas Janet differentiated thoughts from voices based on the content:

> But if it speaks about you, if it says 'you should' or something like that, then that feels like a voice.

Another criterion used by participants to identify an experience as a voice was that of 'unfamiliarity'. That is, if the grammar or vocabulary of the experience felt unfamiliar, then it was deemed to be a voice. This is explained by Tony (who had also described some of his voices as being auditory in nature):

> It's like, em, it just doesn't feel like it's something I've thought of. Or the actual sentence would be a sentence I wouldn't usually use in my dialogue.

These various descriptions of the experience of hearing a voice suggest that there may be different processes involved in how people (even the same person) come to construe experiences as voices. If this is so, this does, of course, have important implications for the kinds of interventions that might be offered to help someone deal with the experience of hearing a voice.

The sense of being connected or disconnected from the world and from other people was an issue of considerable importance for three participants. Those for whom this was an issue tended to see it as being fairly central to the experience. There was some suggestion that the early stages of psychosis are more characterized by feeling 'connected', whereas in the latter stages a sense of 'disconnection' is more evident. This was apparent in Paul's story. He reported that at the earliest stages of his experience:

> I was so connected to everything, to the air, to like throughout the distance, like clouds and stuff, and to music.
> Everything was connected to me, was that . . . like my I don't know, spirit or something, was here, or was there as well. I was spaced out in a way.

However, he characterized his experience later on as consisting of more of a feeling of disconnection:

I would feel like I was put in some box, you know. And like I would just look in through this here, but I'm in a dark box and I'm looking somewhere outside.

John also reported that being psychotic felt like being disconnected from himself and from his past:

I felt disconnected, more disconnected, when I couldn't work out what I was doing in the past.

Janet described her experience as having more a sense of profound, disconcerting social disconnection:

Like I don't know. Like I don't know if I belong here, or what.

Making sense of madness: impact of the experience

The next major category in our analysis relates to the impact of the experience on the individual. Before looking at the variety of ways in which participants spoke about how the experience of madness impacted on them, it's worth noting that this impact was expressed, some of the time at least, as something both pronounced and profound in terms of its magnitude. Isa captures the intensity and seriousness of this:

I feel that my experience was powerful. It, em, it could only have done one of two things my experience: killed me or made me stronger. And it's made me stronger.

Participants spoke at some length about the various ways in which the experience of psychosis affected them. We further subdivided these into major subcategories as shown in Figure 3.6. The major subcategories relate to the part of the person's life most affected, as well as more general issues such as the person's attitude to the experience, and the trauma of the psych-

Figure 3.6 Subcategories within impact of psychosis.

osis itself. Further subdivisions within these major subcategories are shown in the overall map of the experience of psychosis (Figure 3.1).

Among the most profoundly moving of our findings was the impact psychosis had on how participants viewed themselves and their minds. It seemed that the experience of psychosis sometimes shook the very foundations of the person's sense of self, leading the person to question some of the most fundamental aspects of being. One of the most pervasive and troubling features of this was in participants coming to doubt their own perceptions and thoughts about the nature of reality. Often, this extended to feeling quite unsure about the ability to distinguish reality from 'non-reality'. While in the literature this is commonly considered an aspect of psychotic experience itself, here participants are commenting on the impact of having had psychotic experiences. Many participants had, during their period of psychosis, developed ideas about how the world is, or what is going on in the world, that were quite different to the beliefs they had held before becoming psychotic and also different to the beliefs of those around them. For many, when this period passed, and they came to doubt much of what they had held to be true while psychotic, they found themselves confronted by more general doubts about their own ways of making sense of and understanding the world. This commonly led to questions for the individual about his or her own judgements, and a loss of faith in one's self.

For many, the experience of loss of faith in judgements about the world seemed to pervade many aspects of being and cast doubt upon many areas of life, leaving the individual feeling very uncertain and rather fragile. This doubt generally developed shortly after the individual had emerged from a period of psychosis, and lasted for a period of time while the person gradually reacquired confidence in him or her self. The enormity of this loss of faith in oneself is conveyed by Paul, who was troubled by this immediately after having a brief, but pronounced psychotic episode:

I think that's sort of shaken my belief system and my direction in life, you know my purpose in life. Sort of like my belief system, my self, my personality you know.

As he elaborates on this, Paul makes clear that he sees his uncertainty as attributable to the psychosis:

The realization that it was a dream or a made up reality, makes you lose all the foundation, and you don't know what to believe any more. And now you basically seem like you have to start from scratch, your life, because everything was shaken around you.

Mark described feeling in a remarkably similar predicament shortly after emerging from a psychotic episode which had been characterized by his developing quite unusual persecutory beliefs:

> I extremely became very doubtful of my own judgements, my balance, my perceptions. Probably just like starting again and retraining myself, even in the normal things of life like driving and reading. Am I perceiving them right, understanding when I read? Like, life's just completely starting again in primary school [laughs].

Margaret felt troubled about her ability to identify what is 'real' in the world, which she saw as a natural consequence of having been psychotic:

> Suddenly finding out that what they thought was real isn't. That would frighten or disturb anybody. What the hell am I supposed to believe? I can't even trust myself any more.

She went on to ponder a question with profound significance for her:

> How in the future am I going to know what's real and what isn't?

While some expressed general doubts about their judgements, others focused more on one particular aspect of being that felt most affected by this. Michael felt somewhat uncertain and estranged from his own emotional world:

> It's like I'm incapable of feelings. I don't know if my feelings are fake or not.

This contrasts with Margaret, who noted that while she doubted many aspects of her being, feelings were the one thing she could rely on as being accurate:

> I do know feelings are real. You can't create those. That's impossible. That's one thing. I will always rely on how I feel. The mind is a write off as far as I'm concerned.

It would be hard to overstate the significance of the loss of faith in one's self that the comments above express. This issue was of crucial importance to participants who expressed doubts about fundamental aspects of the self, such as trust in one's own perceptions. Having these aspects of life called into question as a result of the experience was, for many, a disconcerting experience where one's foundations were shaken, resulting in great uncertainty. Questions of this nature ('Can I really trust what I perceive?'; 'How do I know who I am?') seem to us to be primarily questions of a philosophical nature, which relate to well-established areas of study within philosophy, such as 'epistemology' (theory of knowledge) and 'ontology' (the nature of being). Given this overlap, we came to see these impacts on self and mind as relating to what we termed 'personal epistemology' (one's views of one's own ability to acquire trustworthy knowledge) and 'personal ontology' (one's personal view about how one can go about 'being in the world': the nature of one's personal being). Both of these were significantly shaken by the experience of psychosis, which often left the person facing quite profound uncertainties about aspects of life and living that most of us, most of the time, simply take for granted.

The usually gradual process of rebuilding trust in oneself was often a focus of therapy, and commonly something that participants spoke about. Mark explains the way in which he managed this, through evaluating how he dealt with situations, and gradually learning to trust himself (at other times he spoke about checking out his perceptions with trusted others as being an important part of this process):

> Well, as life goes by one day at a time and you do the normal things that you should do, it's coming back just by maybe a little repetition of maybe the same thing. Or simply that nothing has actually gone wrong while I have been trying to get myself back on track. And so if I can trust, 'OK that went all right', so I can try doing the next thing. OK that went fine. That means I can trust myself in those two avenues. The next one and the next one, just like steps.

Not all of the ways in which psychosis affected the individual were of a negative nature. Some reported that they felt that as a result of the experience they now had a different and richer awareness and understanding of themselves and of the world. Some reported that as a result of the psychosis they felt that they were now more aware of their own internal experiences in a positive way. Tony commented that as a result of hearing voices, he pays for more attention to himself generally, and more specifically his thought processes:

> I never studied myself that hard until I had the psychosis. I have never really em . . . never really listened to myself talking.

For others, the impact was not only on awareness of internal experience, but on their general understandings. Isa:

> If I hadn't gone into that black hole [psychosis], I truly believe I wouldn't be where I am now. I feel like I know myself better, understand myself

better. And, I know it sounds funny, but I feel like I understand people better too.

Participants also spoke about their relationship with the world in a broad sense (including both the material and the interpersonal world) having been affected through the psychosis. Generally, the direction of this impact was for the person to feel a greater distance between self and world, although this was not always the case. For example, Paul, for whom this issue of feeling distanced was of considerable importance, noted, when reflecting on the time he first had psychotic experiences:

My impression is that my involvement, my experience of the world was increased.

However, this contrasted sharply with how he felt in his post-psychotic state:

It's almost like I've been cut from the world.

One of the more specific interpersonal consequences of having been psychotic was a kind of social stigma, which includes the sense of having been written off by other people; the feeling that others no longer considered the individual to have a valid contribution to make to discussions. Margaret, who was a member of a religious group, felt this acutely. She struggled with feeling that her experiences were seen by other members of the group purely as signs of psychosis, with none of the spiritual significance she believed the experiences to have:

Well, I feel very rejected at the group because I've not been validated when I thought I was having true experience.

Margaret's sense of being invalidated by others extended far beyond just feeling that others did not accept her understanding of her experience. She felt that, as a result of having had a mental health problem, she herself had been written off:

Well, I feel like I've been written off as a bloody nutcase, like my mother was written off too. But my mother was having very profound experience.

Mark also felt that his experience of psychosis had influenced how some friends viewed him:

I meet people they are sort of looking at me like 'he's had a bit of a breakdown; he has had psychosis; he was a bit nutty' [laughs]. So, I have got to put up with the fact of people looking at me and thinking 'Is that strange or is that normal?'

Others reported that one aspect of this was that others would now keep more of a distance. Spencer noticed:

My neighbours have backed off from me since I've been unwell. That's OK.

Despite the fact that the vast majority (although certainly not all) of the comments about the impact of psychosis conveyed negative ways the experience had impacted on the individual, attitudes of participants to the experience of psychosis were not uniformly negative. Every participant experienced some distress associated with the psychosis, which is not surprising since they are clients of a mental health service and people who find psychotic experiences disturbing are far more likely to use mental health services than those who do not. Nevertheless, we see also that some expressed both positive and negative attitudes towards the experience. Sometimes a positive attitude to the experience was expressed in a quite unambiguous fashion, where the experience of psychosis was clearly highly valued. Raj had had an intense, but relatively brief, episode of psychosis, characterized by ideas of reference and delusions which had a strong spiritual theme. While Raj believed that these did develop into psychotic experiences he remained convinced that the initial phases of the experience were spiritual in nature and were a positive experience for him:

It felt so comforting. Like I had done the greatest thing in the world, or I'd been blessed by the greatest thing in the world.

Margaret also viewed much of her experience in spiritual terms, expressing a strongly positive attitude:

I was the happiest I've ever been in my life. It was the best thing in my life that had ever happened to me, that I had experienced.

Others expressed a positive attitude to the experience which implicitly recognizes that there were aspects to the experience which were not viewed so positively. Moana often spoke about how interesting she found her psychotic experiences:

Sometimes I find that there is a part of me that does like it and that's purely because my imagination is quite stimulated. It's like that whole creative side of me is stimulated.

However, illustrating the coexistence of both positive and negative attitudes to the experience, even within the same individual, Moana also found aspects of her 'imaginings' difficult:

> It's really annoying, because em, because nobody wants to sit around imagining cutting people up.

Similarly, Tony had a curiosity about hallucinations which meant he initially welcomed these experiences, though he found that this did not last long:

> The visual hallucinations I just have no concern over, like they can't hurt me, but the audio ones are really distressing to me.

Making sense of madness: responses and coping

Another area of great practical concern to participants was how to respond to and/or cope with the experience of psychosis (see Figure 3.7). This is, of course, to be expected, given that all participants were clients of a mental health service and that these comments come from psychotherapy sessions, where the focus would often be on coping with difficult aspects of the experience. Under this broad heading, we include the individual's own strategies for dealing with the experience, as well as participants' comments on interventions (such as medication and psychotherapy) provided by the clinical team.

The majority (approximately 80 per cent) of participants of the first episode psychosis team will be using psychiatric medication at any one point, with an even higher percentage having been on medication at some point in their involvement with mental health services. It is not surprising therefore to find that participants often spoke about medication matters. Participants expressed a range of opinions about the role of medication, with sometimes the same individual expressing quite different positions at different times.

It was relatively common for participants to express some ambivalence about the use of medication to help cope with their psychosis. This often involved weighing up the perceived benefits and disadvantages of medication,

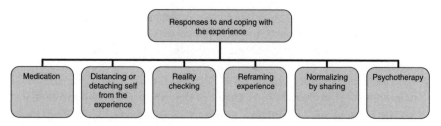

Figure 3.7 Responses to and coping with the experience.

and using this balance in deciding whether or not they would continue using the medicine. Here, Michael explains his decision-making process:

> I've weighed them [pros and cons] up and I think it may as well be better than what it was before I was on drugs [medication].

Leon also used a kind of cost-benefit analysis to govern his decision regarding using medication:

> It's not good, the bad things that happen. It's not good being on medication or anything. But it's quite good em . . . like I feel like I'm better off now than I was before.

Others were clear that the medication had a significant negative impact on them. This did not always translate into the person stopping medication, but was certainly an important influence on how they felt about the medicine. Spencer expressed his concern that the medication is a way of avoiding difficulties, something which he saw as inherently problematic:

> I thought that medication is more of an automatic run away from the situation.

Others, such as Michael, were more negative about how taking the medication made them feel. Although Michael continued to use medication consistently, he complained:

> It's like it's taken my whole self and just dampened everything so nothing can happen. I'm not able to work things out, it's like my brain isn't doing anything.

At other times, a more positive attitude to the medication was expressed. Tony expresses this in a straightforward manner:

> All I really know is the pills work.

Michael, despite feeling that the medication turned him into a 'bit of a zombie', nonetheless noted:

> I'm feeling better. It's because of the medication, I'm pretty sure.

Isa, somewhat like Spencer, felt that the medication did not truly help him tackle his problems and expressed some pride about managing his difficulties without the use of medication:

> I've been feeling quite good about myself, yeah and about not taking medication.

This helps convey a position that many participants expressed regarding medication: namely, that they saw it as one of the ways in which they could cope with the psychosis, though generally a strategy that had some disadvantages.

Of course, those who experience psychosis develop their own ways of dealing with distressing aspects of the experience, and this was also true of participants in this research. One commonly adopted strategy for dealing with psychotic experience was to try to detach or distance oneself from the experience psychologically (this could also be referred to as 'distracting'). For example, Moana was clear that being engrossed in her 'imaginary world' was not good for her, and she endeavoured to distance herself from this:

> It's like when I'm in the moment of imagining things, that's when I think things are real. But when I get some distance from them, then I know they're not.

Other ways of dealing with the experience involved some kind of investigation of the experience, or what we might call 'reality checking'. This consisted of using another frame of reference (either within the self, or from another person) to evaluate the experience. Margaret found that she could check out whether her internal voices were real or hallucinatory by using 'sensory correspondence': that is, by seeing if she also perceived the experience through the more reliable (to her) modality of sight:

> I'm not ever listening to this [points to head] again. I'll never ever in my life listen to another voice. For it to be God or somebody, I have to see it. It's gotta be in front of me. I'll have to see them like I'm seeing you.

Moana sometimes applied what she called a 'scientific perspective' to her experience. This involved her weighing up various pieces of evidence, or deliberately seeking contrary evidence, which helped her decide whether or not the notions she had about harm she feared she had done to others actually corresponded to real events. It did not, and she generally found a lack of evidence to suggest that she had caused any harm:

> I had to sit down and I had actually to tell myself, you know, it's not true. I had to find evidence, I had to find, you know, flaws in, you know, the whole story and just focus on those.

While Moana reported that this approach often helped her, she noted it was not foolproof, as sometimes she found that even when confronted with contrary evidence, this did not persuade her that she could, or should, dismiss her original thoughts about having harmed others:

> Even though things haven't corresponded out here, I find a way of looking at it so that there's an explanation of why that hasn't happened. I can make an excuse to myself. I can alter things to protect my theory.

Another way of checking one's experience was to ask another person to see if they had, or hadn't, perceived what the participant had perceived. Mark explained that when he had ideas that he felt were unusual, he did not find it helpful to try to work these out on his own, but this did not trouble him as he found asking another trusted person worked well for him:

> Because I was starting to think you can't always change the way you feel but you don't have to, do you? You just get a more reliable opinion.

Some participants found that an effective way of dealing with psychosis was by looking at the experience differently, or by reframing the experience. This may have involved, as it did for Moana, trying to develop a whole new way of looking at the world and processing information:

> I feel like I'm reprogramming my brain. I feel like I'm having to reprogramme the way that I used to . . . to get back to the way I used to think.

Margaret was more specific. She came to see her troublesome voices as being an expression of her own guilt about having been sexually abused as a child. While this new understanding did not have an impact on the voices themselves, it meant she was far less troubled by them:

> I found myself sitting on the bed saying to myself this morning, 'don't worry Margaret, it's just the guilt coming up, let it go, focus on something positive'. I'm talking like that to myself 'it's just your past coming up, guilt, just let it go, let it go'.

Some found sharing the experience of psychosis with others very helpful. This sharing sometimes involved simply speaking with a sympathetic friend or hearing about the stories of other service users. The common thread was coming to see psychosis as being a shared human experience, which seemed to help normalize the experience and so make the individual feel less troubled by it. Janet found that telling her friend about her experience had been helpful to her:

> I said to my friend, 'Oh, they've classed me as psychotic'. And she went, she asked like what I mean. And I said, 'Like, I hear voices and I see things and I feel like I could quite easily go out and harm someone'. And she goes, 'Oh, I think everyone can do that'. And it was like, oh well, maybe I just don't have anything wrong with me.

One of the things Moana found most helpful about having had a short stint in hospital was hearing other people talking informally about their own experience:

> And I heard stories about other people; that just brought me back down to earth.

Moana felt quite inspired by others' stories, so much so that she sought out published first-person accounts of psychosis and used these to help her conceptualize her own experience:

> The only reason I wanted to read about other people, was to see some examples that would blend in with mine.

Making sense of madness: Māori issues

As has already been explained (pp. 42–43) while Māori participants were not excluded from the study (and two participants identified themselves as Māori), on advice from Māori mental health services, issues specific to Māori culture were not the focus of the present study. Both Māori participants in the study did have contact with Māori cultural support workers. However, despite this, there were times when aspects of Māori culture in relation to the experience of psychosis were mentioned by participants. Here, we want only to acknowledge the importance of these cultural issues, and to recognize that they did emerge in the clinical interviews with participants. We accept and agree with the advice given that a proper investigation of Māori cultural matters in relation to psychosis needs to be undertaken by someone who has a good understanding of Māori culture. For the purposes of the present report, we wish only to respectfully mention these issues. Examples of the kinds of issues mentioned include references to Māori spirituality, such as this by Moana:

> There was this guy who em, he slept in a marae [meeting house], and he ended up getting possessed. And when he was possessed, he started blurting out all these words of Māori, and he couldn't speak Māori. And, anyway, they basically got rid of the demon or whatever that had possessed him. Apparently, he'd slept under, you know how they have

the Māori carvings, they're actually individual tribal leaders. And apparently, one of them was dark, and so he'd been possessed by, you know.

This now brings us to an end of the first stage of our research findings. What we've presented is essentially a summary of the numerous and diverse ways in which participants in our research spoke about the experience of psychosis. Admittedly, we have imposed some kind of order in terms of how we have presented these comments, by gathering together comments that we saw as similar. We believe that the examples we have given above convincingly convey the complexity and sophistication of how those who experience psychosis can, if given the opportunity, speak about their experience, and further that there is clearly a role for those who have first-hand, lived experience of psychosis to contribute to the debate around what it is and how to assist those who may be troubled by it. Interesting and important as these issues are, this was not the end of our research project.

Another objective of our research was to see if we could, through our deep immersion in the data, find some broader ways of making sense of the experience of madness. What we mean by this is we hoped to develop some explanatory concepts (or 'theoretical constructs') that would capture something of the *essence* of the subjective experience of madness and do so in way that has practical implications for how we work clinically with those who have such experiences. We will now outline this aspect of our research findings.

Making sense of madness: theoretical constructs

We developed three theoretical constructs ('fragmentation–integration'; 'invalidation–validation'; 'spirituality') which, we are proposing here, convey some of the essential elements of the subjective experience of psychosis. These constructs cut across and subsume many of the descriptive categories listed above. We see these three constructs as being more explanatory in nature, in that we are using them here to try to abstract from our participants' accounts of their experience some core features of the experience of psychosis, which might help us develop our theoretical understandings of what is going on when someone experiences psychosis, and by extension, our clinical and research approaches to these experiences. Implications from our research for theory, research and clinical practice will be discussed in the final chapter of this book. We should explicitly acknowledge that these constructs come from us: we developed them as our way of making sense of our participants' accounts of their experience. We believe they offer us new and (we hope) more helpful ways of thinking about the experience of psychosis and that they do so in a way which remains true to the lived experience of the individual.

We chose to refer to these as 'constructs' to acknowledge the influence on our thinking of the American psychologist George Kelly's (1955) theory of personal constructs. For Kelly a 'construct' is a psychological process, bipolar in nature, which we use to make sense of, relate to and navigate our way through various aspects of the universe. Examples of common constructs might include 'good–bad' or 'edible–inedible'. In Kelly's theory each construct has a limited 'range of convenience' (or range of situations in which it tends to be applied). As we shall see, the first two constructs ('fragmentation–integration' and 'invalidation–validation') fit the bipolar format of a construct as described by Kelly, whereas the third, 'spirituality', does not readily fit this format, although we do not see this as problematic. For each construct, we will give a brief definition followed by a consideration of the aspects of the experience of psychosis which this constructs covers (or, in the language of personal construct theory, its 'range of convenience'). As broad-ranging explanatory constructs, these are, necessarily, somewhat abstract in nature. However, we will provide specific examples in the form of quotes from participants which should illustrate the relevance of the constructs to specific aspects of the experience of madness. The order in which we now present our three theoretical constructs is not intended to indicate any particular relationship or hierarchy between the constructs.

Theoretical constructs: fragmentation–integration

The construct 'fragmentation–integration' refers to various aspects of the individual's experience of psychosis. What we hope to convey by this construct is a sense of a loosening (or, less often, tightening) of connections and associations between aspects of experience for the individual. This relates to a sense of 'wholeness', and the notion that a central aspect of psychotic experience is that this sense of wholeness can become 'fragmented', or, at the other end of the construct, that there can be a sense of 'integration', though it seems that this is less pronounced in psychosis. Largely, the experience of fragmentation is associated with a loss of harmony, whereas integration may be associated with a sense of well-being.

The various aspects of the experience of psychosis encompassed by this construct (its 'range of convenience') includes the individual's experience of self, of other people (the interpersonal world) and of the material world. Each of these reflects important aspects of participants' worlds which were implicated in the experience of psychosis in ways that we feel can be subsumed by fragmentation–integration construct.

Fragmentation–integration of self

In terms of the experience of self, participants often spoke about psychosis in ways which suggested that this had important implications for and on the sense of self, commonly conveying a feeling of fragmentation of parts of the self. Here, what we are suggesting is that one of the core features of madness is the individual's experience of self, which is changed in important, often disconcerting ways, reflecting, commonly, a sense of fragmentation of different aspects of the self.

In considering the descriptive categories outlined above, we can see evidence of this fragmentation of self in some of our participants' notions of causes of psychosis. For example, within those causes of psychosis under 'self' we find many which attribute the cause of psychosis in a way that conveys a sense of a self not at one with itself (such as 'disintegration of self' and 'leaky mind') and also the self attacking itself ('self-sabotage'). Similarly, where participants identified emotions as causes of psychosis we find suggestions of discord or loss of harmony within the self. For example, seeing 'guilt' as causing psychosis suggests a person ill at ease with aspects of the self. Many of the metaphors participants used to describe their experience also convey some discord within the self (in fact, one such metaphor, from Leon, was of psychosis as being akin to 'defragmenting' a computer, which contributed to our use of the term here). When considering the impact of experience we find further evidence of fragmentation as illustrated in experiences such as the sense of 'discontinuity of self'. A sense of fragmentation is also conveyed by some of the ways participants coped with psychosis (particularly those involving distancing and detaching self from the experience). The notion of 'spiritual fragmentation' (see below, page 86) also clearly conveys a sense of personal fragmentation.

We can think of this sense of fragmentation of self as related to both the experience of self in the here and now, where the self was felt not to cohere, not to fit together as it once had, as well as to the experience of self over time, where the sense conveyed was of there being discontinuity between the self felt now and the self in the past, as if the continuity which holds the self together had somehow been fractured. The extent of this sense of fragmentation, both in the here and now, and over time, varied from seemingly pervading the experience of self to being more limited to particular aspects of self. Both of these were distressing, troubling experiences for participants who expressed a sense of grappling with the very essence of the self, which was conveyed as ethereal, changing, and failing to provide firm ground upon which to stand.

Fragmentation of self in the here and now

A sense of the self in the here and now being quite out of synchrony with itself in a fairly pervasive way permeated participants' stories. This is captured in Michael's comment that conveys the intense existential discomfort associated with the experience:

> I haven't got a personality or anything. I'm not in sync with my personality and my self or anything.

John expressed this sense of feeling internally disconnected, when he reflected on what had been going on for him when psychotic:

> I felt disconnected, more disconnected, when I couldn't work out what I was doing in the past.

Moana also saw a kind of internal fragmentation as being at the core of psychosis:

> It means that we're actually struggling with ourselves.

Fragmentation of self: lack of continuity over time

Another way in which the self seemed fragmented was over the course of time, where the continuity of the self was broken or interrupted as part of the psychotic experience. This was not delusional in nature (for example, believing that the self had been replaced or altered by an external force), but rather related to the experience of the phenomenology of self and the sense that the individual struggled with the felt experience of continuity, such that the current self felt quite different from the self before psychosis. This sense of loss of continuity of self is expressed by Michael, who laments that he finds it hard to recall how things were before he had his psychotic episode (the context here made clear that he was not literally talking about remembering events, but rather remembering how he used to feel):

> I can't remember anything about what life was like before.

The sense of confusion and loss associated with this disruption to the self is evident in Paul's comment:

> I can see the world and everything, but I don't seem to, you know, see it with the same eyes as I used to before, you know. So, I think that maybe, you know, as a result of what I went through, maybe I have changed, but I don't know what has changed about me.

Integration

At the other end of the 'fragmentation–integration' construct as applied to the self, there was the occasional sense that, through psychosis, the person came to feel more integrated, more at one with the self. This was much less pervasive than fragmentation. Nonetheless, there were elements of participants' stories which did suggest that psychosis was, at times, associated with a sense of integration of the self. As is apparent in the quotes which follow, integration was much less distressing (and often not distressing at all) than the experience of fragmentation. For example, in ways in which participants spoke about causes of psychosis, both 'making sense of things' and 'giving voice to suppressed thoughts' suggest that, in some ways at least, there was a sense of a coming together, or integration, of aspects of the self. Moana noted:

> The way this sickness developed, it was so logical. It just came together and explained everything.

In this context, the 'everything' she referred to included a range of disparate thoughts and feelings she had been experiencing. Tony's comments also suggest that the experience of psychosis was associated with increased awareness of and unity of the self:

> It [psychosis] made me just more aware of the mind I have.

> I never really studied myself that hard until I had the psychosis. I never really, em, never listened to myself talking.

Here, he is speaking of his internal, sometimes hallucinatory, voice as being a part of himself which he had hitherto ignored, but had now come to attend more to.

Fragmentation–integration of interpersonal world

The 'fragmentation–integration' construct can also be applied to how participants spoke about their experience of the interpersonal world in the context of having been psychotic, with there being a sense of social relationships being fractured or breaking up. Some of participants' notions of causes of psychosis, such as 'isolation', 'abuse' and 'interpersonal relationships', seem to indicate some difficulties or fragmentation of the interpersonal world. Similarly, when describing the experience of psychosis, the notion of this constituting a 'personal or different reality' suggests a person cut off somewhat from other people. This fragmentation of interpersonal relationships seemed to vary depending on the particular phase of the psychotic experience. Margaret identified increased distance in relationships and associated isolation as having helped create the conditions within which psychosis could emerge:

> I was going home at night, spending a lot of time on my own, watching TV, shutting myself in the house for weeks and weeks. Now, when you do that you can get quite withdrawn and introverted, and you can . . . that's how I can see that I must have created it.

Paul also noted that in the period leading up to his first contact with mental health services, he had become increasingly isolated, which he felt had contributed to him appearing thought disordered when he tried to communicate. He notes that this situation perpetuated itself as his communication difficulties exacerbated the fragmentation of his interpersonal relationships:

> I guess maybe, probably, the reason for that is probably that I have been isolated maybe for some time, and I have lost that, you know, that touch for people and stuff. And, like, that has put a distance between me and other people.

This sense of finding it difficult to relate to others was reported as an important concurrent aspect of the experience of psychosis. That is, fragmentation of relationships was also part of the psychotic experience itself, not just a precursor to it. Sara expressed this when reflecting on her second psychotic episode and how removed from people around her she felt:

> Yeah, the second time I was feeling that I was the only person. I didn't belong to anyone. I was alone.

Sometimes the feeling of being different from others and therefore struggling to connect persisted beyond the psychotic episode itself and seemed to relate in a more enduring way to how the person had come to see him or herself as a result of having been psychotic. Paul:

> I guess from that moment on I felt much more different from other people.

He went on to explain the impact that this had on his social world:

> It's like something has been taken away from me, that's how it feels. Like it's put a wall between me and you know maybe, in a way, other people.

At the other end of the construct there is much less evidence of integration in the interpersonal worlds of participants. There may be some limited suggestion of integration in some of participants' ways of coping, such as 'reality checking' which for some involved asking other people about experiences. Also, in 'normalizing by sharing' there is some sense of the importance of the interpersonal world and the need for at least a degree of integration for this to occur. There was the occasional comment that through the psychosis the individual felt more connected, or more integrated with the interpersonal world, although how far this translated into actual relationships was unclear.

Michael felt that as a result of having been psychotic, he was now more tuned into aspects of interpersonal relationships that he had been insensitive to before:

> I am more aware now of the unspoken connections between people.

Fragmentation–integration of the material world

Fragmentation also characterizes aspects of how participants spoke about their experience of the material world, describing feelings of being disconnected from the world which seemed at times to be something they witnessed but felt quite cut off from. This sense of fragmentation in relation to the physical world is captured beautifully by Moana:

> I feel everything feels kind of surreal and I feel like I'm floating around in some magical bubble.

Paul felt similarly disconnected (or fragmented) from the material world around him:

> I would feel like I was put in some box, you know. And like I would just look in through this here, but I'm in a dark box and I'm looking somewhere outside.

The seriousness of this sense of being detached from the world is illustrated in the following quote, also from Paul, who explains in a matter-of-fact, detached way that he could easily have killed himself when he felt this way:

> Yeah it was really extreme. You just feel detachment. You just feel detachment. You just don't feel a part of anything. Just feel like maybe you'll go to a building and jump off.

These feelings of detachment for Paul seemed to characterize how he felt towards the end of, or shortly after, a psychotic episode. At other times, he reported that he had felt a much greater sense of connection to the world, a greater integration with the world. Here, Paul reflects on how he felt just as he was becoming psychotic:

> My impression that my involvement, my experience of the world was increased.

He went on to explain how intense this felt:

> I was so connected to everything, to the air, to like throughout the distance, like clouds and stuff, and to music.

Here, Paul's experience of the material world would appear to be located much more towards the integration end of the 'fragmentation–integration' construct, and his quotes above convey movement from one end of this construct to the other, in terms of how the world is experienced. In Paul's case, there seemed to be a temporal effect, where the early phases of psychosis were characterized by a sense of integration with the world, whereas in the latter stages fragmentation was more pronounced. Of course, it is impossible to be certain about this based on the current research, though it does point to the possibility of a relationship worthy of further investigation.

Theoretical constructs: invalidation–validation

The second theoretical construct, 'invalidation–validation', refers to what are, surely, essential and fundamental characteristics of being human: the sense of feeling confident in one's ability to accurately perceive and understand experience and to convey this to one's self and to others. The 'invalidation' end of the construct relates to the experience of having one's authority (or 'authorship') over the interpretation of experience called into question, undermined, ignored or rejected, whereas 'validation' refers to having one's understanding of experience supported, confirmed, or 'validated'. We see this experience of invalidation as relating to both the experience of self and of the interpersonal world.

Invalidation–validation of self

In terms of relationship with self, participants spoke about experiencing a personal loss of faith in their own judgements about the interpretation and meaning of experience. This is clearly a crucial aspect of human existence: the feeling that one can rely on the information received from the senses and can trust what this information means. Personal invalidation can be seen clearly in some of the ways in which participants spoke about the impact of psychosis, such as the 'loss of faith in own judgements'. Personal invalidation incorporates the personal loss of trust in one's own 'personal epistemology' (personal view of one's own ability to acquire trustworthy knowledge) and 'personal ontology' (personal view about how one can go about being in the world) as mentioned earlier (pp. 66–67). Also included here are doubts expressed about various aspects of one's personal ways of understanding and being in the world, including doubts about cognitive, emotional, and perceptual judgements.

Janet expressed doubts about her own cognitive capacities when reporting what was the worst aspect of psychosis for her:

Doubting myself, my own judgements.

Similarly, Paul doubted himself:

I have found myself always questioning my own thought processes.

Michael came to doubt the extent to which he could trust his own emotional responses, feeling uncertain about how 'real' these were:

It's like I'm incapable of feelings. I don't know if my feelings are fake or not.

Perception was also called into question by those who had had perceptual disturbances (generally hallucinations) as part of the psychotic experience. Paul expresses the loss of grounding that this caused for him:

Psychosis is like having your eyes closed. Nothing you see is making you grounded.

Others expressed this sense of invalidation within the self in a more general sense of coming to distrust the self, without specifying particular faculties. Margaret:

What the hell am I supposed to believe? I can't even trust myself any more.

At the other end of this construct, personal validation, we find an expression of a need for this in participants' accounts of their experience. This is evident in the process of 'reacquiring trust in one's own perceptions' as well as in participants' comments about the importance of putting their story together not only for sharing with others, but also as a way of 'self-validating'. John:

I just hope I'll be able to make sense of the whole lot.

Raj:

I just need to know what it is.

Neither of these, as the contexts make clear, is a request for an explanation to be offered, but rather they are expressions of the desire for developing a personal understanding of the experience, a form of self-validation. We see the importance of developing a personal understanding of experience also in Sara's comment:

I want to find out why it has happened and why it has happened to me.

Invalidation–validation in the interpersonal world

In addition to this sense of personal invalidation, participants' accounts expressed a feeling of being confronted with invalidation in relationships with other people. This social (or interpersonal) invalidation consisted of feeling that others questioned or undermined one's capacity to adequately understand and communicate one's experience. As such, this has an overlap here with elements of the descriptive category in Figure 3.3 above, 'Storytelling and authoring', and, in particular, the subsection on 'De-authoring and invalidation' (some of the quotes used here were also used in these earlier sections). This interpersonal invalidation extended beyond the feeling that one's capacity to explain the psychotic experience was being invalidated, to feeling that, more generally, one's entire self was being 'written off' or invalidated. This was how Margaret expressed this feeling:

> Well, I feel like I've been written off as a bloody nutcase, like my mother was written off too. But my mother was having very profound experience.

Raj felt that having his experience labelled as 'psychosis' by others was a form of invalidation:

> Telling me I've gone through psychosis and all this. And I just . . . it's made me worse in the last two years. I haven't done anything. It's got me so down and out.

At the other end of the 'invalidation–validation' construct, some expressed the importance to them of the sense of being validated by self or by others, the sense of being recognized as a valid author of one's own experience. Here, Isa's comment seems to point to the contrast between the two ends of this construct:

> I feel down when I think other people are judging me or categorizing me. I feel good when I feel validated.

In this context, validation referred to a combination of feeling that one's understanding of a given situation was accurate and reliable, and to having others accept, rather than question, one's understanding (that is, it contained aspects of both personal and social validation). This desire for some form of validation from others was an important consideration, expressed in a variety of ways. We could consider the enthusiasm participants had for telling their stories (as well as having them listened to, of course) and the importance they attached to this reflects a desire for validation. In addition to telling their stories, both Isa and Moana specifically asked if they could write down their story and, importantly, that the author (Jim Geekie) would read them. This seems to be a clear expression of the importance of validation. Isa:

> I have never felt so right about anything as I feel about telling my story.

Leon commented on the importance of receiving validation from others also, noting that he felt he obtained this from attending one of the FEP team groups:

> Going to the groups and stuff [helped me] and you hear people having the same sort of things, like people, em, like people talking about you and stuff.

Moana also commented that she enjoyed reading first-hand accounts of psychosis because this helped validate her own experience and understanding.

Theoretical constructs: spirituality

The final of the three theoretical constructs is 'Spirituality'. As already noted, this construct is different from the other two theoretical constructs in that it does not fit within the bipolar structure as, unlike the first two constructs, this does not have an 'opposite' end (at least, we were unable to come up with one which we felt genuinely fitted with the data, rather than just reflecting our desire for uniformity in our three theoretical constructs). Now, 'spirituality' is a term which has different meanings depending on the context, so we should clarify what we mean by it here. What we are referring to here is an inclination to view the experience of psychosis, or aspects of it, in terms of a broad framework of meaning, pertaining to how the individual views his or her relationship with the universe. That is, a tendency to place the psychotic experience in a metaphysical context where it is considered to reflect something of existential or moral significance for the individual (for example, relating to the purpose of life or to the nature of 'Good and Evil'). Generally, this involved moving beyond explanations of psychosis which locate it purely within the material world (though this is not to imply that these explanations were rejected by the individual), to seeing psychosis as having, in one way or another, a bearing on the individual's understanding of the meaning of life and relationship with the universe in the broadest sense. Sometimes this involved the participant referring specifically and explicitly to external spiritual beings (such as God, the Devil, or simply 'spirits', as in spiritual causes of psychosis, which we discussed earlier in this chapter), or to non-physical aspects of self (such as 'the soul'). At other times no such specific beings were invoked, though it was clear from the context that the participant saw the psychotic experience as being of some relevance to metaphysical matters.

Spirituality as an aspect of psychosis was an issue for most participants, though in quite different ways and to differing extents. Relationships between psychotic experiences and spiritual matters were often of central importance to participants. In addition to notions of spiritual contributions to causality, there were other important connections between psychosis and spirituality in participants' stories, which are summarized in Figure 3.8.

The broadest aspect of the spirituality–psychosis connection in participants' accounts was the tendency to view the experience of psychosis in a spiritual framework without necessarily specifying details of the nature of this relationship. Here, psychosis was seen as somehow bound up with the spiritual world, which provided a way of thinking about the experience within a framework which helped render the psychosis meaningful and sometimes more manageable. Moana was particularly interested in spiritual matters, despite holding no clear-cut religious beliefs of her own. When discussing her psychotic experiences she often mentioned spiritual themes. Her perspective on this matter is summarized in her brief comments on her psychosis:

> There's a whole spiritual story surrounding all of this.

In many ways this comment provides a useful summary for the position of many participants, who viewed their experience in broad spiritual terms. Isa:

> Now I see my voice as being like a spiritual journey.
>
> Deep down, I think it's spiritual.

Raj also explained, regarding his 'ideas of reference':

> I was getting a lot of signs everywhere. Everything was for a reason. That there's something out there. Sort of made me believe in a higher power once again.

Figure 3.8 Ways in which 'spirituality' was present in the experience of psychosis.

There were aspects of viewing the experience in spiritual terms that caused some dilemmas for participants. This was particularly the case for Moana. Although she generally found her psychotic experiences troublesome and wished she could prevent these happening, she found herself asking a profound but pragmatic question of her experience:

> But, I keep thinking, what is that? What if that's my soul?

This, not surprisingly, left her feeling very ambivalent about 'treatment'. After all, who would take 'treatment' aimed at altering or even eliminating the soul?

Some participants reported that since having their psychotic experience they felt less 'together' or less integrated spiritually, somewhat out of sorts with themselves on a spiritual level. This was something that seemed not easy to convey, but was clearly a troublesome matter. Michael:

> That's why I sort of say that I am in a zombie state. It's like I'm not conscious to everything, that I don't feel in sync with my spirit, I guess.

Moral matters overlapped with spiritual matters for participants. The perennial issue of 'Good versus Evil' was one which permeated some participants' stories. Sometimes this issue was expressed as a deeply personally matter, where participants found themselves confronted with questions regarding viewing themselves as either 'good' or 'bad'. At other times, these notions were expressed in a more universal fashion, relating to the abstract concepts of 'Good and Evil' often conveyed in terms of 'God' and 'the Devil'.

Participants who held strong spiritual beliefs and who felt that spiritual matters played a major role in their psychotic experience often struggled to clearly differentiate these two domains: the spiritual and the mental. Some flip-flopped in terms of how they construed their experience, at times seeing it in terms of spirituality, at other times in terms of psychosis. Commonly participants found it very difficult to make a clear demarcation between psychosis and spirituality and put forward arguments that it was, in fact, impossible to differentiate these experiences in terms of phenomenology. Margaret was particularly vociferous about this matter. After much thought and discussion, she concluded:

> What is the difference? How do you differentiate between a true schizophrenic and a true spiritual experience? You can't.

This was not a theoretical question for participants, but rather one with practical implications. After all, quite different responses would be indicated depending on whether one viewed the experience as psychosis or spirituality.

Again, Margaret was able to convey the essence of this dilemma, when she posed what was a rhetorical question (as the context made clear: she had already concluded there was no answer to the question):

> You know, do I have to keep coming here forever every time I hear what I think is a spiritual voice? Does that mean every time I have a spiritual experience I'm gonna have to go on more medication?

Finally, we come to participants' reflections on spiritual implications of having been psychotic. This was not a matter of concern for all participants. Most did not appear to consider that there were any personal spiritual implications that derived from the psychosis. However, there were two participants for whom this was an issue, and for those two it was particularly troublesome. No-one expressed this more clearly nor more frequently than Moana. She felt convinced that as a consequence of having had (in her mind) immoral, unethical thoughts while psychotic, there would be a price to pay. The magnitude of her concerns is conveyed in her simple comment, which at the time she meant quite literally:

> I feel really condemned.

This now brings us to the end of what has turned out to be a rather lengthy discussion of our research into the subjective experience of madness. We have outlined our three 'theoretical constructs' which, we believe, go someway towards conveying something of the essence of the experience of madness. We see these constructs as having important practical and theoretical applications and implications, which we will discuss in Chapter 7. We have also shown, in the first stage of our analysis, the diverse ways in which those who experience psychosis talk about the experience. We hope we have provided a convincing case that those who experience psychosis are able to make a unique and valuable contribution to the business of making sense of madness. This is, after all, not at all surprising and should not really be a contentious claim, given that in most, if not all, other areas of life, we fully appreciate that first-hand, lived experience must be acknowledged and listened to if we wish to develop an understanding of the experience in question. The notion that we might be able to make sense of madness *without* attending to the voices of those who know what it's like from the inside strikes us as, frankly, bizarre as well as being damaging in that it silences those who may be struggling within themselves to articulate an aspect of human experience that is sometimes painful, often confusing, but something that we must, surely, listen to more carefully if we genuinely want to understand this particular aspect of what it is to be human.

Before ending this chapter we will discuss briefly other accounts of and research into the subjective experience of madness. We have already outlined (Chapter 2) some of the principles behind research into subjective experience as well as providing arguments to support the position that such research is important in the area of mental health. Here, we wish only to refer to research and personal accounts of psychosis which relate to our research findings outline above. Inevitably, due to constraints of space, our coverage of this literature will be highly selective in nature.

Research into the subjective experience of madness

A study with some similarities to our own research was carried out in Denmark by Larsen (2004), who investigated the experience of fifteen clients of a Danish first episode psychosis service, through three research interviews over a two-year period. Like us, he reports that finding personal meaning in the experience was of central importance to clients who, like the clients in our study, demonstrated flexibility in their ways of understanding the experience. Larsen (2004) emphasizes that meaning-making is an active process and the individual draws on a range of sources available to him or her, including spiritual factors. Similar findings are reported by Wagner and King (2005: 142), who studied psychotic clients in Brazil, and found that for these clients exploring the meaning of their experience was the primary concern: 'Existential needs were the most important and pressing theme for people with psychotic disorders.' They go on to note that this was an issue rarely addressed adequately in clinical settings: 'The overriding issue for patients was dissatisfaction with their existence and a lack of meaning' (Wagner and King 2005: 144).

In yet another corner of the world, this time South India, Corin et al. (2004) report similar findings. They found that the search for significance and meaning was one of the main themes for first episode psychosis clients, although this contrasted with family members who saw this as unimportant. Similar to our research, they report that clients describe a loss of meaning (fragmentation) and loss of position (invalidation) as well as spiritual concerns. They suggest that there is something about the nature of psychosis that makes it resistant to understanding within a single frame of reference.

In the USA, Vellenga and Christenson (1994) interviewed fifteen 'severely mentally ill' out-patients, who were long-term clients of mental health services, and they looked for common themes in participants' accounts of the experience. They identified four themes which they see as characterizing the experience for the individual: a sense of stigmatization and alienation; a feeling of pervasive distress; reaching a form of personal acceptance of the experience; and the desire for this acceptance to be shared by others (family and friends). Again we can see similarities to our findings where the importance of finding meaning, and sharing this with others are major considerations for those who experience psychosis. As such, one might imagine, clinical services designed to assist those who experience psychosis should be sensitive to this issue in how they work with clients. Sadly, this seems not to be the case as research which looks at clients' experiences with mental health services commonly finds that this is an area where clients feel their needs are disregarded. This may be a result of a discrepancy between how mental health workers tend to construe mental health difficulties (in terms of 'illness') and how clients construe their difficulties.

Jenkins (1997) carried out a fairly large-scale study in the USA, involving interviews with eighty patients of Latino and European origins, who had received diagnoses of schizophrenia or depression. Jenkins (1997) notes that in discussing their mental health difficulties, very few participants (16 per cent) invoked the notion of 'mental illness' explicitly and without prompting, with even the more general notion of 'illness' of any sort being used by fewer than half of those in the study. In another research study Knight and Bradfield (2003) looked at how individuals felt about being diagnosed by a health professional as having a 'mental illness'. Although a small-scale study (with only three participants), this study, by paying such close attention to the participants' own accounts of the experience, nonetheless manages to shed light on this experience in ways that quantitative research approaches rarely do. They found that the experience of being diagnosed is overwhelmingly negative for the individual concerned who reports feeling that a part of the self is 'colonized' by the diagnosis. Also there are social implications, with the individual diagnosed reporting a fear of being rejected by others, and a growing sense of alienation and isolation, combined with a sense that there is now a lack of 'validation' from others. This study is a good example of how an in-depth, qualitative investigation can illuminate the area being investigated, even with a small sample size. A similar finding is reported by Barker et al. (2001) who conducted semi-structured interviews with eight clients with a diagnosis of schizophrenia and eight family members. They found that the first episode of psychosis tends to be characterized, by both clients and family members, as consisting of disruption to one's life and difficulty in making sense of the experience. They report that clients complained of finding professional explanations unhelpful and of feeling unheard by professionals.

Closer to home (for us), the New Zealand Mental Health Commission has produced a number of excellent reports which focus on the subjective experiences of mental health service users. These include pamphlets on subjective aspects of mental health difficulties as experienced by Pakeha clients and their families (O'Hagan 2000a), forensic service users and their families (O'Hagan 2000b) and from Māori (Fenton and Te Koutua 2000) and Pacific Island (Malo 2000) perspectives. Common threads which run through this series include a general feeling of discontent with mental health services, associated with the narrow medicalization of the individual's experience to the exclusion of other ways of making sense of madness, such as cultural and spiritual frameworks.

Studies which have looked at the individual's experience of self report findings consistent with our concept of 'fragmentation'. For example, in the study by Jenkins (1997) mentioned above, participants conveyed a sense of being ill at ease with self and the world which Jenkins refers to as being out of step with the 'rhythm of life'. In a study carried out in New Zealand, Walton (1995) investigated subjective experience, using a qualitative methodology involving in-depth interviews with ten long-term clients of mental health services with diagnoses of schizophrenia. She concludes that in terms of subjective experience, schizophrenia can best be characterized as constituting a quite distinct 'way of being in the world' (in the Heideggerian sense). Walton (1995) explains that this consists of the mind-body experience being altered, which she suggests relates to the nature of 'being with self', 'being with others', and more generally 'being in the world'. She concludes that the subjective experience of schizophrenia, rather than consisting of discrete symptoms, effects one's 'whole being in the world'. Again, this seems very similar to our notion of fragmentation, as applied to the self, the interpersonal world and the material world.

What we see, from the research we have outlined above is, we believe, a considerable degree of congruence between our findings and those of other researchers in the field. The subjective experience of psychosis is characterized by the search for a personally meaningful way of making sense of the experience, which may include exploration of spiritual aspects of the experience for the individual, along with a desire to have this meaning at least respected by others ('validation') and feelings of distress ('invalidation') when the individual's capacity to author his or her own experience is undermined by others (or, sometimes, by the experience of psychosis itself). Combined with these experiences, researchers also report that psychosis is commonly associated with the experience of a breaking of personal and interpersonal connectedness ('fragmentation'). This congruence of research findings, along with encouraging feedback we received from participants in our research when we shared our analysis with them, and feedback we have received from other researchers and clinicians (when we have shared our research findings at conferences and such like), suggests to us that our analysis, and our three theoretical constructs are valid and helpful ways of conceptualizing the subjective experience of psychosis.

First-person accounts of the experience of psychosis

The research discussed above gives some indication of the ways in which subjective experience can be the focus of formal research investigations, and demonstrates that these studies can yield important insights about the experience of madness. Such research aims to 'bridge the gap' between the scientific research characterized by remote 'objective' methods and first-hand lived experience. Another important though much less formalized source of information about the nature of subjective experience in schizophrenia is found in the 'first-person' literature: that is, personal accounts of the experience of psychosis. These accounts come in a variety of forms, and can be found in a range of sources. It is, sadly, exceptionally rare for these first-hand accounts to be incorporated (or even acknowledged) within the professional, 'scientific' literature on schizophrenia. A massive gulf exists between the professional, 'objective' accounts of what madness is and the first-hand accounts that have been offered by those who have had these experiences. Before giving further consideration to this first-person literature, it is worth familiarizing ourselves with arguments that have been made regarding the contribution to our understandings of experience that first-hand accounts can provide.

From a philosophical position, writers such as William James and George Santayana have argued that knowledge of an experience from the inside is different from external knowledge. While James' (1902) focus was the nature of religious experience, the philosopher, George Santayana (1948) argued that, in relation to madness, certain aspects of the experience are available only to the person who has the experience:

> The physician knows madness in one way: he collects the symptoms of it, the causes and the cure; but the madman in his way knows it far better. The terror and the glory of the illusion, which, after all, are the madness itself, are open only to the madman or to some sympathetic spirit as prone to madness as he is.
>
> (Santayana 1948)

Greater attention to subjective experience can help correct mistaken assumptions which an over-reliance on 'objective' ways of knowing may entail. Ridgway (2001) argues that first-person accounts can help question the dominant discourse of the times (such as the notion that schizophrenia is an 'incurable deficit' syndrome) as first-person accounts may contradict aspects of this discourse – in particular, the notion that there is no hope of recovery: 'First-person narratives are important source materials that can help us refocus our thinking beyond the myopic and outdated deficit perspective' (Ridgway 2001: 336).

One example of a first-person account which forces us to question our assumptions regarding the treatment of schizophrenia is provided by Tomecek (1990), who first attacks the notion that schizophrenia should be viewed as a brain disease then goes further in suggesting that for him schizophrenia is a way of being in the world that involves an element of choice. Tomecek (1990) acknowledges that this way of being can be problematic, but, for him, it is associated with artistic expression and 'being gifted' and is, in certain respects, preferable to being 'normal'. He expresses anger at the idea that schizophrenia should necessarily be treated with a view to eliminating the condition. Accounts such as this force us to recognize and question the often implicit assumption that madness ought to be 'treated'.

Rufus May (2003), who is a clinical psychologist occupying the rare, though not unique, position of being both a practising clinician and himself having had personal experience of madness, argues that exposure to other people's accounts of the experience of and recovery from madness can have important therapeutic value through helping engender hope in those who may be struggling with their own experience of psychosis: 'Meaningful accounts of psychosis that allow us to connect with others and make choices about our lives are essential to any recovery process' (May 2003).

Attention to subjective experience, either through research which focuses on subjectivity, or through consideration of first-person accounts of madness is an essential requirement in the dual quest to understand the nature of the experience and, where appropriate, to offer hope and assistance to those who may find such experiences troublesome. This is not to deny the importance of 'objective' research into madness, but rather to argue that such research, on its own, is inadequate. Writing in the early 1960s, in his introduction to a collection of first-person accounts of madness, Kaplan (1964: ix) looks to the future and considers the contribution that such accounts may make to psychiatry: 'One is led to speculate that patient psychiatry might make a meaningful contribution to our understanding of mental illness.'

While Kaplan's speculation has taken considerable time to start to bear the fruit promised, as discussed in Chapter 2 there are now signs of a subtle shift within the literature on madness such that subjective experience is coming to be given more attention and the gulf between 'objective' approaches to madness and the subjective experience may be lessening somewhat as research which endeavours to bridge this gap becomes more prevalent, so creating greater opportunities for syntheses of the various ways of understanding madness available to us.

In terms of first-person accounts of madness, there is now a vast literature in this area, where individuals have, in their various ways, documented their own personal experiences of madness and made these available to the public. These are often moving, sometimes painful, sometimes humorous, always informative, deeply individual expressions of the human aspects of the experience of being, or having been, mad. It is worth noting that there is also a growing literature on the experience of psychosis, written by carers and family members (for example, Lachenmeyer 2000; Olson 1994).

Given the vast quantity of first-person accounts that are available, it is impossible to provide an in-depth analysis of the content of this literature here. Instead, we will endeavour to provide an overview that will, hopefully, convey something of the extent and diversity of this literature. This diversity is apparent not only in the content of first-person accounts of madness, but also in the format. While written narratives are by far the most common format, these are by no means the only medium in which expressions of the subjective experience of madness can be found. For example, Gilman (1988) discusses the nineteenth-century British artist, Richard Dadd, who had profound experiences of madness (which appear to have been implicated in Dadd murdering his own father). Dadd spent much of his life incarcerated against his will in mental hospitals, but continued to portray madness in his paintings. Gilman (1988) comments also on van Gogh's images of madness and notes that both Dadd and van Gogh portray madness in a way which conveys the humanity and the passion of the individual, as well as the mundane daily existence of the inmates of mental hospitals. Gilman (1988) notes that these portrayals differ markedly from the images of madness by their 'sane' contemporaries, a difference which Gilman attributes to both Dadd and van Gogh having had personal experience of madness.

Other media that have been used to capture and express the essence of the first-hand experience of madness include cinema, such as the self-directed, award-winning documentary about the experience of madness, *People say I'm crazy* by John Cadigan (2004), as well as poetry, such as that of Sylvia Plath (1965) and others, examples of which can be found in Estroff (2004). Another format in which first-person accounts of madness are presented is through oral presentation, such as at conferences. For example, at the 2005 International Society for the Psychotherapies of the Schizophrenias (www.isps.org) Making Sense of Psychosis conference in Auckland, five presenters related aspects of their own personal experience of psychosis.

However, by far the most extensive record of first-person accounts of madness is in the written narrative form. Here we find a vast and ever-growing collection of diverse stories of the experience of madness. Historically, first-person accounts of madness written in English can be traced as far back as the fifteenth century (Hornstein 2002), with sustained interest developing in mid-nineteenth-century England, when the son of a former Prime Minister published, at his own expense, a booklet outlining his experience of madness and documenting his concerns about the psychiatric treatment he had received against his will (Percival 1840). Percival's account is damning of the treatment he received and makes a heartfelt plea that efforts to understand rather than simply control people who have such experiences would be a more appropriate and helpful response. From the 1960s we see a burgeoning growth in the number of publicly available written accounts of the experience of madness. Joanne Greenberg's (1964) classic account, *I never promised you a rose garden* (also made into an acclaimed film), has been credited as stimulating interest in the area of first-person accounts. This development coincided with the growth of the consumer movement within mental health. See Chamberlin (2004) and O'Hagan (1994) for overviews of this movement.

A number of journals regularly publish first-person accounts of the experience of madness. Not surprisingly, consumer-orientated journals such as the *Journal of the California Alliance for the Mentally Ill* and *Asylum* regularly feature articles about the experience of madness written by those who have had such experiences. Although mainstream scientific journals rarely publish such accounts, there are exceptions to this rule, notably both *Schizophrenia Bulletin* (which from the mid-1980s onward published regular first-person accounts) and *Psychiatric Services* (which did the same on a regular basis from 1994 on). Generally, these are short pieces which focus on particular aspects of the experience of schizophrenia. The soon to be launched ISPS journal, *Psychosis: Psychological, Social and Integrative Approaches*, will publish longer first-person accounts, from both service users and clinicians, on a more equal footing with more traditional research studies (www.tandf.co.uk/journals).

There have been a number of published anthologies of first-person accounts of mental distress (including, but not limited to, the experience of psychosis). The New Zealand Mental Health Commission has been active in this area, having commissioned four booklets which contain the stories of the experience of mental illness from different perspectives (Fenton and Te Koutua 2000; Malo 2000; O'Hagan 2000a, 2000b) as well as one book, *A gift of stories*, a collection of first-person accounts of mental illness (Leibrich 1999). Outside New Zealand there has, of course, also been a number of publications which have collected stories of the experience of madness. Among these, collections by Kaplan (1964) and Romme and Escher (1993) are worthy of particular note. Kaplan's book is of interest both because of the early date of publication as well as its focus on inner experience. Romme and Escher's (1993) collection is of interest because it focuses specifically on the experience of hearing voices and because it contains contributions from those who have been patients of mental health services as well as, unusually, some from voice-hearers who have had no contact with mental health services. Another interesting recent book illustrates how a collection of different perspectives – from services users, carers and professionals – can be brought together to more meaningfully illuminate a particular experience, in this case that of mental health in-patient care (Hardcastle et al. 2007).

Full-length books which explore the experience of madness, by virtue of the fact that they are of greater length than either journal articles or contributions to collected accounts, allow for deeper exploration of the experience and the context within which this experience takes place. This allows the author to explore in more depth the subjective nature of the experience and his or her thoughts about the causes and meaning of these experiences as well as closer examination of factors such as the responses of others, social stigma, and the role of mental health services. These books are now voluminous in number and many are readily available, having been popularized, in part at least, through celebrated and successful movies such as *Girl, interrupted* (1999) and *An angel at my table* (1990), which are based on first-person accounts of madness by Kaysen (1993) and Frame (1984) respectively.

Despite the vastness of first-person literature and the richness of these accounts, the gulf between these and the scientific literature is great. There have been valiant attempts to try to remedy this, most notably by Sommer and his colleagues in the USA, who, over a period spanning some forty years attempted to draw attention to this rich source of data about the experience of mental ill-health. Sommer and colleagues have been champions of the importance of first-person accounts, arguing persuasively that these can provide important insights into a variety of factors including phenomenology, changes within diagnostic practices and the kinds of treatments offered, as well as the ways in which the public respond to people with mental health problems. Sommer and Osmond (1960, 1961, 1983) compiled bibliographies of first-person accounts (limited to those who had spent some time in hospital) and this was developed further by Sommer et al. (1998), who updated this list and proposed a method of classification of such literature, using variables such as demographic factors, diagnosis, treatments and the attitude of the writer to his or her experience of mental ill-health. More recently, a more comprehensive bibliography has been developed by Hornstein (2005), listing more than 300 first-person accounts of madness written in English, dating from the fifteenth century. Hornstein (2002) suggests that we should view first-person accounts of madness as a form of 'protest literature' analogous to slave narratives. She is very critical of the way in which professionals respond to patient narratives, arguing that 'psychiatrists have not simply ignored patients' voices, they have gone to considerable lengths to silence them'. She goes on to point out that given the lack of certain knowledge in our understandings of serious mental illness, 'ignoring accounts by patients seems perverse' (Hornstein 2002). The book edited by Hardcastle et al. (2007), which looks at in-patient care, is a rare example of a book which tries to 'bridge the gap' between subjective experience and professional accounts.

The sudden growth in published accounts of madness since the 1960s has been overtaken and overshadowed by the development of the internet, which has made it relatively easy and affordable for ordinary individuals to make available to others their accounts of the experience of madness. This contrasts with the situation in nineteenth-century England when only those with considerable financial resources, such as Percival (1840), were in a position to make their stories available to the public. The number of web pages which are either totally or largely dedicated to the individual's account of the experience of madness is impressive. For example, the National Association of Mental Illness (NAMI) South Carolina branch website alone lists over 100 links to personal accounts (www.namiscc.org/Experiences/index.htm). There are also innumerable individuals who have documented in some detail various aspects of their experience of schizophrenia (for example, Ian Chovil: www.chovil.com). Each of these sites lists links to other organizations and individuals who have documented their personal experience of psychosis on the internet. Given the nature of the internet, establishing accurately the number of such accounts available may be impossible. However, some indication of the extent of this literature is provided through the following results using the Google search engine (as of June 2008): 'personal account' and 'schizophrenia' yields 29,800 hits, 'personal account' and 'psychosis' yields 19,700, and 'personal account' and 'madness' gives 51,200 hits. Of course, these figures do not necessarily reflect the number of unique web pages, but they do, nonetheless, convey the extent of this growing body of literature. What this shows is that despite the fact that subjective experience occupies a peripheral position in the mainstream literature on schizophrenia, there is a growing body of literature which does attend to the subjective experience of madness. Surely, we believe, it is no longer acceptable (not that it ever was) for this great literature to be ignored by those who approach the study of madness from professional or so-called scientific positions. Making sense of madness requires that we recognize as valid and necessary incorporating observations and reflections from a variety of different positions, and this must include those from the first-hand, lived experience of madness, lest we find ourselves with models of madness bereft of their essence, reduced to caricatures of this complex and confusing aspect of what it is to be human.

The recovery movement

Closely aligned with the growth in the interest in first-person accounts is the 'recovery movement', which may provide a framework that ensures that the first-person perspective occupies a central position in efforts to make sense of madness. The recovery movement is a consumer-driven movement which grew out of the consumer and civil rights movements in the USA in the 1970s (Davidson 2003). Roberts and Wolfson (2004) note that first-person accounts have become the founding story of the recovery movement. This movement was also inspired by outcome studies which demonstrated that recovery from 'severe mental illness' is possible even for the so-called 'chronic' cases, in contrast to the pessimism of traditional conceptualizations of schizophrenia (Harding et al. 1987).

Davidson (2003) provides an overview of the recovery movement (which has variously been referred to as a paradigm, a model, a philosophy, a process and a movement: I will use the latter term here). He identifies key components of this perspective, which include assuming a sense of agency and responsibility for dealing with one's difficulties, as well as maintaining hope regarding a positive outcome. Roberts and Wolfson (2004: 37) report that the recovery movement assumes that those with mental health difficulties 'can recover without the help of doctors, and sometimes even despite them'. They go on to argue that this does not necessarily imply that the movement is anti-psychiatry, but instead reflects consumers reclaiming agency and developing hope for a positive outcome, and may provide a 'potentially unifying goal of recovery' (Roberts and Wolfson 2004: 37), which will allow clinicians and clients to work together towards this common goal, albeit with the need for their roles within this process to be redefined.

Patricia Deegan (1988: 15), one of the foremost advocates of the recovery movement, defines recovery as 'a process, a way of life, an attitude, and a way of approaching the day's challenges'. She stresses that recovery is a deeply personal process and that the definition of 'recovery' is also personal, with the individual being best able to identify his or her own recovery goals, which may or may not include control of symptoms. Deegan (1996: 92) comments that 'The goal of recovery is not to become normal. The goal is to embrace the human vocation of becoming more deeply, more fully human.'

Roberts and Wolfson (2004) note that the process of recovery is often inspired by a 'pivotal moment', which may include, for example, finding personal meaning in the experience of psychosis. The recovery movement has had a significant impact on many aspects of mental health care in many parts of the world. This movement has had a major impact in New Zealand, with public mental health services adopting a recovery-based philosophy since 1998 (O'Hagan 2001).

This brings us now to an end of our discussion of ways of making sense of madness which give emphasis to subjective aspects of the experience. We have shown that those who have first-hand lived experience of psychosis have much to contribute to our understandings of madness, through both their own first-person accounts of the experience and through formal research which investigates subjective experience. While we are advocates of the need for understandings of madness to be informed by, and sensitive to, subjective aspects of the experience, we do not want to suggest that other perspectives are of no importance. On the contrary, our position is that looking and thinking about madness from a number of positions, including, but not limited to the first-person perspective, is a requirement for any serious attempt to make sense of madness. With that in mind, we will now look at other positions from which madness can be understood: the lay perspective (in Chapter 4) and that of the mental health professional clinician and researcher (Chapter 5).

Making sense of madness II

Lay understandings: what does the public think about 'schizophrenia'?

We have now shown that people who experience psychosis have much to say about the experience, although by and large the opinions of people who actually have psychotic experiences are rarely paid much attention in mainstream literature. Let us now move on to a different question. In this chapter, we want to consider the thoughts and opinions of people in general. Specifically, the question we want to answer in this chapter is: how do lay people make sense of madness?

First, a little on terminology. 'Lay public' is an interesting term. It tends to imply ordinary or non-expert. It seems reasonable to ask why should we be interested in what the 'lay public' have to say about the topic of madness. We can think of a couple of reasons. First, we should remind ourselves that users of mental health services do not come from planet Zion. They themselves are, of course, members of the 'lay public', which means that if or when they come to mental health services for support, it seems likely that their views of their experiences and their expectations from mental health services are likely to be informed by the view of the 'lay public'. So, having a better understanding of the views of the so-called lay public about what causes madness might help mental health professionals better appreciate what new clients to their services might be thinking and feeling when first coming into contact with mental health services. Second, keeping in mind that clients of mental health services belong to and live in the same communities as the 'lay public', what the public believe about madness will impact on how those who have mental health difficulties are construed and treated by others in their communities, and will, according to some of the research we summarize here, have a strong influence on prejudice and stigma that individuals who experience psychosis might be subject to.

Were we to read only the views of biologically minded psychiatrists and the promotional materials of drug companies, one might be led to think that believing that madness could be caused by psychosocial factors such as poverty, loneliness, discrimination, child abuse and so on is a minority position that is very controversial, radical even. But, when we look at the research into how lay people make sense of madness, we will see that it turns out that these beliefs are not at all strange to the public. Everywhere that studies have been conducted into lay understandings of madness, we find that the public believes that bad things happening to people are far more important than faulty brains or genes when it comes to who ends up crazy. In terms of treatments, the public also expresses a preference for talking therapies and other non-medical types of support over psychiatric drugs or (less surprisingly) electroshock therapy. In this chapter, we will first summarize the research on which we base those statements and then describe the response of the experts to these findings.

Public beliefs about the causes of madness

We have seen already that those who have experienced madness have a diverse range of beliefs about the experiences (and we will show in Chapter 5 that this is also true of professionals in this field). Similarly, we also find that there is a huge range of beliefs about the causes of madness expressed by lay people. Much of the research in this area is carried out through surveys designed to elicit opinions about the nature of mental health difficulties. Most surveys of the public about what causes 'schizophrenia' reveal that the public hold quite sophisticated conceptualizations, recognizing both social and biological factors as causes, reflecting that the public tend to hold what the experts would call 'multi-factorial' models. When we look more closely at the results we find, however, a very strong pattern in terms of what sorts of causes of madness lay people think are most important. For example, a 1995 survey of over 2000 Australians found that what lay people identified as the most likely cause of schizophrenia was 'Day-to-day-problems such as stress, family arguments, difficulties at work or financial difficulties', which was endorsed as a likely cause by 94 per cent of Australians. 'Problems from childhood such as being badly treated or abused, losing one or both parents when young or coming from a broken home' was rated as a likely cause by 88 per cent. 'The recent death of a close friend or relative' and 'Traumatic events' were both rated as a likely cause by 85 per cent. Furthermore, 72 per cent believed that unemployed people are more likely to have schizophrenia. Only 59 per cent endorsed 'inherited or genetic' factors as a likely cause (Jorm et al. 1997). In a study of changes over time, the same research team found that by 2003–2004, those who endorsed 'inherited or genetic' causes had increased from 59 per cent to 70 per cent. This figure, however, was still exceeded by endorsement of all four psychosocial causal factors: 'problems from childhood' (91 per cent), 'day-to-day problems' (90 per cent), 'death of someone close' (88 per cent) and 'traumatic event' (87 per cent) (Jorm et al. 2005).

Meanwhile, on the other side of the world, when Londoners were asked about the cause of schizophrenia, Furnham and Rees (1988) report that:

Overall subjects seemed to prefer environmental explanations referring to social stressors and family conflicts – e.g. 'being mercilessly persecuted by family and friends' and 'having come from backgrounds that promote stress'.

(Furnham and Rees 1988: 218)

Another London study found that the most endorsed causal model of schizophrenia was 'Unusual or traumatic experiences or the failure to negotiate some critical stage of emotional development', followed by 'Social, economic, and family pressures' (Furnham and Bower 1992). Reflecting on their findings and the relative lack of impact of understandings of madness which promote a biomedical position, they note 'It seems that lay people have not been converted to the medical view and prefer psychosocial explanations' (Furnham and Bower 1992: 207). Further, and consistent with the findings reported in Chapter 3 that those who experience psychosis see finding meaning in the experience as one of their primary concerns, the researchers found that the lay public adopts a similar position:

Subjects agreed that schizophrenic behaviour had some meaning and was neither random nor simply a symptom of an illness.

(Furnham and Bower 1992: 206)

In Ireland a survey found that when the public were presented with a vignette portraying the positive symptoms of schizophrenia (for example, hallucinations and delusions), the most commonly cited causes for the experiences described in the vignette were stressful life events, with only 11 per cent of their sample citing biogenetic causes. When the vignette described negative symptoms (such as social withdrawal) the most frequently cited cause was childhood problems such as 'lack of adequate parental love' (Barry and Greene 1992: 152). Only 5 per cent of the public cited biogenetic causes as explanations for these 'negative symptoms' (Barry and Greene 1992). Moving away from the English-speaking world, a survey of over 2000 Germans found that the most common causes of schizophrenia cited were: isolation (73 per cent), unemployment (72 per cent) and stress in partnership or family (64 per cent). By way of comparison, biological causes were less frequently endorsed, with 'Disorder of the brain' cited by 49 per cent and 'Heredity' by 45 per cent (Angermeyer and Matschinger 1996a).

What this research shows is that in terms of understanding madness, the general public express a clear preference for social causes rather than illness explanations based on faulty genes or brains. Research of this sort, with findings consistent with this claim, has now been replicated in sixteen countries. In addition to the four countries already mentioned above, similar results have been found in China, Ethiopia, Greece, India, Italy, Japan, Malaysia, Mongolia, Russia, South Africa, Turkey and the USA (Read et al. 2006).

It is important to note that the same pattern found when the general public are surveyed also holds true for 'patients' as well as for their family members. Studies of the causal explanations held by people who have been diagnosed with schizophrenia also find a strong preference for psychosocial causes (Holzinger et al. 2002; Pistrang and Barker 1992). The causes espoused as 'likely/very likely' by Germans who experience psychosis were 'recent psychosocial factors' (88 per cent), 'personality' (71 per cent), family (64 per cent) and 'biology' (31 per cent). Germans diagnosed 'schizophrenic' are particularly likely to identify family as a causal factor of their condition (Angermeyer and Klusmann 1988). In this study, the relatives of those diagnosed schizophrenic also strongly favoured psychosocial over biological explanations (Angermeyer et al. 1988). These researchers cite five previous studies (all carried out before 1988) which report similar findings regarding the views of relatives of those diagnosed with mental health problems. However, we should acknowledge that even within Germany, this is not a uniform finding. A subsequent German study found that when asked about causes, relatives who belonged to organizations for the families of 'schizophrenics' believed in brain disorder and heredity more strongly than psychosocial factors (Angermeyer and Matschinger 1996b). The researchers attribute this finding to those family members having had greater exposure to the opinions of psychiatric 'experts', who were more likely to express biologically based explanations for the causes of schizophrenia. This hypothesis is consistent with a study of relatives in Turkey, where there are only 0.6 psychiatrists per 100,000 people (Karanci 1995), meaning that family members are much less likely to be exposed to biomedical explanations for their family member's troubles. Here, we find that relatives cite stressful events (50 per cent) and family conflicts (40 per cent) more often than biological/genetic factors (23 per cent). Similarly, 55 per cent of 254 relatives in India identified psychosocial stressors, whereas 15 per cent cited heredity and 14 per cent brain disorder (Srinivasan and Thara 2001).

Further evidence of public rejection of biogenetic explanations for schizophrenia comes from studies of 'psycho-education' programmes, which are specifically designed to teach the illness model of madness to relatives (Read and Haslam 2004). One study assessed whether relatives retained 'knowledge' about the 'illness' and found 'absolutely no change in the amount of knowledge between pre-tests and post-tests' (Cozolino et al. 1988: 683). Of importance here is that the researchers defined 'knowledge' as, essentially, a biologically based understanding of psychosis. Another study found that before entering a 'psycho-education' programme, only 11 per cent of relatives of those with a diagnosis of schizophrenia believed the problems were caused by a 'disordered brain', a figure which increased to 32 per cent after the training. In the same study, the number of relatives who believed in 'genetic inheritance' increased from 11 per cent to 15 per cent, suggesting that this programme had little of the desired effect of persuading relatives to view the difficulties of their family members as being primarily caused by biological factors. Only 3 per cent of the patients adopted an illness model before or after the attempt to 'educate' them (McGill et al. 1983).

That 'patients' adopt a predominantly social view of the causes of their problems may come as no surprise to many (although some experts continue to dismiss this as proof that they have no 'insight' into the claimed 'fact' that they have an illness). What is perhaps more surprising is that family members, in general, also share a social perspective. It turns out that the very vocal 'family' organizations that promote an illness model, like SANE in the UK and the National Alliance for the Mentally Ill (NAMI) in the USA, are not at all representative of families in general.

Public beliefs about treatments

Given what we have discovered about how lay people understand the causes of madness, it should come as no surprise to hear that research shows that the public also favour psychosocial treatment approaches for schizophrenia over medication (Read and Haslam 2004). This has been demonstrated in Australia, Austria, Canada, England, Germany and South Africa (Read 2007; Read et al. 2006). For example, when Austrians are asked what they would do if a relative became psychotic the most common response is 'talk to them' (Jorm et al. 2000: 403). The most preferred treatment for schizophrenia in Germany is psychotherapy, which is recommended by 65 per cent of respondents, compared to psychiatric drugs, which only 15 per cent see as the best treatment. ECT is supported by a mere 1 per cent of the German public (Riedel-Heller et al. 2005). For Australians, the reasons for rejecting anti-psychotic drugs as a preferred treatment include 'have more risks than benefits', 'lack efficacy because they do not deal with the roots of the problem' and 'are prescribed for the wrong reasons (for example, to avoid talking about problems, to make people believe things are better than they are, as a straight jacket)' (Jorm et al. 2000: 404).

A review of the research in this area by Angermeyer and Dietrich (2006) found eight studies confirming that 'The particular liking of psychotherapy is more developed for schizophrenia than for depression', with one exception. Recent studies in the USA (Croghan et al. 2003) and Germany (Angermeyer and Matschinger 2004) suggest that the rejection of psychiatric drugs may be weakening. Between 1990 and 2001 the percentage of the German public recommending drug treatment increased from 31 per cent to 57 per cent. However, the percentage recommending psychotherapy increased from 68 per cent to 83 per cent (Angermeyer and Matschinger 2005); both of these figures may indicate a growing desire among the public that those who experience psychosis should be offered some support, with the preference for psychotherapy over medicine still in evidence.

The experts' response

The public is not always right of course. One branch of one discipline – biological psychiatry – is absolutely convinced that these millions of people who endorse psychosocial causes of psychosis and see psychotherapy as the preferred treatment are just plain wrong. Some of those who come from this position feel so confident that their particular view of schizophrenia/madness – that it is a biologically caused illness requiring biologically based treatments – is correct, that they have coined the term 'mental health literacy', which is used to measure the extent to which members of the public properly understand (that is, agree with these experts) that schizophrenia is an illness requiring medical treatment.

Vast amounts of money have been spent promulgating the view among the public that hearing voices and other such complaints are symptoms of a brain disease with a strong genetic predisposition and requiring medical intervention. In passing, it is worth noting that much of the financial support for the promotion of this perspective is provided by the pharmaceutical companies, who have much to gain from wider public acceptance of the biological perspective of madness (Mosher et al. 2004; Read 2008). The rationale for promoting the biological perspective through 'educating' the public, so we are told, is to reduce stigma against those who experience psychosis. For decades it has been argued that if the public were to adopt an illness model of psychosis and other mental health problems, then prejudice against those who experience such difficulties would disappear, or at least be greatly reduced. The thinking behind this 'mental illness is an illness like any other' approach to destigmatization is the idea that if you are ill you are not responsible for your actions and if you are not responsible you cannot be blamed. It turns out, however, that this well-intentioned notion is not supported by the research. Of twelve studies examining attitudes to 'mental illness' in general, all but one revealed either that biogenetic beliefs are related to negative attitudes or that psychosocial beliefs are related to positive attitudes (Read et al. 2006). For example, two New Zealand studies compared young adults who hold biogenetic causal beliefs about mental health difficulties with those who have a more psychosocial orientation and found that those with biogenetic beliefs tend to think of 'mental patients' as more dangerous and unpredictable, and they are less likely to interact with them (Read and Harre 2001; Read and Law 1999). This research also found that presenting information about psychosocial causes, and critiquing biological theories significantly improved attitudes held towards people with mental health difficulties (Read and Law 1999).

When we move from studies of 'mental illness' in general to those examining 'schizophrenia' in particular we find similar results are reported. A New Zealand study found that viewing a video of a person describing hallucinations and delusions followed by a biogenetic explanation significantly increased perceptions of dangerousness and unpredictability. When the same video was viewed, but followed by an explanation that emphasizes reactions to adverse life events as causing the difficulties, this led to a small (non-significant) improvement in attitudes (Walker and Read 2002).

In Germany, large-scale studies (with 5025 participants) were conducted to consider whether biological beliefs about schizophrenia are related to attitudes. The researchers found that beliefs in both 'brain disease' and 'heredity' as causes of schizophrenia had no effect on levels of anger felt towards those with the diagnosis, but levels of fear were increased. However, if psychosocial stress was seen as the cause of schizophrenia, then attitudes were more favourable (Angermeyer and Matschinger 2003). Further analysis of the same data has confirmed specific relationships between biogenetic causal beliefs (particularly 'brain disease') and perceived dangerousness, fear and desire for distance (Dietrich et al. 2006).

The same research team (Dietrich et al. 2004) analysed interviews with 745 Russians and 950 Mongolians plus their original sample of 5025 West and East Germans (the survey was conducted prior to the reunification of Germany). They found that belief that 'heredity' is a cause of schizophrenia was associated with a greater desire for distance in all four samples. Belief that it is a 'brain disease' was associated with greater desire for distance in three of the four samples. In Mongolia belief in three of the four psychosocial causes ('stress at work', 'broken home' and 'lack of parental affection', but not recent 'life event') was associated with reduced desire for distance. 'Lack of parental affection' was also found to be related to less desire for distance in Russia and West Germany. A trend analysis of changes in causal beliefs and desire for distance over eleven years (Angermeyer and Matschinger 2005: 333) found that 'Although the endorsement of biological causes increased substantially, the public's rejection of people with schizophrenia increased in the same period'. In both 1990 and 2001 biological causal beliefs were related to greater desire for distance.

Organizations of 'psychiatric patients' have long expressed concern about the effects of a narrow biological perspective on their self-esteem, arguing that this perspective not only increases stigma but also minimizes the complexity of their lives and their capacity for recovery (Campbell 1992; O'Hagan 1992). Presenting a psychosocial explanation to clients induces more efforts to change than a disease explanation, with those who adopt disease explanations tending to use alcohol to relieve their stress more (Fisher and Farina 1979). In the UK, Birchwood et al. (1993) found that in those who experience psychosis 'patients who accepted their diagnosis reported a lower perceived control over illness' and that depression in this client group is 'linked to patients' perception of controllability of their illness and absorption of cultural stereotypes of mental illness' (Birchwood et al. 1993: 387). Similarly, in Spain, among patients diagnosed schizophrenic, those with better 'insight' (that is, who believed they were 'ill') were more depressed

(Rodriguez et al. 2000). This relationship between biogenetic causal beliefs and negative attitudes has also been found in professionals. Staff with a biological perspective assess patients as more disturbed (Langer and Abelson 1974) are less likely to ask them about adverse life events that might have caused their difficulties (Cavanagh et al. 2004) and are less inclined to involve patients in planning or managing services (Kent and Read 1998).

In conclusion then, we hope we have shown in this chapter that lay people hold complex, multi-factorial understandings of the experience of madness. These understandings embrace biological and psychosocial factors as contributing to the cause of psychosis, with greater endorsement of the role of psychosocial causes. Similarly, international research also shows that there is a preference among the public for psychosocial treatments over biological ones. One thing which the research into lay understandings highlights is that there are great disparities between the model that is currently dominant among experts and the model currently adopted by the international public, from whom – of course – the users of mental health services are drawn. It seems that for most people around the world hearing voices and having strange beliefs, when looked at in the context of the complexity of an individual's life history and circumstances, are understandable human phenomenon. Only if looked at from a narrow perspective which posits biological causes such as faulty neurotransmitters or deviant genes as sole or primary causes do these experiences become incomprehensible. We can conclude that a simplistic 'brain disease' or 'genetic illness' model renders these experiences more frightening to all concerned, perhaps precisely because such explanations mean that the experiences themselves make no sense. This chapter shows that how we make sense of madness is important not only for improving our understanding of the experience, but also in reducing prejudice towards those who have such experiences. This book does not seek to resolve the issue about who is right or wrong about the causes of (or treatments for) madness. What we do hope to do is to show that there are various ways that one can go about the business of making sense of madness and that these have implications for how the experience of madness is responded to by the individual and by those around him or her. We have already looked into how those with first-hand experience and the lay public make sense of madness. In Chapter 5 we will look at how one other group – the professional or 'scientific' community – makes sense of madness. While this group (which, by the way, we happily identify as members of) is numerically a relatively small group, it is a group which nonetheless carries considerable influence and power by virtue of its socially sanctioned status as 'experts' in the field. Let us now look at what these so-called 'experts' have to say about madness.

Chapter 5

Making sense of madness III

Scientific/professional understandings of 'madness'

We have now looked at how 'madness' can be made sense of from the perspective of the person who has the experience, as well as from the position of ordinary 'lay' people. It is time now to turn to how professionals working in this field make sense of these experiences. It may seem somewhat odd that we have placed the professional perspectives *after* first-person and lay perspectives. This is a deliberate choice on our part. We believe that the perspectives that we will outline in this chapter are, generally speaking, given prominence in the literature on madness at the expense of the first-person and lay perspectives, with the implicit assumption that the professional perspectives represent the 'true' or 'real' way of making sense of madness. This is an assumption that we do not wish to endorse here. Indeed, our explicit position is that the experience of madness can be – perhaps *must* be, if we are to truly appreciate its complexity – viewed from different perspectives, each of which contributes to our understandings of the experience in different ways. This is not to in any way suggest that the professional perspective is unimportant. After all, we ourselves approach the experience of madness from the positions of being professional clinicians and researchers working in this area. The point we wish to make is that we professionals do not have a monopoly on understandings of madness. Yes, our understandings are legitimate and important, but they are not, as is often suggested or implied, the final, definitive word on what madness really is. With these caveats in mind, let us now have a look at how those in the so-called 'scientific' community make sense of madness.

Our purpose in this chapter is to provide an overview of some of the myriad ways that professionals working in this area make sense of madness. It will be impossible for us to be comprehensive here – the literature is, simply, far too vast for this. But, what we hope to do is to give a flavour of the diversity of 'scientific' models of madness that are, or have been, proposed to account for what madness really is. Our primary aim here is to draw attention to the great extent and variety of theoretical explanations that have been, and continue to be, propounded as accounts of madness. As such, we are less concerned here with the empirical evaluation of these theories. Suffice it to say, that each theory does have an evidence base which proponents of each particular theory call upon to support the theory. Of course, from a scientific perspective, the evidence base of any theory is of critical importance, and we do not wish to imply that each of the theories outlined here has the same quality or quantity of supporting evidence. There is considerable variability in the nature and extent of the 'evidence' that supports each theory. What is clear though is that at the present time there is no single theoretical account of madness which has satisfied the needs of the multitudes of researchers and clinicians working in this field. Our intention in this chapter is to illustrate the diversity of understandings, and the associated debate and disagreement which, we contend, characterizes this area. It is not our intention to make a case for adopting any one particular theory (although we should acknowledge that our sympathies lie more with psychological understandings of madness, which will inevitably colour our presentation of the issues here).

First, we should remind ourselves that 'madness' is a term more associated with the lay literature, rather than with professional/scientific approaches. A central feature of many, though not all, professional accounts of mental health difficulties is the use of formalized systems of categorizing clients' difficulties (according to criteria developed by professionals rather than by clients themselves). The main diagnostic terms of relevance to the present discussion are 'psychosis' and 'schizophrenia'. Although other diagnostic terms (such as 'bipolar disorder', 'manic depression', 'schizophreniform disorder', 'schizoaffective disorder' and 'psychotic depression') are used, these will not be explored in any great depth here. 'Schizophrenia' and 'psychosis' are the most commonly used diagnostic terms in referring to the kinds of experiences that in lay parlance we might call 'madness'. As our interest here is not in the subtle differences between the various diagnostic terms but in the more general issue of making sense of madness, our focus will be on those terms, which can, for the present purposes, serve as exemplars of the scientific/professional approach to making sense of madness.

The notion of 'schizophrenia' is, arguably, one of the cornerstones upon which the current dominant medical model of mental health rests (Kendell and Gourlay 1970). It is a central component of mental health care, as well as being an important social issue. Estimates of the social costs of schizophrenia have suggested that in Western countries schizophrenia accounts for between 1.5 per cent and 3 per cent of total health care budgets, with indirect costs (such as loss of productivity, and other social costs) being three or more times greater than the direct costs (Knapp et al. 2004; Lindstrom 1996). Gunderson and Mosher (1975) estimate that the total costs of schizophrenia in the USA may be as much as 2 per cent of the gross national product.

Historically speaking, the current nosology (system of categorization) of madness is a relatively recent innovation, having its origins in the nineteenth century, when a shift towards a more medical approach to mental health care developed. We can trace the beginnings of our current nosology of madness to the work of German psychiatrist Emil Kraepelin (1919), who broke down the unitary notion of 'insanity' into two supposedly distinct disorders: manic depression and dementia praecox ('senility of the young'; Bentall 2003: 15). In Kraepelin's view manic depression was associated with a more optimistic prognosis, whereas dementia praecox was considered to lead to inevitable and irreversible deterioration. Swiss psychiatrist Eugene Bleuler took up and developed Kraepelin's concept of dementia praecox, within a paradigm influenced, initially at least, by Freudian theory. Bleuler suggested that the common denominator of the various subtypes of dementia praecox was the 'breaking of associative threads' which were deemed to hold thoughts, emotions and behaviour together (Birchwood et al. 1988: 16). Somewhat at odds with Kraepelin's pessimistic view of outcome, Bleuler rejected the term dementia praecox in favour of his own neologism 'schizophrenia' (derived from Greek 'skhizo', split, and 'phren', mind), a term first used by Bleuler in 1908 (Barham 1995). Ultimately, Bleuler's term and concept came to usurp Kraepelin's 'dementia praecox'. Unlike Kraepelin's pessimistic position, Bleuler's view created a basis for a psychotherapeutic approach, and recognized considerable variability in outcome, with many patients recovering from the condition. Despite the fact that there have been continual modifications to the definition of schizophrenia, with an even wider variety of developments in attempts to explain and treat schizophrenia, the basic notion of schizophrenia has remained largely intact, though certainly not unchallenged, since the time of Kraepelin and Bleuler. Jansson and Parnas (2007: 1178) comment that since the introduction of the concept 'psychiatry has produced not less than 40 definitions of schizophrenia'. We have already discussed current definitions of schizophrenia and psychosis as used in clinical and research settings and considered some of the reservations which have been expressed about the usefulness of these terms (see pp. 12–17). We will discuss these issues in greater detail below.

Investigations into the prevalence of schizophrenia have yielded inconsistent results. Though some have argued that the incidence of schizophrenia is consistently and cross-culturally found to be around 1 per cent (British Psychological Society 2000; Carpenter and Buchanan 1995; Sartorius et al. 1986), other studies (as reviewed by Read 2004a) have found quite different incidence rates, thus casting doubt on the claims to uniformity. Among the very few findings in the literature on schizophrenia about which there is any genuine consensus is the repeated finding that it is in late teens and early twenties that a diagnosis of schizophrenia is most likely to be made, with onset commonly being a little earlier for men than for women (Hafner et al. 1993; Harrop and Trower 2003). Figures relating to the incidence of psychosis suggest that around 3 per cent of the population will have psychotic experiences of one sort or another which leads to involvement with mental health services, although recent studies have shown that many people who have psychotic experiences never come to the attention of mental health services (Bak et al. 2003).

Whatever terms we may use to refer to experiences of this sort, and whatever reservations and criticisms may be levied at those terms, it is important that we do not lose sight of the fact that 'madness' is a significant and often highly distressing condition for the individual and for his or her loved ones. Also (as noted above) the social and health implications of schizophrenia are considerable. This is reflected in a *Science* editorial stating quite bluntly – and, we believe, overly pessimistically – that 'schizophrenia is the worst disease known to man' (from Carpenter and Buchanan 1995).

Some difficulties with the term 'schizophrenia'

Before moving on to discuss theories of schizophrenia, we need to acknowledge that this term itself has not been free of controversy. Indeed, the very concept of schizophrenia has been the subject of robust, often highly emotively charged criticism from a range of quarters and for a variety of reasons: ethical, scientific and clinical.

An ethical challenge to the general concept of 'mental illness' as well as to more specific notions such as 'schizophrenia' was put forcefully by American psychiatrist, Thomas Szasz (1961, 1991), who argued that using a medical framework to conceptualize behavioural difficulties was unjustified and unhelpful. He argued that 'mental illness' is a myth which obscures important ethical considerations (such as personal responsibility for behaviour), and which serves to bolster the claims of the medical profession that these problems lie within its jurisdiction.

Serious doubts have also been expressed regarding the scientific standing of the concepts of schizophrenia and psychosis. A clear exposition of this case is found in the work of Bannister (1968), who proposes that schizophrenia is what he termed a 'disjunctive concept', which makes it of little utility to scientific investigations, resting as it does on a 'Chinese menu' type criteria for definition. In the case of schizophrenia, this relates to the 'any two from five' characteristics as adequate to make a diagnosis, making it possible for two people who share none of the five criteria to be grouped together under the same diagnostic concept. Bannister argues that such a concept does not meet the basic requirements to be considered scientific, using a metaphor to convey his negative prognosis for the notion of schizophrenia:

> Schizophrenia, as a concept, is a semantic Titanic, doomed before it sails: a concept so diffuse as to be unusable in a scientific context.
>
> (Bannister 1968: 181)

Bannister's argument has been echoed more recently in the work of psychologists such as Richard Bentall (2003) and Mary Boyle (1990), who suggest that the concept be abandoned on the grounds that it does not meet the basic requirements for a useful scientific construct because it does not satisfy the requirements of 'reliability' (the extent to which agreement can be reached on who is and is not 'schizophrenic') and 'validity' (the extent to which the construct relates to a 'real' condition, with common causes, outcomes and responses to treatment). They conclude that the concept of schizophrenia is not a valid scientific concept, but is little more than an article of faith. Boyle (1990) argues that schizophrenia is a 'scientific delusion' which hinders rather than helps understandings and ways of working with 'madness'.

Though criticisms of medical diagnostic concepts such as schizophrenia are perhaps to be expected from a psychological position, the notion has also come under fire within psychiatry itself. An overview of a century of mental health research and practice by one of the foremost psychiatrists in the field of first episode psychosis and schizophrenia, Pat McGorry (1995), pointed out that 'The concept of dementia praecox is about to turn 100 without any fundamental change.' McGorry (1995), echoing Bentall, Boyle and Bannister, argues that the basic categorical model upon which the concept of schizophrenia is based may be an obstacle to scientific and clinical progress.

The practical and clinical utility of the notion of 'schizophrenia' has also been called into question. Psychiatrists such as McGorry (1994, 1995) point out that over the first few years of a client's presentation to mental health services, there is considerable diagnostic instability, rendering diagnoses like schizophrenia less helpful at this stage. Such factors led McGorry to propose that the more general term 'psychosis' should be employed, rather than schizophrenia, at least in the initial phases of treatment.

Another argument used against the term 'schizophrenia' relates to the stigma which has come to be attached to the term, and hence to the person so diagnosed (Link et al. 2001; Sayce 2000). Birchwood et al. (1988: 17) point out that 'The concept of schizophrenia has become so cemented within the psychiatric (and lay) vocabulary that the label has become attached to the person as well as the disease.'

McGorry's position, favouring the use of a broader term such as 'psychosis' over 'schizophrenia', has gained some support within the clinical and research fields in recent years, as evidenced by the fact that specialist clinical services set up to meet the needs of young people presenting with these difficulties have adopted the term 'psychosis' in preference to 'schizophrenia'. Similarly, the report by the British Psychological Society (2000) also endorses the use of the term psychosis in favour of schizophrenia. This report defines 'psychosis' as 'An umbrella term for unusual perceptions (for example hearing voices), or unusual beliefs. In both cases other people sometimes see the person to be, to some extent, out of touch with reality' (British Psychological Society 2000: 10).

The British Psychological Society report acknowledges that the term psychosis is problematic, but, it proposes, preferable to schizophrenia, which the authors argue carries with it excess pejorative baggage. Thus, while the term psychosis is perhaps less clearly defined than schizophrenia, it is viewed more favourably because it is considered to have fewer negative associations and less of the historical baggage that comes with the term 'schizophrenia'. Further, perhaps because psychosis is a more general term, which is less clearly defined, this, somewhat paradoxically, allows greater attention to be given to the individual symptoms which are subsumed under the heading 'psychosis'. It is perhaps not surprising that such a position finds favour from clinical psychologists, among whom there is a tradition of advocating an approach which focuses on individual symptoms (such as hallucinations, or delusions) rather than putative syndromes (such as schizophrenia or manic depression). This will be discussed in more detail below (pp. 119–121).

However, it is important to note that the term 'psychosis' is certainly not free of negative connotations, being associated with such lay terms as 'psycho', which clearly carry pejorative associations. It would be inaccurate to claim that the term is free of any historical baggage whatsoever. Interestingly, the term 'psychosis' is reported by Barham (1995) as having originally been used by alienists in the first half of the nineteenth century, thus giving it a longer history than the term schizophrenia. An example of some of the baggage that comes with the term is to be found in Jaspers' (1963) influential contention that a defining feature of psychosis is that it is fundamentally 'ununderstandable' and therefore not amenable to psychological intervention. We believe that Jasper's position is untenable: psychosis may be complex and confusing, but, as we demonstrated in Chapter 3, not only is it understandable, but also at least some of those who actually experience psychosis can, if given the opportunity, help contribute to making it so.

An interesting contribution to the debate around the issue of diagnoses of mental health difficulties is made by Gergen and McNamee (2002), who suggest it is useful to consider whose interests are best served by making a diagnosis, and they suggest it is rarely the client's interests which the diagnosis serves. More specifically, they suggest that the single most important question for us to ask is, simply: is the client helped by being classified? They conclude that generally this is not the case, with the drawbacks of being diagnosed far outweighing the advantages. The specific drawbacks of being classified that they refer to include the client being disempowered as authority over his or her experience is taken by the 'expert' clinician.

Theories of schizophrenia

Having considered some of the conceptual limitations of the concepts of schizophrenia and psychosis, we will now move on to look at some of the professional/scientific theories that have been proposed to account for what schizophrenia is and what its causes are. While it is true that a very wide range of variables has been implicated as having a causal role in schizophrenia, attempts have been made to impose some kind of order on the range of theories that have been considered plausible explanations of madness. Siegler and Osmond (1966: 1193), in their classic review of the dominant models of madness in use in the mid-1960s, begin with the blunt statement that 'Schizophrenia is disputed territory.' They argue that the theories of madness at that time could be categorized as falling within one of six categories: medical, moral, psychoanalytic, family interaction, conspiratorial and social. While they acknowledge that there may be differing evidence bases for the different theories, they argue that it is factors *other* than evidence which determines which theory will be adopted in any particular clinical setting when they note: 'We strongly suspect that objective evidence is not the basis on which the models are accepted or rejected as programmes' (Siegler and Osmond 1966: 1201).

This is quite a profound claim they are making: that the different models of care adopted in different clinical settings are determined not by scientific evidence, but by other factors. They suggest that other considerations, such as the moral position of those involved in delivering the service, or the influence of a charismatic individual who promotes a particular way of working, are examples of the factors which determine which model of madness will in fact be adopted in different clinical settings. It is our contention that Siegler and Osmond's (1966) description of schizophrenia as 'disputed territory' remains as true today as it was then, an argument we will develop in Chapter 6. Before developing this argument, let us first discuss some of the currently held theories of psychosis, which we have categorized (according to the primary emphasis of each theory) as biological, evolutionary, neuropsychological, psychological, psychodynamic and psychoanalytic, communication and family, life event, sociological and anthropological, philosophical and existential, and spiritual. This categorization is somewhat arbitrary, and for the sake of convenience, rather than reflecting clear-cut distinctions in the various models of madness, with some theories incorporating elements from more than one of the domains.

Biological theories of schizophrenia

Recent decades have witnessed something of a renaissance and a return to dominance of the biological paradigm in mental health research and care, particularly in the field of psychiatry. However, even within psychiatry, this model of schizophrenia has not achieved universal acceptance, with some notable dissenting voices (for example, Breggin 1991; Mosher 2004; Szasz 1991). Rather than a single biological theory of schizophrenia, what we find is a range of theories, which posit different biological factors as being implicated in the genesis of schizophrenia, including (but not limited to) genetic theories, biochemical theories, brain structure theories, and neurodevelopmental theories.

Genetic theories of schizophrenia posit that inherited genetic factors make a significant contribution to aetiology. This viewpoint is based upon studies which show higher rates of schizophrenia found in the biological relatives of those with schizophrenia. These studies include simple family epidemiological studies as well as more sophisticated twin and adoption studies which endeavour to disentangle genetic and environmental contributions to schizophrenia. A sympathetic overview of this research is provided by Gottesman (1991), whereas Boyle (1990) and Joseph (2004) provide damning critiques, attacking the methodologies and conclusions of genetic arguments. Harrop and Trower (2003: 23) occupy the middle ground in this often heated debate, when they suggest that 'The best conclusion to draw seems to be that, while there may well be a genetic component, it may be substantially smaller than many studies have estimated.' However, even this cautiously optimistic appraisal of genetic theories is called into question by a large-scale study designed specifically to investigate the genetic association between schizophrenia and 'candidate genes' (that is, genes seen as most likely to be implicated in schizophrenia, based on previous research and theory). Despite the size and rigour of this study, the authors are forced to conclude that it is 'unlikely that true associations exist at the population level' for the postulated candidate genes (Saunders et al. 2008).

Biochemical accounts of schizophrenia look to chemical factors within the brain as significant contributors to aetiology. Fujii and Ahmed (2004: 714) support their neurobiological theory with the bold assertion that 'schizophrenia and other psychotic disorders are brain disturbances'. However, despite the apparent certainty of their claim, they then go on to confess that whatever neurobiological circuits may be implicated in this purported 'brain disturbance' are not at all well understood. They suggest that the 'success' of biological treatments is evidence in support of their theory. Many question this claim, including Whitaker (2002) and Ross and Read (2004).

Among the biochemical explanations for schizophrenia, one of the most notable is the so-called 'dopamine hypothesis' (Carpenter and Buchanan 1995). This theory proposes that schizophrenia is caused by either an excess of the neurotransmitter dopamine or of dopamine activity in the brains of those with the condition. Evidence to support this theory is based on the effects of dopamine enhancing drugs (which may exacerbate symptoms) and dopamine inhibiting drugs (which have been found to diminish some symptoms). Critiques of biochemical theories is provided by Bentall (2003) and Read (2004b).

The structure of the brain (as opposed to the chemistry) has also been implicated by those with a biological leaning as having a causal role in schizophrenia. One of the predominant theories within this framework is the notion that enlarged brain ventricles are important causal factors of schizophrenia (Johnstone et al. 1979). The evidence base for this theory is partly from post-mortem studies, which have suggested that those with a diagnosis of schizophrenia do have enlarged ventricles. However, doubts have been expressed regarding the consistency of this finding as well as some of the oversimplified conclusions which have been reached (Chua and McKenna 1995; Dean 2000).

Recent years have seen the emergence of neurodevelopmental theories of schizophrenia, which seem to have acquired some dominance within the biological perspective. Neurodevelopmental theories posit that schizophrenia is the consequence of a subtle neurological defect, acquired early in life, which affects brain development and which manifests itself through the symptoms of schizophrenia as the brain matures (Bloom 1993). This theory is distinguished from earlier neurological theories in that it proposes that the underlying biological defect is non-degenerative in nature. Evidence in support of this theory derives from studies which identify brain abnormalities in newly diagnosed patients that are similar to those found in those who have a longer history of schizophrenia, so lending weight to the argument that the putative neurological defect is non-progressive (Jaskiw et al. 1994).

Neurodevelopmental theories of schizophrenia are commonly differentiated into 'early' and 'late' theories, based on the assumed timing of the neurological insult. 'Early' theories implicate intrauterine or perinatal neurological deficits (Keshavan et al. 1998), whereas 'later' theories propose that this insult is acquired later in life. For example, Feinberg (1982) suggests that exaggerated synaptic pruning during adolescence is the root cause of schizophrenia. Common to both sets of theories is the notion that schizophrenia is the expression of an underlying, non-degenerative neurological defect, which expresses itself with the onset of schizophrenia, possibly triggered, or amplified by environmental stressors. Pantelis et al. (2003) review the evidence for these theories, and conclude that the weight of evidence supports the hypothesis that 'an early neurodevelopmental insult interacts with either normal or abnormal post-pubertal brain maturation to produce further (late neurodevelopmental) brain structural and functional changes' (Pantelis et al. 2003: 399).

Another factor which has been implicated in the cause of psychosis is the use of illicit substances, with cannabis having been perhaps most thoroughly researched in this area. Although drug use, is, of course, a complex behaviour involving more than simply the ingestion of a biological substance, as these theories tend to focus on the biological components of substance use (as opposed to sociological or personality factors for example), we include them in this section as examples of biological theories. The notion most commonly expressed is that psychoactive substances may act as a trigger for an underlying predisposition or vulnerability (such as a neurodevelopmental defect). An association between cannabis use and psychosis is well recognized, but doubts regarding the nature and extent of this relationship have been expressed. Evidence to support this relationship is provided by Henquet et al. (2005). In a prospective study they found that, for vulnerable individuals, exposure to cannabis during adolescence and early adulthood increases the risk of subsequent psychosis in a dose-response fashion, meaning that the more cannabis the person uses, the more likely they are to develop psychosis. However, an earlier review by MacLeod et al. (2004) concluded that evidence of a relationship between cannabis use and psychological harm is inconsistent and less in extent than sometimes assumed. They suggest that whatever relationship may exist may be a non-causal association: 'We found no strong evidence that the use of cannabis in itself has important consequences for psychological and social health' (MacLeod et al. 2004: 1586). However, illustrating some of the uncertainty in this field, a more recent review of substance use and psychosis by Thirthalli and Benegal (2006: 243) concludes 'psychosis in the aftermath of substance abuse is fairly common'.

This does not nearly exhaust the range of biological theories that have been proposed to explain madness. As noted in the British Psychological Society (2000: 26) report: 'A complete list of all the factors that have been identified as potential causes of psychotic experiences would cover every aspect of biological functioning.' Though these theories are varied in their focus, they share the common thread of explaining schizophrenia in terms of purported biological pathologies of one sort or another. One exception is the Traumagenic Neurodevelopmental theory which proposes that the neurological defect may result from early childhood trauma (Read et al. 2001).

As with all models of illness, there are clinical implications which derive from these theories. Biological conceptualizations of madness tend, not surprisingly, to be associated with biological treatment recommendations (such as medication and electro-convulsive treatment). As such, these models have been criticized for being suspiciously close to the business interests of the pharmaceutical industry (Mosher et al. 2004) an issue also addressed by Sharfstein (2005), who was at the time president of the American Psychiatric Association.

Evolutionary theories of schizophrenia

Closely related to the biological theories, in that biological factors tend to be implicated, are the evolutionary theories. In a well-researched, entertaining and highly readable book, Horrobin (2002) argues that between approximately 80,000 to 140,000 years ago, in the evolution of *homo sapiens* there was a genetic mutation that was associated with increased creativity and imagination, giving rise to the development of artistic and technical skills which were central to the evolution of human societies. Horrobin proposes that this genetic mutation reflected a prototype of what we now know as schizophrenia, though in a much less pronounced (and much more positive) form than is now known. Horrobin suggests that the genes associated with schizophrenia are of considerable importance in human evolution, but that changes in diet, where humans tend to eat less fish, have seen an amplification of the 'negative' phenotype of this genotype. Horrobin (2002) calls upon genetic analyses of prehistoric remains, as well as evolutionary biochemistry, in support of this theory. Clinical implications which emerge from this theory suggest that fish oils may help alleviate some of the more troubling aspects of schizophrenia.

An unusual (and difficult to test empirically) theory of schizophrenia which also implicates evolutionary factors was espoused by American psychologist, Julian Jaynes, who proposes that the symptoms of schizophrenia (in particular, hearing voices) reflect a fairly recent stage in the evolution of human consciousness. Jaynes' (1976) thesis is that the human mind has undergone a significant transformation over the past 4000 years or so. He suggests that prior to the second millennium BC, mind was 'bicameral' in nature, with a very limited capacity for self-reflection, which meant that one's own thought processes were commonly experienced as a 'voice'. He proposes that schizophrenia is 'at least in part, a vestige of bicamerality' and that before the second millennium BC, 'everyone was schizophrenic'. From this perspective, the symptoms associated with schizophrenia were a normal aspect of the way in which the mind functioned 4000 years or so ago, and those who experience symptoms such as voices are not in the strict sense 'ill', but rather are simply manifesting an earlier state in the evolution of human consciousness.

A more recent evolutionary theory of schizophrenia has been developed by New Zealand psychiatrists Rudegeair and Farelly (2003) who propose that the symptoms of schizophrenia may be a form of dissociation between different psychological functions. They suggest that integration of psychic functions is a relatively late evolutionary development and that this is vulnerable to disruption by early childhood traumas, which, they argue, may impair psychic integration, leaving the individual with 'dissociated' states, which are, Rudegeair and Farelly (2003) contend, the underpinning cause of schizophrenia.

Neuropsychological theory of schizophrenia

A theory of schizophrenia which seems to cross the biological–psychological divide is that of Frith (1992, 1994) in that it endeavours not only to identify the purported biological substrate of the condition but also to delineate the associated psychological impairments in information processing and representation. Unlike the biological theories, Frith's theory pays considerable attention to the content of psychotic experience. Frith (1992) argues that we can make sense of the wide range of symptoms associated with schizophrenia if we look at a fairly narrow range of deficits or malfunctions in a few important higher-order psychological processes involved in processing information, such as thoughts about thoughts ('metacognition' or 'meta-representation'). Frith (1992: 116) argues that 'All the cognitive abnormalities underlying the signs and symptoms of schizophrenia are reflections of a defect in a mechanism that is fundamental to conscious experience. This mechanism has many labels. I shall use the term metarepresentation.'

An important example of the kind of meta-representational processes that Frith (1994) hypothesizes are implicated in schizophrenia is what he refers to as 'theory of mind'. 'Theory of mind' includes the important social ability to infer what might be going on in other people's minds. Frith (1994: 147) argues that malfunctioning of this mechanism could underlie apparently disparate symptoms of schizophrenia, such as thought disorder, flattened affect, and delusions: 'Many of the signs and symptoms of schizophrenia can be understood as arising from the impairments in processes underlying "theory of mind" such as the ability to represent beliefs and intentions.' Frith (1992) proposes that we view schizophrenia as a disorder of self-awareness, characterized by three principal meta-representational abnormalities which can account for all the major signs and symptoms. These three abnormalities which Frith (1992) argues are biologically based and located in the prefrontal cortex of the brain, are:

- An impairment in willed action associated with an inability to generate spontaneous willed actions.
- A defect in self-monitoring leading to an absence of awareness of one's own intentions.
- A disorder in the monitoring of the beliefs and intentions of others.

Although there is some experimental support for some of Frith's notions (reviewed in Bentall 2003: 316–319), the biological underpinnings of the theory remain unsubstantiated, nor is there much in the way of clinical evidence to support the utility of this theory to guide treatment.

Psychological theories of schizophrenia

In this section we include explanations of madness which give emphasis to psychological processes in the aetiology and/or maintenance of schizophrenia (we will discuss psychodynamic models in a separate section as, to some extent, they derive from a distinct intellectual tradition). It is worth pointing out that psychological perspectives on psychosis are not the sole province of psychologists. Indeed, many approaches to psychosis which are clearly psychological in orientation have been developed by non-psychologists, for example Beck's (1952) seminal work on psychological therapy for delusional beliefs.

From an historical point of view, psychological approaches to psychosis, and in particular cognitive-behavioural perspectives inspired by the work of Beck, have blossomed since the early 1990s. However, prior to this recent resurgence, psychologists did show some interest in schizophrenia in the

1940s and 1950s, generally operating within a behaviourist perspective, for example, with the application of token economies in in-patient settings (reinforcing 'acceptable behaviour'). There followed a period of relative neglect by psychologists of the so-called 'serious mental illnesses', such as schizophrenia, which came to be referred to as 'behaviourism's lost child' (Bellack 1986). With the advent of the cognitive revolution within psychology there came a resurgence of interest in psychological approaches to research and treatment for psychosis and schizophrenia (Miller 2003).

Psychological approaches derive from a perspective which is quite different from the biological perspective on human distress. While the biological framework tends to view psychosis as a symptom of a medical condition which is categorically different from 'normal' human processes, the psychological framework is more likely to question the notion that psychosis is a medical illness, and to employ understandings of normal human processes to make sense of unusual or abnormal presentations such as we find in psychosis. To fully appreciate psychological approaches to psychotic experience it is first necessary to consider the important and distinct aspects of the psychological perspective.

Perhaps the most obvious difference between the biological and the psychological approach is at the level of conceptualization. As already noted, psychologists have been critical of the assumption that human distress can be helpfully viewed through a framework which assumes that symptoms can be grouped together into putative medical syndromes such as 'schizophrenia' (for example, see Bentall 2003; Boyle 1990; Read 2004a, 2004b). This antipathy between the concepts of schizophrenia and psychosis and the tenets of a psychological approach to understanding human behaviour and experience led to the development of a quite different orientation in investigating madness. One such approach has been to look at if and how the experiences associated with 'madness' do in fact group together in the way that diagnostic terms suggest they do. For example, using a statistical procedure called 'cluster analysis', Liddle (1987) found that symptoms of schizophrenia tend to group together in three clusters: positive symptoms (hallucinations and delusions), negative symptoms (poverty of speech, low motivation, etc.) and cognitive disorganization (incongruity of affect, disorganized speech, etc.). This finding has been replicated in other studies (see for example, Toomey et al. 1998), although other researches have suggested the three factors could be further subdivided (McGorry et al. 1998).

Many, though not all (for example, Birchwood et al. 1988) of those working within a psychological framework have argued that rather than studying putative diagnostic categories which incorporate a range of different symptoms, there is more to be gained from investigating (and treating) psychotic experiences at the level of the individual symptom rather than at the level of a putative syndrome (which, as we saw in Chapter 3 is consistent with how participants in our research related to their experiences). This argument has been made most clearly by Persons (1986) and Costello (1992), both of whom outline a range of reasons for adopting such an approach. Bentall (2006: 220) extends this argument and suggests that we 'need to abandon psychiatric diagnosis altogether'.

The individual symptoms approach has proven a particularly useful paradigm for research into psychotic experiences, such that it is now becoming the dominant model for psychological research into psychotic experiences. Another aspect of the focus on individual symptoms – which Bentall (2003) suggests would be more accurately and helpfully referred to as 'complaints', to avoid the implication of 'illness' inherent in the concept of 'symptom' – is that it is more consistent with the well-founded assumption that these experiences lie on a continuum with normal experiences, and hence that normal psychological processes can help us understand the aetiology and/or maintenance of these 'complaints'. Evidence to support this position can be found in research, such as that by Strauss (1969), who demonstrated that both hallucinations and delusions are best thought of as points on a continuum with normal perceptions and beliefs, differentiated by factors such as degree of conviction and preoccupation with the experience. Similarly, research into hallucinations and delusions has found that such experiences are more common than one might imagine in 'normal' populations. For example, Tien (1991) outlines research which suggests that one in ten people may experience hallucinations. Estimates on the prevalence of delusional beliefs in 'normal' populations, including research carried out in Dunedin, New Zealand (Poulton et al. 2000) suggests that as many as 20 per cent of the population may meet criteria for holding delusional beliefs, although a large-scale Dutch study found only 3.3 per cent of the population held 'true' delusional beliefs (van Os et al. 2000). A British study reported that over a period of eighteen months more than 4 per cent of their non-clinical sample reported at least one psychotic experience, although they had reported none at the beginning of the study (Wiles et al. 2006).

Research such as the above lends support to the notion that the 'complaints' which characterize psychosis and schizophrenia do lie on a continuum with normal human experiences, and that investigations which focus on individual complaints may contribute to our understandings of these experiences. We will now outline psychological theories of thought disorder, hallucinations and delusions which derive from this tradition.

Psychological theories of thought disorder

An early example of a psychological approach to psychotic experiences is Don Bannister's investigations into thought disorder, where he proposed that thought disorder can be understood as the consequence of someone having been 'invalidated' so often that he or she goes out of the business of making testable (and hence disprovable) statements about the world, instead reverting to statements which are so loose in their meaning as to be impossible to disprove, as well as being very difficult for others to understand (Bannister 1960; Bannister and Fransella 1966; Bannister et al. 1975). Despite this early research of Bannister's it was some time before research of this nature became more commonplace among psychologists.

Psychological theories of hallucinations

Bentall's theory of hallucinations (2003: Chapter 14) is located firmly within the cognitive tradition in psychology where it is assumed that is not experiences in themselves which cause distress, but rather how the individual evaluates, or appraises, such experiences. Thus, the focus shifts from exclusive attention on the experience to the appraisal processes the individual uses to render the experience meaningful. Bentall (2003: 367) proposes that hallucinations are not, as is often assumed, the result of 'faulty' perceptual processes, but rather they 'arise from an error of judgement rather than an error of perception'. The particular judgement implicated, according to Bentall, is the judgement about where an experience originates from – inside or outside the self: 'People who hallucinate make faulty judgements about the sources of their experiences, and it is for this reason that they mistake their inner speech or visual imagery for stimuli external to themselves' (Bentall 2003: 367).

Bentall (2003) argues that ascertaining whether or not experiences are internally or externally generated is not something that is a 'given' of the experience. Rather, Bentall suggests that identifying the source of experiences is a skill, which, like all other skills, develops over time, is subject to individual variation, and can fail under certain conditions. This skill has been referred to as 'source-monitoring' (Johnson et al. 1993). This source-monitoring theory of hallucinations is supported by Garrett and Silva's (2003) study of the subjective experience of hallucinations, which found that clients' descriptions of hallucinations were congruent with this theory.

Bentall (2003) discusses a range of factors which are important components of the source-monitoring skill, including qualities in the individual (such as expectations and beliefs), aspects of the stimulus (such as how clear it is) and situational factors (such as the degree of urgency or danger involved). A hallucinatory experience is the outcome of failure in the application of this skill when an internally generated experience (such as inner speech) is misattributed by the individual to an external source, which means it will be experienced as a voice. In his exposition of the theory, Bentall (2003: Chapter 14) provides a detailed overview of research and clinical evidence which lends support.

Other research which has investigated the role of the appraisals of experience in psychosis includes the seminal work by Romme and Escher (1989, 1993, 1996). In a series of investigations into the experience of hearing voices, Romme and Escher showed that these experiences are not always distressing to the individual. They found that an important determinant of whether or not voices would be distressing to the individual was the understanding, or 'explanatory model' (Kleinman 1988) that the individual had for such experiences. For example, those who viewed their voices as guides giving useful advice would be much less likely to experience distress than those who viewed their voices as manifestations of a powerful evil force. These findings are similar to those of Chadwick and Birchwood (1994), who point to the role of appraisals of omnipotence and omniscience of voices in influencing levels of distress for the individual.

Psychological theories of delusions

As with the research on hallucinations, research in the area of delusions has been well summarized and synthesized by Bentall (2003). In psychological theories, delusions are seen largely as the product of normal information processing. In particular, processes involved in formation and maintenance of normal beliefs are seen as implicated in the formation and maintenance of delusions. Bentall (1994: 356) argues that 'The reasoning biases exhibited by deluded subjects might be seen as amplifications of normal mechanisms for coping with threat.'

Bentall's theory of paranoid delusions has developed over a number of years, being modified and expanded in light of the growing body of research and clinical practice in this field. Bentall (2003) suggests that a range of cognitive processes may be involved in the development of paranoid thinking, including causal attributions that the individual makes about experiences. Bentall argues that paranoid people have a characteristic attributional style which renders them vulnerable to paranoia. Research by Bentall and others (Candido and Romney 1990; Kindermann and Bentall 1996) suggests that paranoid people have a tendency to make 'external personal' attributions for negative events. That is, they tend to blame negative events (such as not getting a job) on other people's deliberate actions (for example, the government telling the employer not to offer the person a job) rather than on situational factors (for example, too many applicants). Although acknowledging some uncertainty regarding why some people may develop this particular tendency, Kindermann and Bentall (1996) suggest that it may have its origins, at least partly, in experiences which have proved challenging to the individual's self-concept:

> Although the developmental origins of the abnormal attributional style of paranoid patients are not understood, it is possible that such a style develops in the context of chronic threats to the self-concept that predate the appearance of psychosis.
>
> (Kindermann and Bentall 1996: 112)

In his more recent work, Bentall (2003: 305) suggests that paranoia may contain a 'nugget of truth', in so far as it may relate, however obscurely, to earlier experiences which the individual has had which contain similar themes to the content of the delusional beliefs. In addition to the role of attributional style, Bentall suggests that other factors, such as hypervigilance for threat-related material and a difficulty in understanding what other people might be thinking (a 'theory of mind' deficit) may also be implicated in the psychology of delusions.

Other psychological explanations for delusional beliefs include Garety's (1991, 1992) theory which places emphasis on the role of probabilistic reasoning, suggesting that those with delusional beliefs have a tendency to 'jump to conclusions' on the basis of limited evidence. In a review of the various theories of delusions and the evidence to support them, Garety and Freeman (1999) conclude that there is sufficient evidence to suggest that both attributional and probabilistic biases are implicated in the formation and maintenance of delusional beliefs. Another perspective on delusions is Rhodes and Jakes' (2004) idea that delusions are expressions of metaphors which have been 'lost': that is, the metaphorical aspect is no longer conscious to client.

Psychodynamic and psychoanalytic theories of schizophrenia

As with psychological and biological explanations of schizophrenia, psychodynamic accounts subsume a variety of different theories rather than a single unified and universally accepted theory. In clinical practice, psychodynamic approaches are characterized by a close working relationship between the therapist and the client, which may involve meeting several times per week, where the focus is on making sense of the client's experience drawing from psychodynamic theory. Psychodynamic understandings of psychosis emerge from such close working relationships and detailed attention to the client's experience.

Psychodynamic accounts of human experience can be traced to the works of Freud (1957) and are based, to varying degrees, on his model of the workings of the human mind. Freud developed a comprehensive model of human psychological functioning which stressed the structure of self (ego, id and superego) and posited a range of processes which are in operation as the self develops through time. Freud's emphasis was on inner conflicts and ways of dealing with these conflicts ('defences') both at the time of the initial conflict, and subsequently over the course of an individual's life when these conflicts may re-emerge, often in a disguised form. Freud's view can, somewhat simplistically, be summarized as seeing psychological difficulties as being the manifestation of conflicts from past experiences.

Freud (1904) himself discouraged psychotherapy of psychosis. Although in his earlier works he had considered this possible, he later revised his position. Josephs and Josephs (1986) point out that Freud was the first clinician to see meaning in psychotic experiences, as illustrated by his famous case study of Schreber. Despite this, Freud later went on to argue that psychosis (which he at times referred to as 'narcissistic neuroses') is not amenable to psychoanalytic therapy because the client is unable to form a 'transference relationship' – an essential ingredient of successful psychoanalytic therapy (Arieti 1974). This viewpoint was maintained by classical analysts, although an early pupil of Freud's, Paul Federn (1952) questioned this and made several attempts to treat psychotic patients, arguing that poor ego boundaries contributed to psychotic problems, with material from the id invading the ego and being projected onto the external world.

A common thread in many of the psychoanalytic conceptualizations of psychosis is that it reflects the individual's attempts to deal with difficult emotions that relate to an earlier stage of development. An early proponent of the psychoanalytic perspective, Melanie Klein (1946), made significant contributions to the analytic conceptualization of psychosis. She suggested that the basis of psychosis can be found in early development and reflects the use of particular defence mechanisms. In particular, she introduced the concept of 'projective identification', which she describes as 'splitting off parts of the self and projecting them on to another person', a process she viewed as implicated in the development of the 'paranoid-schizoid position'. This position was developed by Bion (1956) who argued that this defence mechanism was a core feature of schizophrenia.

Also operating within a psychodynamic framework, Sullivan (1956) suggested that schizophrenia can be explained as an adaptive strategy by the individual in trying to deal with the cumulative effects of trauma, which threaten to throw him or her into panic and terror. Sullivan (1956) viewed schizophrenia as a defensive strategy for avoiding fragmentation and chaos, and for maintaining a meaningful view of the self, even if that is at some cost to the individual (who retreats into madness). A similar view is espoused by Shapiro (1991), who argues that self-destructive behaviour in schizophrenia reflects an attempt to reverse self-fragmentation brought on by the experience of overwhelming affect.

Searles (1961) agrees that schizophrenia is characterized by fragmentation of experience, which results in a loss of continuity and connection, although he proposes that it is intense fear of change (derived from parental restrictions on autonomy) which is the genesis of psychosis. Modern analysts, such as Symington (2006), suggest that the emotion of shame may be important. He argues that shame fuels the projective process, such as 'projective-identification'. He suggests that psychosis reflects an 'inner jelly-like chaos' which derives from the 'total absence of inner government'.

London (1980) notes that one of the weaknesses of psychoanalytic theories of schizophrenia relates to scientific evaluation, with there having been few scientific studies evaluating the validity of the constructs or the efficacy of psychoanalytic therapies. While there have been claims that the psycho-dynamic perspective on schizophrenia is 'dead' (see for example Mueser and Berenbaum 1990), it is clear that these suggestions of the demise of this model have been somewhat premature. There is a vast and growing psycho-dynamic literature on psychosis. More recent models of madness which can be subsumed under the psychodynamic umbrella include Karon's (1999) view that schizophrenia is an expression of chronic terror and the defences utilized by the individual to live with this terror. Overviews of psychodynamic ther-apy of schizophrenia can be found in Hingley (1997) and Silver et al. (2004). Psychodynamic theories of psychosis have been consistent in their efforts to explore the meaning of psychotic experiences (Hingley 2006; Silver et al. 2004) and to find helpful ways of working psychotherapeutically with those who experience psychosis. Robbins (1993) illustrates, using detailed case studies, how, in clinical practice, psychoanalysts go about the business of exploring the meaning of psychotic experiences.

Communication and family theories of schizophrenia

Though less prominent nowadays than in the 1950s and 1960s, theories of schizophrenia which focus on styles of communication have nonetheless had a significant impact on the literature, particularly in the areas of systemic conceptualizations and family therapy of schizophrenia. Among the earliest proponents of theories of this sort was Gregory Bateson (Bateson 1973; Bateson et al. 1956). Bateson argued that schizophrenia results from the individual being brought up in a family environment characterized by a par-ticular style of communication, wherein the child is repeatedly exposed to a 'double bind' situation which renders him or her vulnerable to schizophrenia. A 'double bind' is a form of communication which operates on at least two logical levels, and contains contradictory commands or requests, thus render-ing it impossible to fully comply: a commonly used illustration of this is that of the mother who holds her child's hand tightly while telling him or her to go off to school. Bateson argued that repeated exposure to such communica-tions leads to problems in understanding the communications and motiv-ations of others (more specifically, to difficulties in discriminating between the literal and the metaphoric aspects of communication). This will result in 'faulty' metacommunication skills in reading the behaviour of self and others which, in turn, leads to the range of symptoms associated with schizophrenia. This deficit, according to Bateson, is the direct consequence of being in a particular family situation characterized by 'double bind' communications. Bateson et al. (1956: 258) argue that 'The child grows up unskilled in his ability to communicate about communication and, as a result, unskilled in determining what people really mean and unskilled in expressing what he really means.'

In support of this view, Wynne and Singer (1963) found that families of those diagnosed schizophrenic consistently score higher than 'normal' families on measures of 'communication deviance'. Further empirical support for the role played by family communication is found in the UCLA Family Project, which followed families prospectively for fifteen years and found that both expressed emotion (hostility, criticism and emotional over-involvement) and 'communication deviance' are predictive of schizophrenia (Doane et al. 1981; Goldstein 1987).

Although these theories came to be associated with theories which 'blame' the family (and in particular the mother) for causing schizophrenia (Johnstone 1999) and dropped out of fashion when such approaches came under fire, we can see a more enduring influence of the theory in clinical approaches to schizophrenia which focus on the importance of styles of communication within the family, such as is found in the literature on expressed emotion (Goldstein et al. 1994; Vaughn and Leff 1976).

Life event theories of schizophrenia

The family communication theories outlined above point to the importance of the interpersonal environment the individual finds him or herself in. In the current section we consider accounts of schizophrenia which have implicated life events (such as childhood trauma) in the aetiology of schizophrenia. We have already referred to Rudegeair and Farelly's (2003) theory which identifies trauma as critical; for convenience I have located this under 'evolutionary' theories, though it could, clearly, also be included here. It is worth pointing out that theorists from a wide range of perspectives (for example, psychodynamic, psychological etc.) have argued that life events play an important role in psychotic experiences.

The role of life events in the aetiology of mental health problems is a topic which has generated, and continues to generate, considerable controversy. Both sides of this debate can be traced to the work of Freud. Freud's earliest (circa 1896) theory on this matter proposed that early childhood sexual experiences are a crucial aetiological factor in the development of mental health problems in later life (Freud 1962). Famously, and controversially, Freud revised this theory some years later to suggest that the early sexual experiences he had considered of such importance were fantasies the child had created, rather than actual experiences. This shift in Freudian theory has been the subject of much analysis in recent years where it is often argued that Freud first uncovered, only to subsequently deny, the important role of actual sexual abuse in the development of mental health problems in later life: see Masson (1984) for a critical review of this change in Freud's theory. Though Freud's interest was more in the so-called 'neuroses' than the 'psychoses', we can see in this about-turn a parallel in the current literature, where the role of sexual abuse and other adverse events in childhood as contributory factors to the causes of psychotic experience is hotly debated.

In the realm of theories of psychosis and schizophrenia, we find an early example of emphasis being given to the role of life experiences (not limited to sexual abuse) by Harry Stack Sullivan (1956, 1962) who encouraged his patients to see their difficulties as being related to life experiences. Pinpointing a more specific relationship, Frieda Fromm-Reichmann (1948, 1958) argued that the symptoms of psychosis can be seen as the client repeating early traumas and past interpersonal relations, which come to manifest themselves in a somewhat distorted form in present relationships. She argued that such traumatic early interpersonal relationships set the client on a solitary path, where trust is particularly difficult, leading to the loneliness of the schizophrenic position.

Interest in the role of early traumatic experiences in schizophrenia has been the subject of considerable empirical investigation since the mid-1990s, with mounting evidence that people who have psychotic experiences are more likely than the general adult population to have been subject to abuse (sexual, physical and/or emotional) as children (Bebbington et al. 2004; Janssen et al. 2004; Read 1997; Read et al. 2004). However, as in Freud's day, the literature in this field is imbued with controversy, which has not yet been resolved by empirical investigations. Some large-scale studies (Bebbington et al. 2004; Janssen et al. 2004; Spataro et al. 2004) reached quite different conclusions about the putative relationship between psychosis and early childhood abuse. While the study by Janssen et al. (2004) concludes that 'childhood abuse predicts psychotic symptoms in adulthood in a dose-response fashion', Spataro et al. (2004) argue that their results 'do not support an association between child sexual abuse and psychosis'. Methodological differences in these studies may account for at least some of the inconsistencies in findings. Spataro et al.'s (2004) study includes only those cases of sexual abuse which came to the attention of the authorities at the time, which are unlikely to be representative of all cases of childhood sexual abuse. Another potential weakness of this study, acknowledged by the authors, is that the average age of subjects at follow-up (in their early twenties) may have underestimated the incidence of psychosis, which commonly does not emerge until the mid-twenties. Similarly, criticism can be levied at the Janssen et al. (2004) study. While this is a large-scale study (n = 4045), their conclusions about the relationship between abuse and psychosis are based on only seven participants who reached their 'need for care' criteria level of psychotic disturbance. Bebbington et al.'s (2004) research was also large scale (n = 8580), with the evidence convincingly pointing to a positive relationship between psychosis in adulthood and a range of 'victimization experiences' (sexual abuse, bullying, violence, being taken into care, etc.), with the association being strongest in the case of those who report sexual abuse. At present, there is a lack of consensus in this field regarding the nature of the relationship between early trauma and psychosis in adulthood, which continues to generate the kind of controversy aroused by Freud's original exposition of this theory. Helpful discussions of the range of theories that might be proposed to account for a association between sexual abuse and psychosis are provided by Bebbington et al. (2004), Larkin and Morrison (2006), Morrison et al. (2003) and Read et al. (2008).

Other investigations which hope to shed light on the nature of the relationship between trauma and psychosis include studies which have considered the relationship between abuse and severity of psychiatric disturbance (Read 1998) and others which have looked into associations between different types of abuse (sexual and physical) and particular symptoms (hallucinations, delusions and though disorder: Read et al. 2003). Although the literature delineating relationships between specific forms of abuse and specific psychotic symptoms is tentative rather than conclusive, it does, nonetheless, provide hope that if such specific relationships are indeed found consistently, this may allow advances to be made in identifying particular mechanisms that may be implicated in the development of psychotic experiences.

Such is the interest in the relationship between trauma and psychosis that an entire issue of the scientific journal *Acta Psychiatrica Scandinavica* (November 2005) was dedicated to this matter. This issue included an updated review of the literature in this field (Read et al. 2005) and further consideration of possible mechanisms (biological and neurodevelopmental) which could explain relationships between trauma and psychosis. Bak et al. (2005) put forward the notion that early trauma may predispose people to experience more distress associated with psychotic experiences through diminishing coping responses.

An example of how the literature in this field can encompass more than one conceptualization of schizophrenia is found in the Traumagenic Neurodevelopmental Model (Read et al. 2001). This model proposes that childhood abuse is an important causal factor in the development of schizophrenia and that this is entirely consistent with findings showing abnormalities in the brains of adults diagnosed with schizophrenia. Though biological correlates of schizophrenia are commonly used to support the idea the schizophrenia is biologically caused, Read et al. (2001) argue that many of the brain abnormalities found in schizophrenia are also found in the brains of those who have been abused as children. That is, they suggest that the experience of abuse causes particular abnormalities in the brain which render people vulnerable to travelling down a neurodevelopmental pathway which may lead to psychotic experiences such as those found in schizophrenia. They also acknowledge that other factors are likely to be involved in the aetiology of such a complex picture as schizophrenia, cautioning against overly simplistic models which posit a single (usually biological) factor as *the* cause of schizophrenia.

While our focus in this section has been mostly on sexual abuse as a possible causal contributor to schizophrenia, this is not the only life event which has been implicated in schizophrenia. Other life events which have been found to be associated with schizophrenia include physical abuse and bullying (Janssen et al. 2004); poverty (Faris and Dunham 1939; Harrison et al. 2001); belonging to an ethnic minority (Hutchison et al. 1996); experiences of racial discrimination (Janssen et al. 2003); recent stressful experiences (Birley and Brown 1970). Other variables which have been considered important in understanding schizophrenia include the notion that urban environment may contribute to psychosis (van Os 2004). Sundquist et al. (2004) discuss evidence consistent with this view and consider the possibility that factors such as poor social networks and lack of support may contribute to the condition.

The theories considered so far in this chapter have developed largely from clinical disciplines, whether they be primarily medical in their orientation, or more inclined to a psychotherapeutic perspective. However, this does not exhaust the range of professional and scientific theories that have been proposed as explanations of what schizophrenia is. Other disciplines have also investigated schizophrenia, and come up with quite different conceptualizations. We will now consider some of these theories.

Sociological and anthropological theories of schizophrenia

The theories discussed so far (with the exception of communication and family theories) have in common that they take a largely individualistic approach to schizophrenia. By this, we mean that they take as their starting point the assumption that schizophrenia can be understood by looking to the individual who receives this diagnosis, and identifying what it is that is unusual about this individual that explains how it is that he or she has developed this complaint. In contrast, sociological and anthropological approaches tend to adopt quite a different starting position, in that their focus is much more on the social context within which a diagnosis of schizophrenia is made. As such, the social and cultural practices involved in the process of identifying someone as 'deviant', and then labelling the person as mentally ill, are given greater prominence in sociological and anthropological accounts of schizophrenia.

Writers such as Littlewood (1991) and Eisenberg (1977) have argued that to understand schizophrenia, we must look not only at those so diagnosed, but also at the process of diagnosis itself, not overlooking the frameworks adopted by those who do the diagnosing. Littlewood (1991) draws our attention to the fact that any complex behaviour can be viewed in a range of ways, and how it is that we view the behaviour will be influenced by many factors, including culturally embedded points of view. Littlewood (1991) points out that concepts such as 'schizophrenia' are not 'natural facts', about which we are compelled to agree, but rather reflect a particular way of construing experience, influenced by our own interests, or those of the culture/subculture to which we belong. Though it might be argued (and indeed often is) that the various models of schizophrenia are supported by empirical evidence, it is important to recognize that this 'evidence' is not independent of the model adopted in the first place. As Eisenberg (1977) points out:

> Once in place, models act to generate their own verification by excluding phenomena outside the frame of reference the user employs. Models are indispensable but hazardous because they can be mistaken for reality itself rather than as but one way of organizing that reality.
>
> (Eisenberg 1977: 18)

Both Eisenberg (1977) and Littlewood (1991) seem to be stressing that our models of madness and the evidence we may call upon to support these models are not independent of one another. That is, particular ways of viewing schizophrenia will lead to particular research endeavours, designed to gather particular types of evidence (and thereby ignore other evidence) which in turn are used as support for the theory. The point being made is that we must recognize that factors other than, or in addition to, 'evidence' are also implicated in our adopted models of madness and we would do well to recognize this.

Within the sociological tradition attention is also given to how and why it is that individuals come to be identified as deviant, and the impact that this has on the person. This work, which has its roots in classic works such as those of Goffman (1961) and Becker (1963), has come to be referred to as 'labelling theory', focusing as it does on the process and impact of being labelled. Looking at the social context writers such as Becker (1963: 9) argue that deviance is actually created by the social group through rules adopted for deciding who is 'inside' and who is 'out': 'Social groups create deviance by making rules whose infraction constitutes deviance, and by applying those rules to particular people and labeling them as outsiders.' Ivan Illich (1975) argues that this process serves a function of social control, whereby those who do not fit easily into conventional social categories are rendered less threatening to society by being categorized as deviant:

> People who look strange or behave oddly threaten any society until their uncommon traits have been formally named and their uncommon behaviour has been slotted into a recognised role. By being assigned a name and a role, eerie and upsetting deviants are turned into well-defined and established categories.
>
> (Illich 1975: 56)

Clearly one such category of deviance, and one that has received considerable attention, is that of mental ill-health in general, and schizophrenia in particular. In addition to the process through which individuals come to be labelled, sociologists have also examined some of the effects of such labelling, arguing that there is an 'iatrogenic effect', whereby the individual will be treated differently by others and will come to see him or herself differently as a consequence of this labelling process. Thus, it is argued, an individual, once labelled as say, schizophrenic, may come to see themselves in this way, and this will have the effect of amplifying the original deviant behaviour and excluding alternative behaviours (Turner 1987). The individual comes to be stigmatized by the label 'mental patient', which in turn will determine how others react to the person. Should the person accept this label, then he or she will act accordingly, thus reinforcing the social role of 'mental patient' (Doherty 1975). This process has been referred to as entering into a 'career of deviance' through 'role-playing' the sick person. Scheff (1984) suggests that once an individual is labelled 'ill', this can lead to a self-fulfilling prophecy, in which accepting the label of illness can actually have an impact on the disease process itself, as he saw in his study of tuberculosis sufferers, where he found that patients who accepted the rules of the hospital ward made a slower recovery than those who rejected these rules. Similarly, there is some research into the impact on the individual of accepting the labels of 'mental illness' or 'schizophrenia': those who accept such labels have been shown to fare worse in certain measures of mental health, such as dependence (Morrison et al. 1977) and sense of control and associated depression (Birchwood et al. 1993).

Another interesting study into the impact of labelling is the infamous study by Rosenhan (1973). His study, which involved 'stooges' falsely reporting that they had heard a voice uttering a single word, demonstrated how easy it was to be labelled as schizophrenic, and also how difficult it was, in the USA in the 1970s at least, for the pseudo-patients to lose the label once diagnosed, despite showing no further signs or symptoms of mental ill-health during their time in hospital. Thirty years later, a replication of this study (Slater 2004) reported similar findings, despite supposed increased reliability and validity of psychiatric diagnoses.

Philosophical and existential theories of schizophrenia

Given the profound, and at times profoundly confusing, aspects of the experiences associated with schizophrenia, it is perhaps not surprising that we also find theories of schizophrenia which have a distinctly philosophical orientation. The historical overlap between psychology and philosophy means that, for many of the earlier writers in this area (such as Jaspers, Freud, and William James), distinctions between philosophy, psychology and psychiatry were far from clear cut. For example, though Karl Jaspers is generally regarded as one of the founding fathers of modern psychiatry, he spent most of his working life as a philosopher. In his classic text, Jaspers (1963: 309) points out that 'in psychotic reality we find an abundance of content representing the fundamental problems of philosophy'.

Philosophical theories may strive to account for schizophrenia in philosophical terms, and/or may focus on the philosophical implications of having such experiences. Although much of modern psychiatry and psychology pays little heed to the philosophical aspects of psychotic experiences, there is nonetheless a significant, if marginalized, literature which addresses these issues. Perhaps one of the most vocal and influential writers in this tradition was the Scottish psychiatrist, R. D. Laing, a major figure in the 'anti-psychiatry' movement of the 1960s and 1970s, who himself had personal experience of psychosis (Clay 1996). Laing (1960, 1967) argued that schizophrenia can be seen as the manifestation of existential despair, reflecting a division in the patient's psyche, which is brought upon by the conflicting demands of living in a world which alienates us. For Laing, madness is a kind of voyage, through which the person comes to more fully appreciate the nature of existence. Schizophrenia, to Laing (1967: 93), was 'a natural way of healing our own appalling state of alienation called normality'. Laing suggested that schizophrenia reflects a kind of 'ontological insecurity' where the individual feels uncertain about his or her very way of being in the world and that appropriate 'treatment' for those suffering from schizophrenia is to provide an environment which allows the individual to work through these philosophical crises (Laing 1967).

Others who have written in the philosophical tradition include the Finnish psychiatrist, Siirala (1961), who argues that people diagnosed schizophrenic are, in some ways, prophets who express the underlying malaise in society. Siirala (1961) sees those with this diagnosis as both victims of a harsh society, and prophets (to whom nobody really listens, unfortunately) who have a particular sensitivity to our 'collective sickness'. This collective sickness reflects the accumulated evil acts committed by members of a society, which have come to be hidden from view for, and by, 'normal' people. He argues that those working in this area have a responsibility to reveal to society the prophecies of patients, given that these are, according to Siirala (1961), insights into the madness that exists not only within the individual psyche of the client, but also within the society to which the client belongs. Arguing along similar lines, Arieti (1974, 1979) proposed we should view schizophrenia as more than simply an unfortunate illness that happens to afflict some members of the human race. Rather, he argues, the experiences characteristic of schizophrenia are such that they can provide us with unique insights into human nature. Of schizophrenic experience, Arieti (1979: 220) proposes 'we can learn from it about human life in general and the human predicament'.

More recently, Louis Sass (1992) has further developed philosophical conceptualizations of madness, drawing on the works of both Heidegger and Wittgenstein. Sass proposes that we can comprehend schizophrenia as a complex and perhaps convoluted attempt by the individual to grapple with issues relating to the very nature of Being itself (that is, with 'ontological' issues). Sass suggests that schizophrenia reflects a particular 'way-of-being-in-the-world' that indicates a shift in how the individual deals with the basic frameworks we use for making sense of the world, such as the nature of 'self' and the nature of 'reality' (Bracken and Thomas 1999; Sass 2004). Sass and Parnas (2003) elaborate this theory, proposing that disturbances of self may be the central feature of schizophrenia. They suggest that this conceptualization can help unify an otherwise disjointed concept (schizophrenia) and also suggest that this theory may help identify prodromal schizophrenia by identifying the subtle changes in self that may precede the condition itself.

The focus on the role of self in schizophrenia is also considered by Landrine (1992: 405), who suggests that psychiatric symptoms, especially those associated with schizophrenia, are 'violations of Western cultural assumptions about how the self ought to be experienced'. Lysaker and Lysaker (2004) add a further perspective, when they suggest that schizophrenia results from what they refer to as 'disturbances in dialogical capacity'. This notion is based on the philosophical position of self as 'subjective multiplicity', as proposed by Nietzsche (1966) and others, and proposes that schizophrenia results from a breakdown within the individual's relationship between different 'selves'.

Spiritual theories of schizophrenia

Spiritual theories of schizophrenia in the modern age can be traced to the works of Carl Jung, who, like R. D. Laing, had a personal experience of a psychotic breakdown (see Jung 1995). Also like Laing, Jung has been an influential figure in this area, though one who has been marginalized by mainstream theorists and clinicians. One wonders if somehow having a personal experience of psychosis, as both these writers have, in some way contributes to being seen somewhat as 'outcasts' by their professional peers. Drawing heavily on Eastern philosophical and theological writings, Jung (1936) proposed that psychosis can be viewed as the result of the disintegration, or fragmentation, of consciousness brought on by a failure to recognize the psychic importance of the spiritual realm of experience. Similarly, William James (1902) considered there to be a close relationship between 'mysticism and insanity'.

There has been a recent resurgence of interest in spiritual conceptualizations and spiritual implications of psychotic experiences. For example, an attempt to examine the relationship between psychosis and spirituality has been developed by British psychologist Isabel Clarke. Using the personal construct framework of George Kelly (1955), Clarke (2000a, 2000b, 2001) proposes that psychosis and spirituality are alike in being a unified area of human experience, both of which reflect attempts by the individual to make sense of the world without use of their usual constructs for navigating reality. Clarke (2000b) argues that the differences between psychosis and spiritual experiences have been exaggerated and further, that what differences there are, reside in the experiencer rather than the experience. This perspective has been elaborated by New Zealanders Randal and Argyle (2005), who suggest the normal process of spiritual development is a gradual one, but certain individuals may experience sudden 'growth spurts' in their spiritual development which can give rise to a 'spiritual emergency' (Grof and Grof 1986). Randal and Argyle argue that phenomenologically there is little to distinguish between what is classed as 'spiritual emergency' and what is considered 'psychosis'.

Issues relating to spirituality are often more readily addressed by non-Western cultures. In 2007 a New Zealand study of Māori understandings of what Westerners call psychosis confirmed that many Māori hold to their traditional views that such experiences are readily and commonly understandable from a spiritual perspective. Voices, for instance, are frequently experienced as support or warnings from ancestors (Taitimu 2007).

Finally, in this section, we must also consider the work of British psychologist, Peter Chadwick, whose writings cover both professional and personal perspectives on schizophrenia, Chadwick himself having been diagnosed with the condition (Chadwick 1992, 1997). Chadwick explores the strong spiritual aspect of the experience for the individual, arguing that this is a crucial part of psychosis. Echoing Siirala (1961, see above), Chadwick (1997: 172) suggests that direct experience with psychosis may provide us with unique and important insights into the nature of existence: 'It may be that many insights had at the outer limits of sanity, shining like a sun to the receptive mind, will yet transform our world and save the minds of others who still live without hope.'

Stress–vulnerability models of schizophrenia

Given the diverse range of theories that have been proposed to account for schizophrenia (only some of which have been considered here), it should come as no surprise that there have also been attempts to integrate these various theories within a broader framework, which can subsume the various theories, and ideally, generate greater consensus among those working in the field. We will conclude this chapter by discussing one such approach, which has gained significant support in both clinical and research settings.

The most widely promulgated of these broad frameworks is what is referred to as the 'stress–vulnerability' model of schizophrenia. Developed from a framework first articulated by Meehl (1962), the notion of 'stress–vulnerability' as a model for schizophrenia was first explicitly expressed by Zubin and Spring (1977) and later expanded by Nuechterlein and Dawson (1984). Essentially, stress–vulnerability models propose that episodes of psychosis can be understood within a heuristic framework which recognizes contributions from both 'vulnerability' factors and from 'stress' factors. Nuechterlein and Dawson (1984) suggest that certain characteristics of individuals may serve as more enduring 'vulnerability' factors and environmental 'stressors' may precipitate psychotic periods in such vulnerable individuals. It is worth noting that within the model as originally outlined by both Zubin and Spring (1977) and Nuechterlein and Dawson (1984), 'vulnerability' factors include pre-existing, enduring characteristics, which are products of both genetic and non-genetic variables (including early physical and social environmental influences). We can see the model as an attempt to conceptualize episodes of schizophrenia in terms of combinations of enduring characteristics of the individual which render him or her vulnerable and more transient stressors in the environment which act as triggers for episodes in such vulnerable individuals.

This model of schizophrenia is rather unusual in that it has achieved a degree of consensus among clinicians and researchers. However, on closer inspection, we may note that this model is in fact open to a variety of interpretations regarding what constitutes a 'vulnerability' factor. For example, there has been some disagreement around whether 'vulnerability' refers specifically to inherited biological factors, or whether other factors (such as being abused as a child) should also be considered as part of the 'vulnerability' that an individual may have to psychosis (see Read et al. 2001, 2008). In their original exposition of the model, Zubin and Spring (1977: 109) were clear that vulnerability included 'acquired vulnerability', and provided specific examples, including 'the influence of trauma, specific diseases, perinatal complications, family experiences, adolescent life experiences, and other life events'. Interestingly, this model is commonly referred to in medical texts as the 'stress–diathesis' model, with the more medical and biological 'diathesis' ('constitutional predisposition toward a particular state or condition and especially one that is abnormal or diseased': Merriam-Webster online dictionary) replacing the more general notion of 'vulnerability' of the original expositions. This is a subtle, yet significant, alteration in the original argument, which is rarely, if ever, acknowledged as having an impact on what the model conveys.

Whatever position one may adopt regarding what is and is not 'vulnerability', we can ask to what extent the 'stress–vulnerability' model is in fact a theoretical explanation of psychosis or schizophrenia. It seems to us that this model simply states that those who have episodes of psychosis must have those factors (whatever they may be) that render the individual vulnerable to psychosis, along with those factors (whatever they may be) which trigger this vulnerability. That is, the model proposes that only those people who have an underlying vulnerability to psychosis are vulnerable to psychosis, and that among those individuals, only those whose vulnerability has been activated (through 'stressors') will become psychotic. We can see that there is a certain tautology to this argument: only those who *can* develop psychosis will do so, and only when their propensity for doing so is actualized. Such an argument could be proposed for every aspect of human behaviour. It is perhaps not at all surprising then that this model has achieved a degree of consensus.

Although it has proven to be fairly useful within the clinical setting (for example, by helping clients identify their own 'triggers') we can see that this is not so much a theoretical explanation for what 'madness' is, but rather it is a broad, all-encompassing framework (or what Bentall (2004) refers to as a 'meaningless generalization') that may have some clinical utility, even if it falls short as a theoretical conceptualization of schizophrenia. This is not to decry the already acknowledged clinical value of this framework, but it is to propose that it is not, in fact, a theory which helps explain what schizophrenia is, or what it is caused by.

Another important attempt to develop an integrative perspective on psychosis, incorporating aspects of a range of different models, including biological, psychodynamic and psychological factors was expounded by Cullberg (2006). Cullberg uses the principles from the stress–vulnerability model and expands on these to develop a biopsychosocial model of psychosis, informed by a broad and impressive grasp of diverse literature in this field. Following this exposition, Cullberg (2006) goes on to consider implications for treatment from this biopsychosocial approach.

This brings us to an end of our three chapters discussing the diverse ways of making sense of madness, from personal, lay and professional perspectives. We are now confronted with the difficult questions of what to make of and what to do with this dizzying array of models of madness generated from these various positions. This is a situation which we ourselves have grappled with in our own attempts to make sense of madness. We outline our response in Chapter 6, where we delineate our efforts at bringing it all together.

Bringing it all together
What 'schizophrenia' really is

What we have covered over the previous three chapters is a complex and possibly confusing assortment of perspectives on how we can go about the business of making sense of madness. Our expedition over the literature in this field has included ways of looking at madness from first-person, lay and professional perspectives. In none of these areas has our coverage been comprehensive or exhaustive. Nor do these three perspectives cover all possible perspectives one could take to approach the topic of madness: for example, we have already acknowledged that we have largely overlooked a large and important literature on cross-cultural understandings of madness. Despite the limited extent of our coverage, we have nonetheless seen that there are myriad ways in which madness can be, has been, and indeed continues to be made sense of from the different perspectives we have included in our overview of the literature in this area. We've shown also that even within each of these broad perspectives – first-person, lay and professional – there is considerable variety in how people make sense of madness. There is no one model of madness on which we can all agree. There is not even one standard word to refer to the experiences that is universally accepted. What should we call it? Madness? Schizophrenia? Psychosis? Does it even make any sense to think of it as an 'it' or are we really talking about a disparate group of experiences which some of us just happen to find convenient to lump together under a single unifying term?

These are just some of the puzzling questions that one might be confronted with when exposed to the mind-boggling selection of accounts of what psychosis is, and what it might be caused by, that we find in the literature in this area. While it would be tempting to think that this confusion could be cleared up by appealing to the scientific evidence, which, one might imagine, must surely indicate which conceptualization of schizophrenia is the 'correct' one, it is not possible at the current time, based on empirical evidence alone, to arrive at any final conclusions regarding what schizophrenia 'really' is, what it is caused by or how best to treat it, if in fact it is something to be 'treated' in the medical sense of this word. Indeed, as we saw in Chapter 5, there is little agreement among the scientists/professionals themselves on what to make of the experience of madness, despite the fact that these professionals are all privy to the same empirical research evidence on schizophrenia. The confusion in this area is exemplified by an argument put forward by a prominent British researcher and psychiatrist Professor Tim Crow (1984) who, using a somewhat twisted logic, proposes that the lack of clear evidence for any particular theory of schizophrenia is good grounds for considering his own 'viral' theory well founded, despite the fact that, as he acknowledges, there is little direct evidence to support his theory either.

It is fairly well recognized and accepted, even in mainstream psychiatric textbooks, that the literature on schizophrenia is characterized by a confusing plurality of theories, each competing for dominance. For example, in a chapter from one of the standard teaching texts of psychiatric medicine (McGlashan and Hoffman 1995: 957, in Kaplan and Saddock 1995) we find the following quote, acknowledging this very diversity: 'Schizophrenic madness has had more explanations thrown at it and been the object of more attempts to render it meaningful than has any other mental illness.'

Also, from the same volume, in a chapter on the problems of studying the epidemiology of schizophrenia, we find a suggestion that the personalities of theoreticians have played a role in this debate: 'The clinical diagnosis of schizophrenia has been a veritable battleground of competing personalities and concepts throughout most of this century' (Karno and Norquist 1995: 903). It is important to stress that the two quotes above do not come from a critical anti-psychiatry text. Far from it: they come from a mainstream psychiatric textbook.

We see then that here is consensus about one thing: namely, that schizophrenia has been, and continues to be, subject to a wide range of explanations. Despite an abundance of empirical investigations into all aspects of schizophrenia, this situation shows no signs of abating. From a more critical position, Whitaker (2002: 291), after reviewing theories of schizophrenia and the available evidence, concludes: 'Thus, if we wanted to be candid in our talk about schizophrenia, we would admit to this: Little is known about what causes schizophrenia.'

This state of affairs might lead us to consider the importance of factors other than simply empirical data in keeping alive this controversy regarding schizophrenia. This case is made succinctly by the psychiatrist-anthropologist, Littlewood (1991: 699), who states that 'Schizophrenia, like left handedness, can be perceived in a variety of ways depending on our own frame of reference, our personal identification and sympathies, our compelling social urgencies.' The point Littlewood seems to be making is that the notions of schizophrenia held by researchers, clinicians and lay people depend on and reflect a whole range of personal and social factors which influence which particular model of schizophrenia is adopted. It has been suggested (for example, British Psychological Society 2000) that some of the difficulties which come with the term schizophrenia may be averted if we use instead the concept of psychosis.

Whatever value there may be in this proposal, it seems that it will not solve the predicament we are discussing here, as definitions and explanations of psychosis have proved just as problematic as those of schizophrenia. Even within the diagnostic 'bible', the DSM IV-R (APA 2000: 297), it is noted that 'The term psychotic has historically received a number of definitions, none of which has achieved universal acceptance.' That this situation is not merely historical is made quite apparent when we find, in the very same manual (which is, we should remember, an effort to standardize such terms) this rather vague attempt at a definition (p.297): 'In this manual the term psychosis refers to the presence of certain symptoms.' This quote is followed immediately by the following, which seems to be midway between a confession and an acknowledgement of defeat, given the purpose of the book: 'The specific constellation of symptoms to which the term refers varies to some extent across the diagnostic categories.'

So, even within a single text, which has the express purpose of standardizing definitions of terms such as psychosis, we once again find inconsistencies. There would appear to be no good reason to assume that the term 'psychosis' offers any hope of resolving the difficulties outlined here which permeate the literature on schizophrenia. It is our contention that both terms are subject to having various definitions, explanations and attempts to render them meaningful, making it unlikely that any single definition will achieve universal acceptance. The same holds true, we believe, for the ordinary language term 'madness', although as this makes no pretence to being a scientific term, inconsistencies in its usage and definitions do not pose the same problems.

How then are we to respond to this situation? It seems that empirical data alone is unlikely to resolve the debate which surrounds the notions of schizophrenia, psychosis and madness. At the very least, looking at the history and current state of conceptualizations of madness, and the evidence base that is used to bolster these competing conceptualizations, we can find absolutely no evidence to suggest that some form of consensus is about to be established. Quite the contrary: notions of madness are as keenly contested today as they ever have been. The scientific method may have led to somewhat clearer requirements regarding what is to be considered 'evidence', but this has not prevented the advocates of the various competing notions of madness from developing a body of evidence supporting their own favoured theory while disputing the evidence of competing theories. Each of the theories of schizophrenia outlined in Chapter 5 has a body of empirical evidence which advocates of the theory call upon in support of their particular theory.

What we would like to suggest therefore is that a conceptual rather than an empirical approach to the notions of schizophrenia, psychosis and madness may be required to help us shed more light on this situation. Jansson and Parnas (2007: 1194, original italics) make a similar suggestion after reviewing schizophrenia studies, proposing that what is needed is 'serious and systematic reflection on the *conceptual validity* of schizophrenia, i.e., *what we take this illness to be* in the first place'. This call for conceptual clarity is echoed by Zachar and Kendler (2007: 564) in their review of psychiatric taxonomy, when they conclude that 'struggling with conceptual and philosophical issues is a legitimate and, indeed, necessary part of the nosological process'. To this end, it is appropriate that we now turn to philosophy, and in particular linguistic philosophy, in order to consider what kinds of concepts 'schizophrenia', 'psychosis' and 'madness' are. Perhaps philosophy, where issues such as conceptual clarity are given greater attention, might help us navigate this murky, perplexing state of affairs we find ourselves in when we try to make sense of madness.

As a bit of preamble to our main argument, it is necessary at this point to delve briefly into the general philosophical framework within which our argument fits. Now, as neither of us can make any claims to being a professional philosopher, our treatment of these philosophical issues may be somewhat superficial, although hopefully we will not be guilty of distorting the philosophical principles purely to meet the needs of our own argument. The philosophical tradition from which we wish to borrow here is what has been referred to as 'ordinary language' or 'linguistic' philosophy, most commonly identified with the work of Austrian philosopher, Ludwig Wittgenstein, particularly his *Philosophical investigations* (1953) published only after his death in 1951, and commonly cited as one of the most influential philosophical texts of the twentieth century. The specific aspect of Wittgenstein's philosophy with which we are concerned here is that of the relationship between words and meaning, a central consideration of the linguistic philosophers. Two seemingly simple principles of Wittgenstein's are of relevance to our argument. First, that words have many different functions, and second, that if we want to know the meaning of a word we should look to how that word is used, rather than to how it is defined.

The issue of words having many different functions is crucial to the argument we will develop below. Essentially, the position that Wittgenstein seems to be articulating is that we should appreciate that while words all look alike, this should not lead us into assuming that they all function in the same way. The common mistake to make here would be to think of all words as having the same function, namely to pick out aspects of the world in a 'correspondence' fashion (where, for example, 'dog' refers to all animals that match the species). Of course, this is indeed one of the functions of words, but we would be mistaken to think of all words as functioning in the same way. Wittgenstein makes an analogy here to convey his position

> Think of the tools in a tool-box: there is a hammer, pliers, a saw, a screwdriver, a ruler, a glue-pot, glue, nails and screw. The functions of words are as diverse as the functions of these objects. (And in both cases there are similarities.)
>
> (Wittgenstein 1953: 11)

He goes on to list some of the variety of functions that words might have, including 'giving orders, and obeying them; describing the appearance of an object, or giving its measurements; constructing an object from a description (a drawing); reporting an event; speculating about an event' and ending his list of examples with 'asking, thanking, cursing, greeting, praying'. The point is that words can have many functions, and if we want to understand a particular word we must consider how it functions, which we can discover by looking at how the word is used. Usage, not definition, is what determines meaning.

So, we want to use both the principles outlined above in our analysis of schizophrenia (remembering that our position is that what we say of 'schizophrenia', is also true of 'psychosis' and 'madness'). We want to argue that if we want to understand what kind of thing schizophrenia is, what 'schizophrenia' means, we should look *not* to how it is defined in diagnostic manuals such as the DSM IV-R, but to how we actually use the word. We should, to quote Wittgenstein (1953: 220) himself on this topic, 'Let the use of words teach you their meaning.'

At this point, we need to introduce a new concept, one which is central to the understanding of schizophrenia that we are about to elaborate. Although it is a rather abstract notion, which requires us to consider a way in which language functions which is not immediately intuitive, it is so central to our argument here, that we feel it is worth labouring this point. What we want to propose is that given the plethora of explanations for what schizophrenia is and the absence of any kind of consensus among researchers or clinicians in this field, we might well consider the possibility that schizophrenia is what the philosopher W. B. Gallie (1955–1956) referred to as an 'essentially contested concept'. This concept of Gallie's fits firmly within the tradition of linguistic philosophy, based on the notion that if we want to understand the meaning of a term we should look not (or not only) at putative definitions, but rather we should look at the usage of the term. The position we want to put forward here is that the multiplicity of competing theories on the nature of schizophrenia are not incidental, nor do they simply reflect a stage in the evolution of the concept (as has been argued), but rather they are an *intrinsic* quality of the concept itself. Certainly, given that the concept has been imbued with controversy since its very inception, and that this controversy shows no signs of abating, on logical or empirical grounds there is a good case to be made that this is a quality of the notion of madness itself, regardless of which particular term (schizophrenia, psychosis, madness, and so on) we may choose to adopt. For our argument here to make sense, we will need to expand further on Gallie's notion of essential contestedness.

Gallie's notion of essentially contested concept

Writing in the 1950s, Gallie (1955–1956: 169; 1964: Chapter 8) proposed that 'There are certain concepts which are essentially contested, concepts the proper use of which inevitably involves endless disputes about their proper uses on the part of their users.' His argument is based upon the 'usage determines meaning' notion and he proposes that there are certain terms which are used in such a way that the meaning of the very term is contested, and that – this is where it gets tricky – this contesting of the meaning is an *integral* part of the meaning of the term. Gallie (1955–1956: 172) goes on to propose that these terms are used in an explicitly competitive fashion: 'To use an essentially contested concept means to use it against other uses and to recognize that one's use of it has to be maintained against these other uses.'

What he seems to be arguing is that there are certain terms for which contesting the meaning of the term *constitutes* (or, at the very least, significantly contributes to) the meaning of this term. As a philosopher, Gallie was concerned with concepts such as 'beauty', 'justice' and 'democracy', which have dogged Western philosophers since at least the time of Socrates. He proposed that these concepts may usefully be considered as essentially contested concepts in that their use – their proper use – involves contesting their meaning, and this constitutes the meaning of the terms.

In his original expositions of the concept, Gallie (1955–1956, 1964) argued that there are five conditions of 'contestedness'. These are, briefly, that the term is (1) appraisive in nature, (2) internally complex in character, (3) that explications of the concept can emphasize different components of the complexity, (4) that the appraisive aspect of the concept can be modified in the light of changing circumstances and (5) that those who use the term recognize the contested nature of the term, and have some appreciation of competing uses of the term.

These conditions would seem to be well met by the concept of schizophrenia: it is a complex, appraisive concept, which is used in such a way that emphasis is placed on different components of the concept by different people (some might emphasize biological components, whereas others give emphasis to environmental factors). The concept has changed to meet different circumstances, and those who use the term do so in a way which implicitly recognizes that it is indeed contested, in that they acknowledge the existence of other theories of schizophrenia, even if alternative theories are summarily dismissed. However, there is one aspect of Gallie's criteria which is not so consistent with schizophrenia. Gallie argues that essentially contested concepts are not only appraisive in nature, but he goes further to suggest that they are positively appraised. To quote Gallie (1964: 161) once again: 'The concept in question must be *appraisive* in the sense that it signifies or accredits some kind of valued achievement.'

Clearly, it would be difficult to make a case that schizophrenia is such a 'valued achievement'. Unfortunately, Gallie does not explain why he believes essentially contested concepts must be positively appraised, which makes it difficult to evaluate his inclusion of this as one of the criteria. If we accept Gallie's argument that terms such as 'beauty' or 'justice' meet the criteria for being considered essentially contested then one would assume that their opposites (say 'ugliness' and 'injustice') must, surely, also be essentially contested concepts. Thus, we want to argue that essentially contested concepts are, as Gallie argues, 'appraisive concepts', but that this appraisal can be either positive or negative in nature. If we accept this modification to Gallie's original criteria, then it seems that 'madness', in whatever fashion we may refer to it, meets the criteria for essential contestedness (as, of course, does its opposite, 'sanity', an equally contested concept).

In sum, what we are proposing is that we consider schizophrenia to be an essentially contested concept, which is to claim that the disputed nature of the concept is neither accidental, nor transitional, but rather reflects a central component of the very meaning of the concept. This is to suggest that the controversy and debate which surround notions of madness are integral to these notions. That is, 'madness' is something which, in Western societies at least, we inevitably dispute the 'true and proper' meaning of. Further, disputing the true and proper meaning of the term *constitutes* the meaning of the term. If meaning derives from usage, and if schizophrenia is, as we contend, a term the meaning of which has always been contested, then a logical conclusion to reach from this is that it is through this contested usage that schizophrenia gets its meaning. To dispute what schizophrenia, madness and psychosis are, what causes them and how we should respond to them is to use these terms properly. The function of these terms (and therefore their meaning) is to occupy a position in an ongoing debate that we have about who and what these terms actually refer to.

This conceptualization is, we believe, a radically different way of making sense of madness, which operates at quite a different level of logical and conceptual analysis. Rather than developing a new theory of madness, or adopting an already developed theory, this approach is an endeavour to develop a 'meta-theory' which looks at how terms for madness function in our language and to take this usage as central to the meaning of the term. That is, madness is, quite simply, something about which we argue the meaning of, inevitably, and interminably. This argument constitutes and sustains the meaning of madness, which suggests that this debate cannot be resolved. Though not expressed in these terms, this is a position expressed by a few other writers in this field. Estroff (2004: 284), for example, suggests that 'Disagreement and contestation about meaning, reality, and identity may represent the quintessence of schizophrenia.' Further, Leudar and Thomas (2001: 208) following their review of historical and current accounts of voice-hearing, conclude that 'hearing voices has always been an experience with a socially contested meaning'.

Outside of the strictly philosophical domain, Gallie's concept of essential contentedness has been used, albeit rarely. Of most relevance to the current discussion, McKnight (2003) suggests that the practice of medicine itself is a prime candidate for being considered an essentially contested concept, pointing out that we cannot simply define the problem area to resolve this dispute as this begs the question given that it is definitions that are being contested (McKnight 2003: 262): 'To claim that a concept is essentially contested is to claim that disputes over its use are not resoluble even in principle.'

Implications of viewing schizophrenia as an essentially contested concept

Although this may seem, initially at least, a somewhat pessimistic position to adopt as it points to the impossibility of the debate regarding the meaning of 'madness' ever being resolved, we want to propose that adopting this position may, in fact, enhance our understandings of how concepts such as 'schizophrenia' and 'psychosis' operate in our culture and thereby enhance our understandings of people so diagnosed as well as informing our efforts to help clinically. In addition, recognizing these terms as being essentially contested may actually provide clarity which will in turn improve the quality of the debate. This is a point made by Gallie (1964: 188) himself when he argues that 'One desirable consequence of the required recognition in any proper instance of essential contestedness might therefore be a marked raising in the level of the quality of arguments in the disputes of the contestant parties.'

It is reasonable to ask how it is that viewing notions of madness as essentially contested concepts would enhance the quality of debate. Gallie does in fact outline a range of implications which emerge from recognizing essential contestedness and discusses how this might improve the quality of the debate. These can be summarized as:

- recognition and acceptance of plurality
- acknowledgement of social, cultural and psychological factors which contribute to the position in the debate that individuals, groups, or institutions adopt
- drawing attention to the purpose and function of the debate.

Before outlining these positions more fully, we would like to stress that this is not a mere philosophical or linguistic point. Notions of madness not only inform research into such experiences, but also significantly influence the kinds of clinical services that individuals who find themselves so labelled receive. The 'contestedness' of schizophrenia is not something we can find only in theoretical treatises on the nature of madness. It is something which permeates most, if not every, clinical encounter between those so diagnosed and their clinicians, where disputes (between clinician and client) about the nature and meanings of the experiences being discussed are commonplace. As such, we believe that enhancing our understandings of the debate around the nature of madness will provide us with not only greater conceptual clarity, but ultimately, and more importantly, the potential to enhance our ability to provide sensitive, respectful and helpful clinical services to clients with a diagnosis of schizophrenia.

Recognition and acceptance of plurality

One of the most obvious implications of accepting that a given term is an essentially contested concept is to recognize that there is a multiplicity of ways in which the term can be defined and used. If we come to see that a given concept is essentially contested, we are, by definition, accepting that there are a number of ways in which this term can be and is used. Gallie goes further than this, by suggesting that recognizing, and to some extent accepting (rather than simply trying to refute or disprove), competing uses of the term may actually enhance our understanding of our own, as well as our rivals' positions:

> Recognition of a given concept as essentially contested implies recognition of rival uses of it (such as oneself repudiates) as not only logically possible and humanly 'likely', but as of permanent potential critical value to one's own use or interpretation of the concept in question; whereas to regard any rival use as anathema, perverse, bestial or lunatic means, in many cases, to submit oneself to the chronic peril of underestimating the value of one's opponents' positions.
>
> (Gallie 1955–1956: 193)

Gallie suggests that failure to recognize valid uses of the concept other than one's own particular use will encourage futile debate around which particular use is the correct or best use of the term. Ironically, and presumably coincidentally, Gallie makes this point using the language of psychiatry, suggesting that those who hold that their use of the term is the correct use may be delusional:

> So long as contestant users of any essentially contested concept believe, however deludedly, that their own use of it is the only one that can command honest and informed approval, they are likely to persist with argument and discussion in the hope that they will ultimately persuade and convert all their opponents by logical means.
>
> (Gallie 1964: 189)

So, if we recognize a term as essentially contested this may make it easier for us to consider alternative uses of the term without feeling the need to refute them. In the area of schizophrenia, this could have very important implications in clinical settings, where, commonly, different clinicians working within the same team may bring different, often competing, and sometimes contradictory, perspectives on schizophrenia to the clinical setting. Similarly, and perhaps more importantly, clients also, of course, have their own understandings of their experiences, and these are often quite different from professional or clinical understandings (as we have already seen in previous chapters). Were clinicians able and willing to allow for a plurality of perspectives on schizophrenia, they may find it easier to work with clients and colleagues who hold a view quite different from their own. This is a position espoused by Gergen and McNamee (2002) who propose that within mental health, acceptance of a multiplicity of possible explanations is preferable to diagnosis because it allows and embraces the voices of various parties, thus empowering the voices of the client.

Acknowledgement of social, cultural and psychological factors

Another related implication of adopting the view that schizophrenia is an essentially contested concept is to draw our attention to factors that may contribute to the position we adopt towards it. If we recognize that there is a range of potential perspectives we can adopt vis-à-vis the essentially contested concept, then we may want to look at which factors influence, either consciously or subconsciously, the position we find ourselves taking. That is, if we want to understand why a particular individual adopts a particular notion of schizophrenia, we must look not only at the notion adopted, but also at factors within or acting upon the individual which draw that particular person to that particular perspective on psychosis. Of course, this analysis can operate at other levels as well as that of the individual; we might also find it fruitful to ask why certain groups, or institutions, or cultures, at certain times or in certain situations, promote and defend particular views on how schizophrenia is to be perceived and explained. Gallie puts it thus:

> At any given stage in the history of the continued uses of any essentially contested concept, it will no doubt be necessary to call upon psychological or sociological history or the known historical facts of a person's or group's background to explain their present preferences and adherences.
> (Gallie 1955–1956: 192)

This might more explicitly draw our attention to a whole range of factors which influence the position, or positions, we adopt in construing schizophrenia. Among other things this might help elucidate some of the underlying assumptions (or what the sociologist Gouldner (1970) calls 'background assumptions') which may underpin our position. Of course, the range of such factors that we could investigate in this regard is myriad, but may include things like sociopolitical position, economic interests, the role of gender, social class, cultural orientation, personal history with madness, religious leanings, and philosophical assumptions regarding the nature of personhood. Investigating if and how factors such as these influence how each of us (researcher, client and clinician alike) makes sense of madness may be an interesting source of study in its own right as well as something which could make an important contribution to our ways of understanding and relating to (or 'treating') those who are so diagnosed. This approach obliges us to look more closely at the role of the person (or group) construing and not only at the person being construed. Rather than simply explaining schizophrenia, or madness, as an illness that resides solely within the individual, we may come to see that how we choose to view schizophrenia, from the range of perspectives on offer at any given time, is, at least in part, a reflection of our own particular history, interests and assumptions about the nature of life and what it is to be human. Further, if we find ourselves released from the dogma of trying to explain what schizophrenia 'really' is (a debate which has failed after a hundred years or more to yield a satisfactory answer) we may instead be able to consider more pragmatically which way of viewing schizophrenia – if that is the term we still use – is helpful for *this* particular client at *this* particular time.

Drawing attention to the purpose and function of the debate

A further important implication of viewing schizophrenia, or any other concept, as essentially contested is that this can draw our attention to why such debates are perpetuated, or what particular functions these debates may serve. Although this is not a point made directly by Gallie, it is, we believe, implicit in his discussion of such concepts. This point is made more explicitly by Pell (1999) in discussing the contested nature of racial differences: 'Part of understanding what it means to be an essentially contested term is understanding the social purposes served by debate about moral or evaluative terms.' This argument suggests that essentially contested concepts are primarily moral and evaluative in nature. Though we may not agree with this fully, there does seem a case to be made for there being a moral component to judgements about who is and is not 'mad'. This point is made clearly, and with some humour, by Bentall (1992) in a paper where he points out that if all moral judgements are withdrawn from psychiatric diagnoses, this does not allow us to make a clear distinction between these diagnoses and experiences such as 'happiness'. The point he is making is that certain considerations, moral in nature, must also inform our judgements about what we consider to be 'abnormal'.

Whether or not we accept the argument that there is a moral aspect to making such a diagnosis, viewing schizophrenia as an essentially contested concept would allow us to question what purpose or function the contestedness may serve. Might it be that this contestedness allows for flexibility in our definitions of madness, which, given the changing nature of society, may indeed be of greater benefit than having a static, unchanging and unquestioned definition? Also, if we see schizophrenia as an attempt to define 'insanity', then clearly this cannot take place in isolation from our definitions of 'sanity'. Might it be that for our society to function effectively and to be open to change, both these notions need to be negotiated, and renegotiated under changing circumstances? No doubt there are many other questions which might emerge from considering what purposes and functions the contested nature of any concept may serve, and whose interests might be best served. But, recognizing the concept as being essentially contested invites us to consider such questions, which in turn might help us to better understand the matter at hand.

So, the invitation we want to extend here, for the reasons we have outlined above, is for us to view schizophrenia as an essentially contested concept. We believe that there is a good case to be made for why we should view schizophrenia in this way. Our discussion over the previous three chapters, when we looked at the various ways in which madness can be and is made sense of by professionals, by lay people, and by those who have first-hand, lived experience of it substantiates our position. Further, we believe that viewing schizophrenia as an essentially contested concept rather than being a nihilistic or pessimistic position is one which opens up new ways of thinking about, relating to and working with the kinds of experience that come to be labelled schizophrenic, psychosis, or just plain 'mad'. In the final chapter of this book, we will consider the question of where we might go to from here, taking into account our argument in this chapter, as well as the findings from our research into the subjective experience of psychosis (as presented in Chapter 3).

Chapter 7

Where to from here?

Now that we are coming to the end of this book, it is time for us to think about where our discussion up to this point takes us in terms of practical and theoretical implications. Of course, the theoretical and the applied fields are, or at least should be, closely related in that our practical approaches to madness – in research, clinical work, and in training, for example – should be informed by our theoretical models, which, in turn, should be responsive to what we find when we listen to and work with those who have experienced madness. So far in this book we have looked at a number of topics, including a selection of the wide range of theories and explanations we find for the experience of madness, from the individual's way of making sense of their own experience to the scientific theories held by researchers and clinicians. We have – we acknowledge – paid greater attention to what those who have subjective experience of psychosis make of the experience, and in discussing this, we clearly gave extra emphasis to our own research in this area. We have also looked at some issues which we think help us understand this great diversity of opinion (and research) about psychosis: we explained that we find the concept of 'storytelling' a helpful one when we look at the diverse range of stories we encounter when we look at how various parties make sense of madness. In Chapter 6, we outlined our response to the situation we find ourselves confronted with when we look into the literature on schizophrenia; we suggested that thinking of schizophrenia (or psychosis or madness) as an 'essentially contested concept' might give us a way of understanding and appreciating the assorted opinions we encounter when we look into madness, and so prevent us from feeling completely overwhelmed and baffled by the mind-boggling range of theories we come across as we explore this area.

However, even if we accept all of the above, we are still left with the all-important question of what this means in practical terms. As clinicians and researchers working in the field of psychosis, we are particularly concerned with how the ideas we have developed in this book might relate to the clinical and research settings, which, we believe, one cannot (and should not) ever fully separate from the theoretical and conceptual field. In this final chapter therefore our focus will be on what we consider to be the important applied implications which emerge from our analysis of schizophrenia, with particular emphasis being given to the two sections which lie at the heart of this book: our research into subjective experience (Chapter 3) and our proposal that we view schizophrenia (psychosis, madness) as an essentially contested concept (Chapter 6).

You may recall that we started this book with a story of a young woman who seemed touched by madness, yet struggled to find support to help her deal with this, from her family, and from the health care system. Briefly, to recap, she experienced visual and auditory hallucinations which involved the experience of talking to her head which she 'saw' floating in a corner of her room. The content of her conversations with her head included considering ways she could escape from her physically and emotionally abusive relationship and led to her developing a plan to kill herself and her two children. She also developed what we can think of as delusional beliefs about her family conspiring against her and her having a tendency to walk at a strange angle, leaning over to the side. We will, where it seems fitting, refer back to this young woman's story to help illustrate the points we wish to make, as we now move on to consider some of the practical implications which emerge from our analysis of schizophrenia.

Acknowledging uncertainty

One of the striking features of much of the literature on schizophrenia is the certainty with which many contributors to this field make their claims about what schizophrenia is, what it is caused by, and how best to treat it. What makes this so striking is that when we look into the literature in this area (as we did in Chapter 5) we find that the range of theories which are claimed with such certainty is immense and the so-called evidence is at best confusing and hard to integrate within any single model, and at worst inconsistent and contradictory. It seems hard to imagine that a dispassionate observer could look into this literature and come away with any firm conclusions about schizophrenia. And yet, firmly held and confidently expressed positions permeate the literature in this field. It seems almost as if every contributor to the discussion on schizophrenia *knows* what it is, how it is caused, and how best to treat it. And yet, when we explore the literature in just a little bit more depth, we find that what these contributors claim to know with such confidence rarely, if ever, generates much consensus among other experts in the field, many of whom claim to *know* something very different about the nature of schizophrenia.

What are we to make of this situation? Why, we ask ourselves, when we are confronted with such uncertainty, do we respond with such confident assertions? Such questions are open to conjecture, which we will not enter into here. The point we wish to make is simply that we know much less about schizophrenia than we claim to know. This is not to say that we know nothing; only that we do not know enough to make such confident assertions about what schizophrenia 'really' is. What we want to propose therefore is that we (professionals, researchers and clinicians in this field) need to acknowledge our uncertainty in this area. We need to temper our claims with the recognition that our theories, and our treatments, are provisional in nature. Yes, we have some ideas about what might help, and yes, we can make some reasonable contributions to discussions about which factors – biological, psychological, social and even spiritual – may have contributed to causing the psychotic experiences. But, our knowledge here is limited and tentative and we believe we need to accept and acknowledge that.

Perhaps, if we work in the clinical area, we can share some of our uncertainties with our clients, rather than – as is often the case – asserting with such confidence that we know what is wrong with the client and what treatment will work. A rare example of explicitly recognizing this uncertainty is found in the work of Seikkula et al. (2006) from Finland. They identify 'tolerance of uncertainty' as one of the seven guiding treatment principles in working with first episode psychosis clients and they note how this promotes dialogue about ways of making sense of the experience. Acknowledging our own limitations in this way might help create quite different working situations, and so have important practical implications clinically. For example, if we return to the story of the young woman, had her family doctor felt and expressed a genuine curiosity about what was going on for her, shared his uncertainty about how to explain her experiences, and then invited her to explore this with him, this may have led to a far more fruitful discussion where the woman was willing to share more of her story, as well as her thoughts about what was going on. Perhaps too, she would then have been more willing to hear the doctor's perspective and understanding of her experience, and more receptive to his ideas about what kind of treatments might have helped. So, to put it simply, acknowledging the uncertainty, which we believe characterizes this field, would have important practical implications for both clinical practice and research.

The role of subjective experience

Another important practical implication from our discussion relates to the role of subjective experience. We have already stated that we believe that one of the major failings of research and clinical approaches to schizophrenia is the neglect of the first-person perspective. This is a state of affairs which, we contend, is ethically, clinically and scientifically unjustifiable and is indeed a hindrance to making progress in this area. Incorporating, respecting and valuing contributions which give greater prominence to lived experience is an essential requirement if we wish to develop ways of understanding schizophrenia which are both true to the lived experience of the individual who receives this diagnosis and sensitive to the needs of those who we seek to offer support to in our clinical services. There is, we believe, a compelling case to be made that in all areas of understanding and working with psychosis, a greater – much greater – role needs to be given to the voice of lived experience if we truly want to advance our understandings of the complex, confusing set of experiences that we refer to as madness. First-person accounts of psychosis are littered with insights into the experience; it seems to us a tragedy that such insights should be so overlooked (as they have been), despite the fact that researchers and clinicians in the field struggle to come up with helpful ways of understanding and working with those who are troubled by psychosis. This is a situation that is, ultimately, to the detriment of clients of mental health services as well as researchers and clinicians in this field as our understandings of the experience are impoverished as a consequence of this exclusion of the first-person perspective.

In addition to the role of first-person accounts, there is also a growing body of research, such as our own (Chapter 3), which looks more closely at subjective aspects of the experience of psychosis. Research such as this provides a very clear indication that people who experience psychosis can be articulate commentators on many different aspects of the experience, and can (if allowed to do so) share those reflections. Further, research into subjective experience can help provide important insights into the understanding of madness by tapping into aspects of the experience which are available only to those who have first-hand acquaintance with the phenomena being investigated. This, in turn, can inform our clinical approaches and so render them more likely to be helpful. Incorporating the perspective of those who have first-hand lived experience with the phenomenon being investigated is a pressing need within the area of psychosis which, as our own research indicates, is feasible and has much to offer our understandings of psychosis. Thinking again about our young woman from Chapter 1, it is clear that if her family doctor had been willing to entertain the notion that she could contribute to making sense of the experiences that were troubling her and if he had invited her to share her thoughts on the matter, she may well have told him about her abusive domestic situation, which she herself saw as significantly contributing to her distress. This would not, in itself, have altered her situation, but it may have provided her with some relief and might have led to the development of a more helpful relationship between the young woman and her doctor.

Conceptual issues: making sense of madness

The current dominant models of schizophrenia do not readily lend themselves to the inclusion of the first-person perspective. Conceptually, therefore, a shift is required in how we approach research and practice into psychotic experience, such that we recognize that those who experience psychosis have a major role to play in our developing understandings of these experiences. We believe that were we to conceptualize schizophrenia as an essentially contested concept (as we argued in Chapter 6), this might provide an overarching framework which, by explicitly acknowledging multiple perspectives, positions and understandings of psychosis, helps us recognize that those who view the experience from a perspective other than our own nonetheless have valid contributions to make to the debate on how we make sense of madness. We are not so naive as to believe that simply persuading others of the essential contestedness of schizophrenia would somehow, magically and on its own, eliminate factors such as the vested interests of professional groups and pharmaceutical companies in the current status quo. We discuss obstacles to implementing changes in theory and practice in mental health care below.

Implications from our research findings

A large section of this book was dedicated to describing our own research into the subjective experience of psychosis. In Chapter 3 we presented our findings from this research, with emphasis being given to the three theoretical constructs (fragmentation–integration; invalidation–validation; spirituality) which we developed to encapsulate the central features of the subjective experience of psychosis as expressed by participants in our research. Similar notions to these three constructs have been reported by other researchers in this area. We will now consider some of the implications from our research findings, beginning with the general clinical implications before moving on to specific implications relating to the three theoretical constructs. The implications we present here are, of course, somewhat tentative in nature and are suggested as guidelines based on the findings of this research. Further empirical evaluation of these constructs as well as evaluation of the impact of these clinical implications would be required before one could be confident about their utility.

One of the most significant findings from the present research is that at least some of those with a first episode of psychosis welcome the opportunity to discuss the nature and meaning of their experience in some depth and see this as an important component of understanding and coming to terms with the experience. This is a consistent finding in research which asks clients about what they would like from clinical services. There is, therefore, sufficient evidence from both our own research and from other research findings to state with some confidence that finding personal meaning in the experience is an important part of dealing with psychosis for many of those who have such experiences. Clinical services should, therefore, ensure that clients are offered the opportunity to explore the personal significance of their experience with suitable clinical staff who may help clients develop helpful ways of understanding and relating to their experience. The corollary of this is that services should be careful not to close down clients' efforts to express what their experience means to them, through ignoring this or, worse, informing the client bluntly that his or her way of thinking about the experience is, simply, wrong, commonly expressed as 'lacking insight'. The opportunity to explore the meaning of the experience in a safe and helpful way should, therefore, be routinely offered to clients, many, if not all, of whom see this as important. Had our young woman's doctor been sensitive to this concern, he might have invited her to share her thoughts about what her experience might mean – or, if this lay outside his realm of expertise, he may have suggested that going to see a mental health specialist would be an opportunity for her to explore the meaning of her experience, rather than describing this as a veiled threat which is how it came across to the woman. Of course, this would require that mental health services did indeed operate in this kind of fashion, which was almost certainly not the case at the time.

Another general implication from our research derives from the finding that a number of clients report positive aspects to their experience of psychosis and hold a positive attitude to the experience, at least some of the time. This is an important clinical consideration which services need to respect and address in clinical settings. It means that clinicians would be mistaken were they to assume that the experience is wholly negative in the client's perspective. This could be of crucial importance in many aspects of the client's care. For example, if the client views some or all of the experience positively he or she may be ambivalent about the offer of 'treatments' aimed at eliminating this experience. Going back once more to our young woman, we recall that her conversations with her disembodied head actually provided her with some solace, in that they allowed her to feel less distressed than she had been when these thoughts were simply going around and around in her mind. We could understand therefore that she might have had some ambivalence about treatment aimed only at taking these experiences away from her. If clinicians are cognisant of this possibility, at the very least this could help them understand the client's ambivalence. So, another clinical implication from our research is that clinicians should explore the client's attitude to the experience of psychosis as it may prove to be unhelpful and inaccurate to assume that the client views the experience wholly negatively. Let us now move on to look at some of the implications which emerge from the three theoretical constructs from our research.

Fragmentation–integration

The clinical implications from the 'fragmentation–integration' construct essentially relate to promoting 'integration' while preventing further 'fragmentation' for the client. Support for the importance of promoting integration clinically is found in Rufus May's (2003) account of his experience of madness. As a clinician with his own personal experience of psychosis he is in an excellent position to comment. On his own experience he describes what sounds like fragmentation when he says 'My own "madness" was about disconnecting from a world I struggled to identify with.' He goes on to suggest that 'The way to combat this isolation is to create safe spaces where unusual experiences can be shared and made sense of.'

Other researchers have also identified integration as an important component of coping with psychotic experiences. Romme and Escher (1993) refer to the importance of 'integration' as central to accepting and coping with voices, and Roe and Ben-Yashi (1999) found 'integration' of self and illness to be helpful in recovery. In New Zealand, Lapsley et al. (2002) report that those who have recovered from mental health problems identify rebuilding of relationships (social integration) as being central to the recovery process.

So, clinical implications from this include the need to try to promote integration on an individual level as well as interpersonal or social integration. For example, integration on a personal level could be promoted through exploring congruence between the psychotic experiences and other life events (see Brabban and Turkington 2002). In terms of therapy, the Trauma Model (Ross 2006) may be a useful therapeutic framework here as it delineates ways of working sensitively with traumatic experiences to help the individual integrate these in ways which help reduce distress. A central consideration in the recommendations we make here is that these interventions take place within a reliable and enduring therapeutic relationship, which provides the context within which these interventions can be incorporated.

In terms of interpersonal and social integration, therapeutic interventions which encourage integration within the family may be particularly useful as these can help the family identify and tackle dynamics within the family, so promoting a greater sense of integration (Aderhold and Gottwalz 2004). Looking back to our young woman, she was clearly experiencing both personal and interpersonal fragmentation, and her brief encounter with her family doctor did nothing to alleviate this. We can imagine that – in an ideal world – her fractured relationships with her family members may have been something a clinical team could have addressed, with a view to reducing her sense of isolation and distance from her family, and maximizing her family's potential support. So, clinical services need to consider the issue of fragmentation within the family, or other social support networks, and aim to offer clinical services (such as family support, or family therapy) which may help promote integration at this level.

Group programmes run by clinical services may also be a useful way of enhancing integration, both on an individual and an interpersonal level. These can include groups which aim primarily to provide opportunities for social contact through social activities, as well as discussion groups which foster integration. Groups which encourage clients to construct and share their stories of psychosis in an open and supportive environment can promote integration by helping clients see commonalities in their experience (Rook and Geekie 2004, 2006; these 'storytelling' groups are described further below).

In terms of service delivery, clinical services may reduce the risk of further fragmentation by ensuring continuity of care for the client. This is particularly relevant as many newly developed 'early intervention' services for psychosis operate with time limits (typically eighteen months to two years) on their availability to clients after which clients may be discharged or transferred to the another team. While there are practical and financial reasons why early intervention services operate in this way, it does run the risk of contributing to the client's experience of fragmentation. Further, it is important for clinical teams to model integration to clients by operating in a consistent way. Given the diversity of ways of understanding psychotic experience held by professionals who work in this area, teams may need a framework which allows them to hold and respect this diversity of understandings (which is likely to be manifest in any multidisciplinary clinical team), while working effectively clinically. A 'meta-theory', such as viewing schizophrenia as an essentially contested concept, may provide a framework which fosters an acceptance of this diversity within the team in an integrative fashion.

Another aspect of service delivery which may contribute to fragmentation of the individual's social network is the use of hospitalization. One of the ingredients of Mosher's effective Soteria House approach was that by living in an ordinary house in the community rather than being hospitalized, people were more able to maintain their usual contacts with family, friends, work, etc. (Mosher et al. 2005), and so, one assumes, experience less social fragmentation. Clinical services need, therefore, to consider the possible impact of hospitalization on the client in terms of fragmentation of social support and should consider looking into alternatives to hospital (such as the Soteria model) which explicitly aim to foster integration of social supports.

Invalidation–validation

The clinical implications which derive from the 'invalidation–validation' construct relate to services doing what they can to prevent further experiences of invalidation while endeavouring to promote validation for the client. Participants in our research expressed the sense that invalidation was a central feature of their experience of psychosis, and that this had both personal and interpersonal aspects. These findings regarding the roles of invalidation and validation in psychosis are reported by others who have investigated the client's experience of psychosis (Lapsley et al. 2002; Romme and Escher 1993; Vellenga and Christenson 1994).

Promoting validation while avoiding invalidation may not always be an easy path to follow when working clinically with clients who experience psychosis, who may express some unusual ideas. There is a risk that services may, inadvertently, replicate the experience of invalidation for clients. This could include, for example, informing the client that he or she simply does not accurately understand his or her experience ('you lack insight'). On a more subtle level, challenging how the client construes the experience runs the risk, if done insensitively, of further undermining the client. Challenges to the client's explanatory model (Kleinman 1988), however well intentioned, may be experienced as further invalidation. At the other end of the spectrum, there are also risks associated with validation, particularly as this relates to the content of the experience of psychosis. For example, it would clearly be clinically inappropriate to validate a client's belief that he should harm himself, or others, in response to command hallucinations. This tension is expressed nicely by Power and McGorry (1999: 159) when they recommend that 'A balance needs to be struck between respecting the patient's interpretation of their psychotic experiences while conveying to the patient one's own clinical judgement and advice regarding treatment.'

The clinical implications begin with the need to be aware of this tension then to aim to find ways of achieving a balance where the client can feel personally validated while aspects of the psychotic experience may be open to questioning. This is a tension that is well recognized within Dialectical Behavioural Therapy, now used extensively in the treatment of Borderline Personality Disorder, where invalidation is seen as a risk within therapy and validation of the person and his or her distress is seen as a prerequisite for change (Linehan 1993). In the area of psychosis, mutual, respectful exploration of the meaning of psychosis within the context of a trusting relationship and with recognition of the plurality of perspectives on schizophrenia may help clinicians achieve this balance. Genuine collaboration in exploring the nature and meaning of the experience may be a requirement here. This may necessitate a shift on the part of clinicians, away from the position of believing that we already know what the experience means, to recognizing that we bring one way of understanding psychosis, and that this is but one among many useful and valid ways of construing the experience. If clinicians were to embrace the notion of 'essential contestedness' this may reduce the risk of invalidating the client in clinical encounters. Roe and Davidson (2005: 91) also suggest that accepting plurality may help avoid unnecessary and unhelpful invalidation by clinicians: 'Acknowledging the existence of multiple, diverse views may be a necessary precondition for encouraging people with schizophrenia to compose and share their narratives.' A specific aspect of this relates to the issue of being diagnosed, which can have a negative impact on clients. The important point here is that clinicians should recognize that offering a diagnosis runs the risk of undermining the client's own attempts to make sense of the experience. This is not to say that clinicians should avoid using diagnostic terms if that happens to be how they make sense of the client's experience, but that sharing thoughts about diagnosis with the client needs to be done in a way that does not further damage the client through invalidation. Perhaps if this was done in the spirit of plurality, seeing the diagnosis as one way, though not the only possible way, of construing the experience, this risk would be reduced. Of course, this would entail the person doing the diagnosing to see their diagnosis as just one among many possible ways of making sense of madness, rather than being a definitive and conclusive statement of fact.

May (2003) proposed that one way to approach the tension between validation and invalidation is for clinicians to recognize the importance of 'emotionally validating' the client's experiences, by acknowledging the impact of the experience, and through exploring the personal meaningfulness of the client's beliefs and their relevance to the individual's life history. This can be done without necessarily validating other aspects of the content of the client's psychotic experiences. Cognitive-behavioural approaches to psychosis recommend a similar approach, where the importance of establishing a therapeutic relationship (which provides a form of validation) is a prerequisite for introducing gentle challenges to the client's beliefs (Fowler et al. 1998; Turkington et al. 2006). Again, this must be done in the context of a supportive and trusting relationship which may take some time to develop.

We can see how the above notions might translate into the kinds of help that our young woman might benefit from. These could include validating the woman's sense of distress and confusion regarding her experience, although one would, of course, have to be wary of inadvertently validating other aspects of her experience (in particular, her thoughts about killing herself and her children). This is a good illustration of the delicate balance between validation and invalidation that may need to be established in working with this client group. Achieving this in the clinical arena would require the development of a firm therapeutic relationship to negotiate this potentially difficult area while providing a form of containment for the client.

Our research findings also point to the importance of one particular aspect of validation: being 'author' of one's own experience (Shotter 1981). This was conveyed by participants through the importance they gave to the issue of narrating one's own story. Others in this field have also noted the importance of clients' being author of their own experience. Roe and Davidson (2005) argue that the process of regaining ownership of 'narrative competence' is a central part of recovery. Clinical services therefore have to provide opportunities for clients to maintain or regain this 'narrative competence'. Putting this into practice may involve providing the client with opportunities to explore and express the meaning of the experience, which could be done in individual and/or in group therapy. In the clinical setting where the current research was undertaken, a 'storytelling' group is offered, developed partly in response to the findings from this research. This group has the explicit purpose of promoting the notion of client as author of his or her experience and provides clients with an opportunity to construct their own 'story' using a variety of formats (narrative, pictorial, musical etc.) and to share this with others in the group, who are asked to provide feedback to those who share their stories. Such a group provides opportunities for both personal and interpersonal validation (Rook and Geekie 2004, 2006) through the constructing and sharing of one's own personal narrative.

Another clinical implication here is the need to address some of the fundamental implications of the client feeling personally invalidated, in particular the client's loss of faith in his or her ways of perceiving and making sense of the world. Interventions need to help the client identify ways of reliably checking out perceptions and understandings of experience, a strategy found helpful by some of our participants. This may involve encouraging the client to use trusted individuals (possibly including the therapist) to test out perceptions: where there is congruence between the client's and the trusted individual's perceptions or understandings, this may help the client build confidence in his or her own perspective. Other ways of evaluating the client's perceptions and understandings of experience may include considering some of the practical implications of particular ways of understanding experience and/or developing 'behavioural experiments' to test out competing understandings. If this process of evaluation takes place within a trusting relationship, this may make less threatening the re-evaluation of certain perceptions without risking a sense of invalidation of self. That is, the therapeutic relationship may validate the client's sense of self while simultaneously allowing the client to test out unhelpful perceptions and understandings of the world.

One way of addressing some of the issues above in clinical settings may be through the use of the 'philosophical inquiry method' (Clayton 1996): a process of philosophical reflection, designed to encourage clearer analytic skills through the guided exploration of philosophical issues. A group for clients which aims to encourage such skills has been trialled in the service where this research was undertaken, where joint clinician–consumer facilitated philosophical inquiry groups have been run for clients, with feedback from participants being encouraging (Burdett 2001; Burdett and Geekie 2003).

Spirituality

The issue of spirituality was a prominent theme for participants in our research, a finding consistent with other research into the subjective experience of psychosis. This is the aspect of psychosis most neglected by Western clinicians and researchers, as indicated by the literature in this field. In terms of clinical implications, perhaps the most obvious and most simple implication is that clinicians need to acknowledge spirituality as an important and legitimate aspect of the experience for clients and provide an opening for this to be discussed safely, without risk of further invalidation. Mutual exploration of these issues may enhance the relationship between clinician and client as well as point to avenues of intervention that would otherwise be overlooked. While formal ways of assessing spirituality have been developed and are of potential use in research settings, Culliford and Johnson (2003) suggest that a straightforward way to open discussion about religion and spirituality in clinical work is simply to ask, 'What sustains and keeps you going in difficult times?'

While a question such as this may help provide an opportunity for clients to express some of their spiritual concerns, there remains the question of how clinicians should respond, given that this may be an area with which they have little expertise. A rare exception to the tendency to overlook this matter in the literature is the work of Randal and Argyle (2005). They provide some guidelines for clinicians in this area, suggesting that the client could be supported in expressing the content of their experience and inner world at their own pace and time, and that the psycho-spiritual roots of the problem could be explored in the clinical setting. One reason why this might not be done routinely could be that clinicians do not feel confident in this area. It may be that clinicians could consider using outside agencies, such as chaplaincy services, or other appropriate experts (sometimes from other cultures) in the particular form of spirituality of concern to the client, where the client's spiritual musings lie beyond the clinician's level of expertise.

Training implications

This brings us to the related issue of training implications from our research. We will touch only on two issues here. Following on from the previous paragraphs, it seems clear that clinicians working in the field of psychosis need some training in assessing and responding to clients' spiritual concerns. This was exactly the point made by one of the participants in our research, Moana, when she commented:

> But you guys [clinicians] have to educate yourselves [about spiritual matters] to some degree, because when I was in hospital there were a lot of people who were spiritual, who had become spiritual and who believed that their experience had some kind of spiritual element to it.

The form and content of this training would need to be given considerable thought. Based on our research, there are indications that this should include assessing spirituality, exploring spiritual meanings in psychotic experience, recognizing the spirituality/psychosis overlap (and, if possible, differentiating these) and the experience of feeling spirituality fragmented. No doubt there are other matters that need consideration too. The point we wish to make here is simply that training for clinicians needs to give more attention to the issue of spirituality.

Another implication for training, related to our research, concerns the more general issue of attending to subjective experience. It may be that training courses for clinicians have a role to play here. Generally, clinical training involves first providing trainees with a professional framework for making sense of mental health difficulties (this may be medical, psychological, psychotherapeutic, occupational, social, etc.) and then instructing the trainee to look at and make sense of the clients' experiences through this framework. It may be that this approach leads to the development of clinicians who can easily lose sight of the client's subjective experience as the professional frameworks come to dominate how the clinician construes the client's experience. Perhaps, were trainee clinicians exposed *first* to clients' stories of their experience (through having more service users involved in their training, through meetings with clients, or if that is not possible, through reading first-hand accounts) and only later to their chosen profession's way of construing these experiences, this might reduce the likelihood of clinicians losing sight of the client's subjective experience. Kaplan (1964: vii) made this point some time ago in the introduction to his compendium of personal accounts of mental illness when he commented that 'There is no better starting point for those seeking to understand this strange and baffling phenomenon than accounts of the experience.' This is certainly a recommendation that is consistent with our research findings.

Obstacles to overcome in implementing these recommendations

We have now outlined some of the implications which emerge from our conceptualization of schizophrenia and from research, including our own, into subjective experience. These implications derive, essentially, from viewing those who have psychotic experiences as authors of their own experience, whose expertise can contribute to the more general tasks of making sense of and dealing with psychosis. There are, no doubt, a number of obstacles which would be faced in putting these implications into practice.

Existential and human obstacles

One such obstacle may be at the existential level. Many of the implications above rest on the assumption that psychotic experiences are an aspect of our humanity, and, as such, not something to be feared or avoided. However, as Mosher (2001) has pointed out, many of our clinical approaches to psychosis seem to have been designed 'to allow the rest of us to avoid having to deal with these persons' humanity – that is, their subjective experience of psychosis and its effect on us'. Mosher suggests that this may reflect a fear of the unknown and the unpredictable, as well as our own fear of our own 'disintegration'. Searles (1961) made a similar point when he suggested that working clinically with psychotic patients may induce intense anxiety in the therapist and may lead to a tendency to avoid aspects of the experience. This tendency to avoid coming close to the subjective experience of psychosis is likely to prove an obstacle in implementing some of the implications from the present research. Possibly, ways around this obstacle might include ensuring that clinicians are adequately trained and supported: perhaps having greater involvement on training programmes by those who have experienced psychosis might help reduce fears associated with becoming close to those who experience psychosis. Similarly, a 'normalizing' framework which identifies the commonalities between psychotic experience and normal experience may help reduce the fear associated with approaching those who experience psychosis.

Financial obstacles

There are also financial obstacles to the implementation of some of the implications from this research. This applies in particular to the clinical implications. The bulk of clinical services for those who experience psychosis depend on public funding for their survival. This, inevitably, imposes limits on the kinds of services which will be funded. The provision of services which provide clients with opportunities to explore the meaning of their experience in the context of a reliable and enduring relationship with appropriate clinicians is a potentially costly exercise (although taking anti-psychotic medication long term and repeated hospital admissions are also expensive undertakings). Tackling this issue may require further research in this area, to evaluate the clinical utility of different clinical interventions. Such research may be helpful in lobbying for further funding for particular services. This raises the question of whether research funding is as readily forthcoming for this kind of investigation as it is, say, for drug-efficacy studies.

Political obstacles

There are also powerful political issues which provide significant obstacles to the implementation of some of the suggestions in this research. The contest for the meaning and control of schizophrenia takes place within a social environment where particular groups have strong interests in maintaining their positions of power and influence. Two such groups merit mention here: professional clinicians and the pharmaceutical industry.

Many of the implications from the present research revolve around clients of mental health services having greater say in the services they receive and, on an individual level, being seen as actively involved in, rather than passive recipients of, the 'treatment' offered by the clinical team. This poses a threat to the position of professionals who have traditionally exercised control in this area. Implications outlined above point towards a redressing of the power imbalance that has existed between clinicians and consumers of mental health services. Resistance to this is likely from those who enjoy privileges under the current arrangement.

Another, perhaps even more powerful group with an interest in maintaining the status quo, is identified by Mosher et al. (2004) and Sharfstein (2005), who discuss the role of the pharmaceutical industry, 'Big Pharma', in mental health research and service provision. Developing and providing services which are less medically oriented, as well as ensuring that consumers have greater say in the services they receive, poses a serious challenge to the position of dominance occupied by the pharmaceutical industry. Similarly, in the area of changes in the kinds of services offered, where we are recommending greater attention to psychosocial interventions, we may expect challenges from those whose positions of power may be threatened by this. As noted by Holmes (2000: 93) 'resistance to the implementation of psychosocial interventions in schizophrenia arises in the context of a pharmaceutical industry which invests vast sums in order to influence doctors to prescribe its neuroleptic treatments'.

Tackling both of these issues may involve political activity aimed at supporting the role of the consumer moment in mental health and advocating for a greater role for consumers in mental health services (Chamberlin 2004). Research shows clearly that users of mental health services who experience psychosis are keen to have an active say in understanding and tackling psychosis, and further, as our research shows, they have much to offer these endeavours. Similarly, there is greater need for mental health workers to recognize the pervasive – and sometimes pernicious – influence of the pharmaceutical industry on models of understanding and treating madness, and this recognition needs to include an awareness that the interests of the pharmaceutical industry may not always coincide with the interests of clients of mental health services, nor even with the longer-term interests of those who provide such services.

Concluding comments

This brings us now to the end of our book, a journey where we have traversed many different stories, many different ways of making sense of madness. We feel privileged to have made this journey with the participants in our research, who were willing to share with us their lived experience of psychosis. We are grateful to them for being so generous with their precious experience, and we hope we have treated their stories with the respect that they deserve. We also hope that our analysis of these stories, along with our reflections on the literature in this area, might mean we have gone some way towards meeting the challenge that we undertook at the outset: to make some contribution to the important but challenging business of making sense of madness. That this is important – at times crucially so – is made clear by Isa, one of our research participants, with whose profound and moving words we end this book:

> It is only through me understanding it that allows me to carry on living. Otherwise it would just be a void.

References

Aderhold, V. and Gottwalz, E. (2004) Family therapy and schizophrenia: Replacing ideology with openness. In Read, J., Mosher, L. R. and Bentall, R. P. (eds) *Models of madness: Psychological, social and biological approaches to schizophrenia.* Hove, UK: Brunner-Routledge.

American Psychiatric Association (APA) (2000) *Diagnostic and statistical manual IV: Text revision.* Washington, DC: APA.

Angermeyer, M. and Dietrich, S. (2006) Public beliefs about and attitudes towards people with mental illness: A review of population studies. *Acta Psychiatrica Scandinavica*, 113: 163–179.

Angermeyer, M. and Klusmann, D. (1988) The causes of functional psychoses as seen by patients and their relatives. I: The patients' point of view. *European Archives of Psychiatry and Neurological Sciences*, 238: 47–54.

Angermeyer, M. and Matschinger, H. (1996a) The effect of diagnostic labelling on the lay theory regarding schizophrenic disorders. *Social Psychiatry and Psychiatric Epidemiology*, 31: 316–320.

Angermeyer, M. and Matschinger, H. (1996b) Relatives' beliefs about the causes of schizophrenia. *Acta Psychiatrica Scandinavica*, 93: 199–204.

Angermeyer, M. and Matschinger, H. (2003) Public beliefs about schizophrenia and depression: Similarities and differences. *Social Psychiatry and Psychiatric Epidemiology*, 38: 526–534.

Angermeyer, M. and Matschinger, H. (2004) Public attitudes towards psychotropic drugs: Have there been any changes in recent years? *Pharmacopsychiatry*, 37: 152–156.

Angermeyer, M. and Matschinger, H. (2005) Causal beliefs and attitudes to people with schizophrenia: Trend analysis based on data from two population surveys in Germany. *British Journal of Psychiatry*, 186: 331–334.

Angermeyer, M., Klusmann, D. and Walpuski, O. (1988) The causes of functional psychoses as seen by patients and their relatives. II: The relatives' point of view. *European Archives of Psychiatry and Neurological Sciences*, 238: 55–61.

Arieti, S. (1974) *Interpretation of schizophrenia.* London: Crosby, Lockwood, Staples.

Arieti, S. (1979) *Understanding and helping the schizophrenic.* New York: Basic Books.

Bak, M., Myin-Gemeys, I., Hanssen, M., Bijl, R. V., Vollebergh, W., Delespaul, P. and van Os, J. (2003) When does experience of psychosis result in a need for care? A prospective general population study. *Schizophrenia Bulletin*, 29: 349–358.

Bak, M., Krabbendam, L., Janssen, I., de Graaf, R., Vollebergh, W. and van Os, J. (2005) Early trauma may increase the risk for psychotic experiences by impacting on emotional response and perception of control. *Acta Psychiatrica Scandanavica*, 112: 360–366.

Bakhtin, M. (1986) *Speech genres and other late essays*. Austin, TX: University of Texas Press.

Bannister, D. (1960) Conceptual structure in thought-disordered schizophrenics. *Journal of Mental Science*, 106: 1230–1249.

Bannister, D. (1968) The logical requirements of research into schizophrenia. *British Journal of Psychiatry*, 114: 181–188.

Bannister, D. (1985) The patient's point of view. In Bannister, D. (ed.) *Issues and approaches in personal construct theory*. London: Academic Press.

Bannister, D. and Fransella, F. (1966) A grid test of schizophrenic thought disorder. *British Journal of Social and Clinical Psychology*, 5: 95–102.

Bannister, D., Adams-Webber, J., Penn, W. and Radley, A. (1975) Reversing the process of thought disorder: A serial invalidation experiment. *British Journal of Social and Clinical Psychology*, 14: 169–180.

Barham, P. (1995) Manfred Bleuler and the understanding of psychosis. In Ellwood, J. (ed.) *Psychosis: Understanding and treatment*. London: Jessica Kingsley Publishers.

Barker, S., Lavender, T. and Morant, N. (2001) Client and family narratives on schizophrenia. *Journal of Mental Health*, 10: 199–212.

Barry, M. and Greene, S. (1992) Implicit models of mental disorder. *Irish Journal of Psychology*, 13: 141–160.

Bateson, G. (1973) *Steps to an ecology of mind*. St Albans, UK: Paladin.

Bateson, G., Jackson, D. D., Haley, J. and Weakland, J. (1956) Toward a theory of schizophrenia. *Behavioural Science*, 1: 251–264.

Beavan, V. (2007) Angels at our tables: New Zealanders' experiences of hearing voices. Unpublished PhD thesis, University of Auckland.

Bebbington, P. E., Bhugrah, D., Brugha, T., Singleton, N., Farrell, M., Jenkins, R., Lewis, G. and Meltzer, H. (2004) Psychosis, victimisation and childhood disadvantage: Evidence from the second British National Survey of Psychiatric Morbidity. *British Journal of Psychiatry*, 185: 220–226.

Beck, A. T. (1952). Successful outpatient psychotherapy of a chronic schizophrenic with a delusion based on borrowed guilt. *Psychiatry*, 15: 305–312.

Becker, H. S. (1963) *The outsiders*. New York: Free Press.

Bellack, A. S. (1986) Schizophrenia: Behaviour therapy's forgotten child. *Behaviour Therapy*, 17: 199–214.

Bentall, R. P. (1992) A proposal to classify happiness as a psychiatric disorder. *Journal of Medical Ethics*, 18: 94–98.

Bentall, R. P. (1994) Cognitive biases and abnormal beliefs: Towards a model of persecutory delusions. In David, A. S. and Cutting, J. C. (eds) *The neuropsychology of schizophrenia*. Hove, UK: Lawrence Erlbaum Associates.

Bentall, R. P. (2003) *Madness explained*. London: Allen Lane.

Bentall, R. P. (2004) Abandoning the concept of schizophrenia: The cognitive psychology of hallucinations and delusions. In Read, J., Mosher, L. R. and Bentall, R. P. (eds) *Models of madness: Psychological, social and biological approaches to schizophrenia*. Hove, UK: Brunner-Routledge.

Bentall, R. P. (2006) Madness explained: Why we must reject the Kraepelinian paradigm and replace it with a 'complain-oriented' approach to understanding mental illness. *Medical Hypotheses*, 66: 220–233.

Bion, W. (1956) The development of schizophrenic thought. *International Journal of Psychoanalysis*, 37: 344–346.

Birchwood, M., Hallett, S. and Preston, M. (1988) *Schizophrenia: An integrated approach to research and treatment*. London: Longman.

Birchwood, M., Mason, R., MacMillan, F. and Healy, J. (1993) Depression, demoralization and control over psychotic illness: A comparion of depressed and non-depressed patients with chronic psychosis. *Psychological Medicine*, 23: 387–395.

Birchwood, M., Iqbal, Z., Chadwick, P. and Trower, P. (2000a) Cognitive approach to depression and suicidal thinking in psychosis. 1: Ontogeny of post-psychotic depression. *British Journal of Psychiatry*, 177: 516–521.

Birchwood, M., Iqbal, Z., Chadwick, P. and Trower, P. (2000b) Cognitive approach to depression and suicidal thinking in psychosis. 2: Testing the validity of a social rank model. *British Journal of Psychiatry*, 177: 522–528.

Birley, J. L. T. and Brown, G. W. (1970) Crises and life changes preceding the onset or relapse of acute schizophrenia: Clinical aspects. *British Journal of Psychiatry*, 116: 327–333.

Bleuler, E. (1911) *Dementia praecox or the group of schizophrenias*. New York: International Universities Press.

Bloom, F. E. (1993) Advancing a neurodevelopmental origin for schizophrenia. *Archives of General Psychiatry*, 50: 224–227.

Boker, H., von Schmeling, C., Lenz, C., Eppel, A., Meier, M. and Northoff, G. (2000) Subjective experience of catatonia: Construct-analytic findings by means of modified Landfiled categories. In Scheer, J. W. (ed.) *The person in society: Challenges to a constructivist theory*. Giessen, Germany: Psychosozial-verlag.

Boyle, M. (1990) *Schizophrenia: A scientific delusion?* London: Routledge.

Brabban, A. and Turkington, D. (2002) The search for meaning: Detecting congruence between life events, underlying schema and psychotic symptoms. In Morrison, A. P. (ed.) *A casebook of cognitive therapy for psychosis*. Hove, UK: Brunner-Routledge.

Bracken, P. and Thomas, P. (1999) Science, psychiatry and the mystery of madness. *Openmind*, 100: 10–11.

Breggin, P. R. (1991) *Toxic psychiatry: Why therapy, empathy, and love must replace the drugs, electroshock, and biochemical theories of the new psychiatry*. New York: St Martin's Press.

British Psychological Society (2000) *Recent advances in understanding mental illness and psychotic experiences*. Leicester: British Psychological Society.

Bruner, J. (1990) *Acts of meaning*. Cambridge, MA: Harvard University Press.

Budd, R. J., Hughes, I. C. T. and Smith, J. A. (1996) Health beliefs and compliance with antipsychotic medication. *British Journal of Clinical Psychology*, 35: 393–397.

Burdett, J. (2001) Using group philosophical inquiry as a means of promoting recovery for people who experience mental illness. Unpublished MA thesis, Deakin University, Victoria, Australia.

Burdett, J. and Geekie, J. (2003) Philosophical inquiry groups for clients of a first episode psychosis service. Paper presented at Fourteenth ISPS (International Society for the Psychological Treatments of the Schizophrenias and Other Psychoses) Conference, Melbourne, Australia, September 2003.

Cadigan, J. (2004) *People say I'm crazy*. Film, available online: http:// www.peoplesayimcrazy.org/index.html.

Campbell, P. (1992) A survivor's view of community psychiatry. *Journal of Mental Health*, 1: 117–122.

Candido, C. L. and Romney, D. M. (1990) Attributions style in paranoid versus depressed patients. *British Journal of Medical Psychology*, 63: 355–363.

Carpenter, W. T. and Buchanan, R. W. (1995) Schizophrenia: Introduction and overview. In Kaplan, H. I. and Saddock, B. J. (eds) *Comprehensive textbook of psychiatry*, 6th edn. Baltimore, MD: Williams and Wilkins.

Carr, V. (1988) Patients' techniques for coping with schizophrenia: An exploratory study. *British Journal of Medical Psychology*, 61: 339–352.

Cavanagh, M., Read, J. and New, B. (2004) Sexual abuse inquiry and response: A New Zealand training programme. *New Zealand Journal of Psychology*, 33: 137–144.

Chadwick, Paul and Birchwood, M. (1994) The omnipotence of voices. I: A cognitive approach to auditory hallucinations. *British Journal of Psychiatry*, 164: 190–201.

Chadwick, Peter K. (1992) *Borderline: A psychological study of paranoia and delusional thinking*. London: Routledge.

Chadwick, Peter K. (1997) *Schizophrenia: The positive perspective*. London: Routledge.

Chamberlin, J. (2004) User-run services. In Read, J., Mosher, L. R. and Bentall, R. P. (eds) *Models of madness: Psychological, social and biological approaches to schizophrenia*. Hove, UK: Brunner-Routledge.

Chua, S. E. and McKenna, P. J. (1995) Schizophrenia: A brain disease? A critical review of structural and functional cerebral abnormality in the disorder. *British Journal of Psychiatry*, 166: 563–582.

Clarke, I. (2000a) Psychosis and spirituality: Finding a language. *Changes*, 18: 208–214.

Clarke, I. (2000b) Madness and mysticism: Clarifying the mystery. *Network: The Scientific and Medical Network Review*, 72: 11–14.

Clarke, I. (ed.) (2001) *Psychosis and spirituality: Exploring the new frontier*. London: Whurr.

Clay, J. (1996) *R. D. Laing: A divided self*. London: Trafalgar Square.

Clayton, C. (1996) *PETE: The practice of philosophical inquiry as a therapeutic experience*. Lymington, UK: Owl of Minerva.

Corin, E., Thara, R. and Padmavati, R. (2004) Living through the staggering world: The play of signifiers in early psychosis in South India. In Jenkins, J. H. and Barrett, R. J. (eds) *Schizophrenia, culture and subjectivity: The edge of experience*. Cambridge: Cambridge University Press.

Costello, C. G. (1992) Research on symptoms versus research on syndromes: Arguments in favour of allocating more research time to the study of symptoms. *British Journal of Psychiatry*, 160: 304–308.

Cozolino, L. J., Goldstein, M. J., Nuechterlein, K. H., West, K. L. and Snyder, K. S. (1988) The impact of education about schizophrenia on relatives varying in expressed emotion. *Schizophrenia Bulletin*, 14: 675–687.

Croghan, T. W., Tomlin, M., Pescosolido, B. A., Schnittker, J., Martin, J., Lubell, K. and Swindle, R. (2003) American attitudes toward and willingness to use psychiatric medications. *Journal of Nervous and Mental Disease*, 191: 166–174.

Crow, T. (1984) A re-evaluation of the viral hypothesis. *British Journal of Psychiatry*, 145: 243–253.

Cullberg, J. (2006) *Psychoses: An integrative perspective*. Hove, UK: Routledge.

Culliford, D. L. and Johnson, R. D. S. (2003) Healing from within: A guide for assessing the religious and spiritual aspects of people's lives. Spirituality and Psychiatry Special Interest Group of the Royal College of Psychiatrists: Publications Archive. Available online: www.rcpsych.ac.uk/pdf/CullifordJohnson Healing.pdf.

Davidson, L. (2003) *Living outside mental illness: Qualitative studies of recovery in schizophrenia.* New York: New York University Press.

Dean, B. (2000) Signal transmission, rather than reception, is the underlying neurochemical abnormality in schizophrenia. *Australasian and New Zealand Journal of Psychiatry*, 34: 560–569.

Deegan, P. (1988) Recovery: The lived experience of rehabilitation. *Psychosocial Rehabilitation Journal*, 11: 11–19.

Deegan, P. (1996) Recovery as a journey of the heart. *Psychiatric Rehabilitation Journal*, 19: 91–97.

Denzin, N. K. and Lincoln, Y. S. (eds) (2000) *Handbook of qualitative research.* Thousand Oaks, CA: Sage.

Dietrich, S., Beck, M., Bujantugs, B., Kenzine, D., Matschinger, H. and Angermeyer, M. (2004) The relationship between public causal beliefs and social distance toward mentally ill people. *Australian and New Zealand Journal of Psychiatry*, 38: 348–354.

Dietrich, S., Matschinger, H. and Angermeyer, M. (2006) The relationship between biogenetic causal explanations and social distance toward people with mental disorders: Results from a population survey in Germany. *International Journal of Social Psychiatry*, 52: 166–174.

Dillon, J. and May, R. (2002) Reclaiming experience. *Clinical Psychology*, 17: 25–77.

Dittmann, J. and Schuttler, R. (1990) Disease consciousness and coping strategies of patients with schizophrenic psychosis. *Acta Psychiatrica Scandanavica*, 82: 318–322.

Doane, J. A., West, K. L., Goldstein, M. J., Rodnick, E. H. and Jones, J. E. (1981) Parental communication deviance and affective style: Predictors of subsequent schizophrenia spectrum disorders in vulnerable adolescents. *Archives of General Psychiatry*, 38: 679–685.

Doherty, E. G. (1975) Labeling effects in psychiatric hospitalization. *Archives of General Psychiatry*, 32: 562–568.

Drayton, M., Birchwood, M. and Trower, P. (1998) Early attachment experience and recovery from psychosis. *British Journal of Clinical Psychology*, 37: 269–284.

Eisenberg, L. (1977) Disease and illness: Distinctions between professional and popular ideas of sickness. *Culture, Medicine and Psychiatry*, 1: 9–23.

Escher, S., Romme, M., Buiks, A., Delespaul, P. and van Os, J. (2002) Independent course of childhood auditory hallucinations: A sequential 3-year follow-up study. *British Journal of Psychiatry*, 181 (suppl. 43): s10–s18.

Estroff, S. (2004) Subject/subjectivities in dispute: The poetics, politics and performance of first-person narratives of people with schizophrenia. In Jenkins, J. H. and Barrett, R. J. (eds) *Schizophrenia, culture and subjectivity.* Cambridge: Cambridge University Press.

Falloon, I. R. H. and Talbot, R. (1981) Persistent auditory hallucinations: Coping mechanisms and implications for management. *Psychological Medicine*, 11: 329–339.

Faris, R. and Dunham, H. (1939) *Mental disorders in urban areas*. Chicago, IL: University of Chicago Press.

Federn, P. (1952) *Ego psychology and the psychoses*. New York: Basic Books.

Feinberg, I. (1982) Schizophrenia: Caused by a fault in programmed synaptic elimination during adolescence? *Journal of Psychiatric Research*, 4: 319–334.

Fenton, L. and Te Koutua, T. W. (2000) *Four Maori korero about their experience of mental illness*. Wellington, NZ: Mental Health Commission.

Fisher, J. and Farina, A. (1979) Consequences about the nature of mental disorders. *Journal of Abnormal Psychology*, 88: 320–327.

Flanagan, E. H., Davidson, L. and Strauss, J. S. (2007) Issues for DSM-V: Incorporating patients' subjective experiences. *American Journal of Psychiatry*, 164: 391–392.

Foucault, M. (1980) Body/power. In Gordon, C. (ed.) *Power/knowledge: Selected interviews and other writings, 1972–1977*. New York: Pantheon.

Fowler, D., Garety, P. and Kuipers, E. (1998) Cognitive therapy for psychosis: Formulation, treatment, effects and service implications. *Journal of Mental Health*, 7: 123–133.

Frame, J. (1984) *An angel at my table: An autobiography*. New York: George Braziller.

Freud, S. (1904) *On psychotherapy*. London: Hogarth Press.

Freud, S. (1957) *The standard edition of the complete psychological works of Sigmund Freud*. London: Hogarth Press.

Freud, S. (1962) The aetiology of hysteria. In Strachey, J. (ed.) *The standard edition of the complete psychological works of Sigmund Freud*. London: Hogarth Press.

Frith, C. D. (1992) *The cognitive neuropsychology of schizophrenia*. Hillsdale, NJ: Lawrence Erlbaum Associates.

Frith, C. D. (1994) Theory of mind in schizophrenia. In David, A. S. and Cutting, J. C. (eds) *The neuropsychology of schizophrenia*. Hove, UK: Lawrence Erlbaum Associates.

Fromm-Reichmann, F. (1948) Notes on the development of treatment of schizophrenia from a psychoanalytic perspective. *Psychiatry*, 11: 263–273.

Fromm-Reichmann, F. (1958) Basic problems in the psychotherapy of schizophrenia. *Psychiatry*, 21: 1–6.

Fujii, D. E. and Ahmed, I. (2004) Is psychosis a neurobiological syndrome? *Canadian Journal of Psychiatry*, 49: 713–718.

Fulford, K. W. M. and Hope, R. A. (1993) Psychiatric ethics: A bioethical ugly duckling? In Raanon, G. (ed.) *Principles of health care ethics*. New York: Wiley.

Furnham, A. and Bower, P. (1992) A comparison of academic and lay theories of schizophrenia. *British Journal of Psychiatry*, 161: 201–210.

Furnham, A. and Rees, J. (1988) Lay theories of schizophrenia. *International Journal of Social Psychiatry*, 34: 212–220.

Gallie, W. B. (1955–1956) Essentially contested concepts. *Proceedings of the Aristotlian Society*, LVI: 167–198.

Gallie, W. B. (1964) *Philosophy and the historical understanding*. London: Chatto and Windus.

Garety, P. A. (1991) Reasoning and delusions. *British Journal of Psychiatry*, 159 (suppl. 14): 14–18.

Garety, P. A. (1992) Making sense of delusions. *Psychiatry*, 55: 282–291.

Garety, P. A. and Freeman, D. (1999) Cognitive approaches to delusions: A critical review of theories and evidence. *British Journal of Clinical Psychology*, 38: 113–154.

Garrett, M. and Silva, R. (2003) Auditory hallucinations, source monitoring and the belief that 'voices' are real. *Schizophrenia Bulletin*, 29: 445–457.

Geekie, J. (2004) Listening to what we hear: Clients' understandings of psychotic experiences. In Read, J., Mosher, L. R and Bentall, R. P. (eds) *Models of madness: Psychological, social and biological approaches to schizophrenia*. Hove, UK: Brunner-Routledge.

Geekie, J. (2007) The experience of psychosis: Fragmentation, invalidation and spirituality. Unpublished PhD thesis, University of Auckland.

Geekie, J. and Read, J. (2008) Fragmentation, invalidation and spirituality: Personal experiences of psychosis. Ethical, research and clinical implications. In Gleeson, J. (ed.) *Psychotherapies for the psychoses: Theoretical, cultural, and clinical integration*. Hove, UK: Routledge.

Geertz, C. (1983) Blurred genes: The refiguration of social thought. In Geertz, C. (ed.) *Local knowledge*. New York: Basic Books.

Gergen, K. J. (1977) The social construction of self-knowledge. In Mischel, T. (ed.) *The self: psychological and philosophical issues*. Oxford: Blackwell.

Gergen, K. J. and McNamee, S. (2002) From disordering discourse to transformative dialogue. In Neimeyer, R. A. and Raskin, J. D. (eds) *Constructions of disorder: Meaning making frameworks for psychotherapy*. Washington, DC: APA.

Gilbert, K. R. (2002) Taking a narrative approach to grief research: Finding meaning in stories. *Death Studies*, 26: 223–240.

Gilman, S. L. (1988) *Disease and representation: Images of illness from madness to AIDS*. New York: Cornell University Press.

Glaser, B. G. and Strauss, A. L. (1967) *The discovery of grounded theory*. Chicago, IL: Aldine.

Goffman, E. (1961) *Asylums*. New York: Doubleday.

Goldstein, M. (1987) The UCLA high-risk project. *Schizophrenia Bulletin*, 13: 505–514.

Goldstein, M., Rosenfarb, I., Woo, S. and Nuechterlein, K. (1994) Intrafamilial relationships and the course of schizophrenia. *Acta Psychiatrica Scandanavica*, 90 (suppl. 384): 60–66.

Good, B. (1986) Explanatory models and care-seeking: A critical account. In McHugh, S. and Vallis, M. T. (eds) *Illness behaviour: A multidisciplinary perspective*. New York: Plenum.

Gottesman, I. I. (1991) *Schizophrenia genesis*. New York: Freeman.

Gould, L. N. (1949) Auditory hallucinations and subvocal speech. *Journal of Nervous and Mental Disease*, 109: 418–427.

Gouldner, A. W. (1970) *The coming crisis of Western sociology*. New York: Basic Books.

Greenberg, J. (1964) *I never promised you a rose garden*. New York: Holt, Rinehart and Winston.

Grof, S. and Grof, C. (1986) Spiritual emergency: The understanding of treatment of transpersonal crises. *Re-Vision*, 8: 7–20.

Gunderson, J. G. and Mosher, L. R. (1975) The cost of schizophrenia. *American Journal of Psychiatry*, 132: 1437–1440.

Hafner, H., Maurer, K., Loffler, W. and Riecher-Rossler, A. (1993) The influence of age and sex on the onset and course of schizophrenia. *British Journal of Psychiatry*, 162: 80–87.

Hardcastle, M., Kennard, D., Grandison, S. and Fagin, L. (eds) (2007) *Experiences of mental health in-patient care*. London: Routledge.

Harding, C., Brooks, G. W., Ashikaga, T., Strauss, J. S. and Breier, A. (1987) The Vermont longitudinal study of persons with severe mental illness. I: Methodology, study sample, and overall status 32 years later. *American Journal of Psychiatry*, 144: 718–726.

Harré, R. (1994) *The discursive mind*. London: Sage.

Harré, R. (1998) *The singular self*. London: Sage.

Harrison, G., Gunnell, D., Glazebrook, C., Page, K. and Kwiecinski, R. (2001) Association between schizophrenia and social inequality at birth. *British Journal of Psychiatry*, 179: 346–350.

Harrop, C. and Trower, P. (2003) *Why does schizophrenia develop at late adolescence? A cognitive-developmental approach to psychosis*. Chichester: Wiley.

Healy, D. (2002) *The creation of psychopharmacology*. Cambridge, MA: Harvard University Press.

Helman, C. G. (1981) Disease versus illness in general practice. *Medical Anthropology*, 31: 548–552.

Henquet, C., Krabbendam, L., Spauwen, C., Kaplan, C., Lieb, R., Wittchen, H. and van Os, J. (2005) Prospective cohort study of cannabis use, predisposition for psychosis and psychotic symptoms in young people. *British Medical Journal*, 330: 11–16.

Heron, J. (1981) Philosophical basis for a new paradigm. In Reason, P. and Rowan, J. (eds) *Human inquiry: A sourcebook of new paradigm research*. Chichester: Wiley.

Hingley, S. M. (1997) Psychodynamic perspectives on psychosis and psychotherapy. 1: Theory. *British Journal of Medical Psychology*, 70: 301–312.

Hingley, S. M. (2006) Finding meaning within psychosis: The contribution of psychodymanic theory and practice. In Johanneson, J. O., Martindale, B. V. and Cullberg, J. (eds) *Evolving psychosis: Different stages, different treatments*. Hove, UK: Routledge.

Holmes, J. (2000) Narrative in psychiatry and psychology: The evidence? *Medical Humanities*, 26: 92–96.

Holzinger, A., Loffler, W., Muller, P., Priebe, S. and Angermeyer, M. (2002) Subjective illness theory and antipsychotic medication compliance by patients with schizo-phrenia. *Journal of Nervous and Mental Disease*, 190: 597–603.

Hornstein, G. A. (2002) Narratives of madness as told from within. *Chronicle of Higher Education*, 48: b7–b10.

Hornstein, G. A. (2005) *Bibliography of first-person accounts of madness in English*, 3rd edn. Available online: http://webtest.mtholyoke.edu/acad/assets/Academics/Hornstein_Bibliography.pdf.

Horrobin, D. (2002) *The madness of Adam and Eve: How schizophrenia shaped human-ity*. London: Corgi.

Husserl, E. (1962) *Ideas: General introduction to pure phenomenology*. New York: Collier.

Hutchison, G., Takei, N., Fahy, T. A., Bhugra, D., Gilvarry, C., Moran, O., Mallett, R., Sham, P., Leff, J. and Murray, R. M. (1996) Morbid risk of schizophrenia in first degree relatives of white and Afro-Caribbean patients with psychoses. *British Journal of Psychiatry*, 164: 474–480.

Illich, I. (1975) *Medical nemesis: The expropriation of health*. London: Calder and Boyars.

James, W. (1890) *The principles of psychology*. New York: Dover.

James, W. (1902) *The varieties of religious experience*. New York: Longmans, Green.

Janssen, I., Krabbendam, L., Bak, M., Hanssen, M., Vollebergh, W. and De Graaf, R. (2003) Discrimination and delusional ideation. *British Journal of Psychiatry*, 1: 71–76.

Janssen, I., Krabbendam, L., Bak, M., Hanssen, M., Vollebergh, W., de Graaf, R. and van Os, J. (2004) Childhood abuse as a risk factor for psychotic experiences. *Acta Psychiatrica Scandanavica*, 109: 38–45.

Jansson, L. B. and Parnas, J. (2007) Competing definitions of schizophrenia: What can be learned from polydiagnostic studies? *Schizophrenia Bulletin*, 33: 1178–1200.

Jaskiw, G. E., Juliano, D. M., Goldberg, T. E., Herzman, M., Urow-Hamell, E. and Weinberger, D. R. (1994) Cerebral ventricular enlargement in schizophreniform disorder does not progress: A seven year follow-up study. *Schizophrenia research*, 14: 23–28.

Jaspers, K. (1963) *General psychopathology*. Manchester: Manchester University Press.

Jaynes, J. (1976) *The origin of consciousness in the breakdown of the bicameral mind*. Boston, MA: Houghton Mifflin.

Jenkins, J. H. (1997) Subjective experience of persistent schizophrenia and depression among US Latinos and Euro-Americans. *British Journal of Psychiatry*, 171: 20–25.

Jenkins, J. H. (2004) Schizophrenia as a paradigm case for understanding fundamental human processes. In Jenkins, J. H. and Barrett, R. J. (eds) *Schizophrenia, culture and subjectivity: The edge of experience*. Cambridge: Cambridge University Press.

Jennings, D. (1986) The confusion between disease and illness in clinical medicine. *Canadian Medical Association Journal*, 135(8): 865–870.

Johnson, M. K., Hashtroudi, S. and Lindsay, D.S. (1993) Source monitoring. *Psychological Bulletin*, 114: 3–28.

Johnstone, E. C., Crow, T. J., Frith, C. D., Husband, J. and Kreel, L. (1979) Cerebral ventricular size and cognitive impairment in schizophrenia. *Lancet*, 2(7992): 924–926.

Johnstone, L. (1999) Do families cause 'schizophrenia'? Revisiting a taboo subject. In Newnes, C., Holmes, G. and Dunn, C. (eds) *This is madness*. Ross-on-Wye, UK: PCCS Books.

Jorm, A., Korten, A. E., Jacomb, P. A., Christensen, H., Rodgers, B. and Pollitt, P. (1997) Public beliefs about causes and risk factors for depression and schizophrenia. *Social Psychiatry and Psychiatric Epidemiology*, 32: 143–148.

Jorm, A., Angermeyer, M. and Katschnig, H. (2000) Public knowledge of and attitudes to mental disorders: A limiting factor in the optimal use of treatment services. In Andrews, G. and Henderson, S. (eds) *Unmet need in psychiatry*. Cambridge: Cambridge University Press.

Jorm, A., Christensen, H. and Griffiths, K. (2005) Public beliefs about causes and risk factors for mental disorders. *Social Psychiatry and Psychiatric Epidemiology*, 40: 764–767.

Joseph, J. (2004) Schizophenia and heridity: Why the emperor has no genes. In Read, J., Mosher, L. R. and Bentall, R. P. (eds) *Models of madness: Psychological, social and biological approaches to schizophrenia*. Hove, UK: Brunner-Routledge.

Josephs, L. and Josephs, L. (1986) Pursuing the kernel of truth in the psychotherapy of schizophrenia. *Psychoanalytic Psychology*, 3: 105–119.

Jung, C. G. (1936) *The psychology of dementia praecox*. Nervous and Mental Disease Monograph Series no. 3. Washington, DC: Nervous and Mental Disease Publishing.

Jung, C. G. (1995) *Memories, dreams, reflections*. London: Fontana.

Kaplan, B. (ed.) (1964) *The inner world of mental illness: A series of first-person accounts of what it was like*. New York: Harper and Row.

Kaplan, H. I. and Saddock, B. J. (eds) (1995) *Comprehensive textbook of psychiatry*, 6th edn. Baltimore, MD: Williams and Wilkins.

Karanci, A. (1995) Caregivers of Turkish schizophrenic patients: Causal attributions, burdens and attitudes to help from the health professions. *Social Psychiatry and Psychiatric Epidemiology*, 30: 261–268.

Karno, M. and Norquist, G. S. (1995) Schizophrenia: Epidemiology. In Kaplan, H. I. and Saddock, B. J. (eds) *Comprehensive textbook of psychiatry*, 6th edn. Baltimore, MD: Williams and Wilkins.

Karon, B. P. (1999) The tragedy of schizophrenia. *The General Psychologist*, 34: 1–12.

Kaysen, S. (1993) *Girl, interrupted*. New York: Random House.

Kelly, G. A. (1955) *The psychology of personal constructs, volumes I and II*. New York: Norton.

Kemp, R., David, A. and Hayward, P. (1996) Compliance therapy: An intervention targeting insight and treatment adherence in psychotic patients. *Behavioural and Cognitive Psychotherapy*, 24: 331–350.

Kendell, R. E. and Gourlay, J. A. (1970) The clinical distinction between the affective psychoses and schizophrenia. *British Journal of Psychiatry*, 117: 261–266.

Kent, H. and Read, J. (1998) Measuring consumer participation in mental health services: Are attitudes related to professional orientation? *International Journal of Social Psychiatry*, 44: 295–310.

Keshavan, M. S., Schooler, N. R., Sweeney, J. A., Hass, G. L. and Pettegrew, J. W. (1998) Research and treatment strategies in first episode psychoses. *British Journal of Psychiatry*, 172 (suppl. 33): 60–65.

Kindermann, P. and Bentall, R. P. (1996) Self-discrepancies and persecutory delusions: Evidence for a model of paranoid ideation. *Journal of Abnormal Psychology*, 105: 106–113.

Kirmayer, L. J. (1988) Mind and body as metaphors: Hidden values in biomedicine. In Lock, M. and Gordon, D. (eds) *Biomedicine examined*. Dordrecht, Netherlands: Kluwer.

Klein, M. (1946) Notes on some schizoid mechanisms. *International Journal of Psychoanalysis*, 27: 99–110.

Kleinman, A. (1986) Illness meanings and illness behaviour. In McHugh, S. and Vallis, M. T. (eds) *Illness behaviour: A multidisciplinary model*. New York: Plenum.

Kleinman, A. (1988) *The illness narratives: Suffering, healing and the human condition*. New York: Basic Books.

Kleinman, A. (1993) Concepts and a model for the comparison of medical systems as cultural systems. In Currer, C. and Stacey, M. (eds) *Concepts of health, illness and disease*. Oxford: Berg.

Knapp, M., Mangalore, R. and Simon, J. (2004) The global costs of schizophrenia. *Schizophrenia Bulletin*, 30: 279–293.

Knight, Z. G. and Bradfield, B. C. (2003) The experience of being diagnosed with a psychiatric disorder: Living the label. *Indo-Pacific Journal of Phenomenology*, 3: 1–20.

Kraepelin, E. (1919) *Dementia praecox and paraphrenia*. Edinburgh: Livingstone.

Kring, A. M. and Germans, M. K. (2004) Subjective experience of emotion in schizophrenia. In Jenkins, J. H. and Barrett, R. J. (eds) *Schizophrenia, culture, and subjectivity: The edge of experience*. Cambridge: Cambridge University Press.

Kupper, Z. and Tschacher, W. (2008) Lack of concordance between subjective improvement and symptom change in psychotic episodes. *British Journal of Clinical Psychology*, 47: 75–93.

Lachenmeyer, N. (2000) *The outsider: A journey into my father's struggle with madness*. New York: Broadway.

Lafond, V. (1998) The grief of mental illness: Context for the cognitive therapy for schizophrenia. In Perris, C. and McGorry, P. D. (eds) *Cognitive psychotherapy of psychotic and personality disorders*. New York: Wiley.

Laing, R. D. (1960) *The divided self: A study of sanity and madness*. London: Tavistock.

Laing, R. D. (1967) *The politics of experience*. New York: Random House.

Laing, R. D. and Esteron, A. (1970) *Sanity, madness and the family*. New York: Basic Books.

Lakoff, R. T. (1995) Cries and whispers. In Hall, K. and Buchotz, M. (eds) *Gender articulated: Language and the socially constructed self*. London: Routledge.

Lally, S. J. (1989) 'Does being in here mean there is something wrong with me?' *Schizophrenia Bulletin*, 15: 253–265.

Landrine, H. (1992) Clinical implications of cultural differences: The referential versus the indexical self. *Clinical Psychology Review*, 12: 401–415.

Langer, E. J. and Abelson, R. P. (1974) A patient by any other name: Clinician group difference in labelling bias. *Journal of Consulting and Clinical Psychology*, 42: 4–9.

Lapsley, H., Nicora, L. W. and Black, R. (2002) *'Kia Mauri Tau!' Narratives or recovery from disabling mental health problems*. Wellington, NZ: Mental Health Commission.

Larkin, W. and Morrison, A. (eds) (2006) *Trauma and psychosis: New directions for theory and therapy*. London: Routledge.

Larsen, J. A. (2004) Finding meaning in first episode psychosis: Experience, agency and the cultural repertoire. *Medical Anthropology Quarterly*, 18: 447–471.

Leibrich, J. (1999) *A gift of stories: Discovering how to deal with mental illness*. Dunedin, NZ: University of Otago Press and Mental Health Commission.

Leudar, I. and Thomas, P. (2001) *Voices of reason, voices of insanity: Studies of verbal hallucinations*. London: Brunner-Routledge.

Leventhal, H., Diefenbach, M. and Leventhal, E. A. (1992) Illness cognition: Using common sense to understand treatment adherence and affect cognition interaction. *Cognitive Therapy and Research*, 16: 143–163.

Liddle, P. F. (1987) The symptoms of chronic schizophrenia: A re-examination of the positive-negative dichotomy. *British Journal of Psychiatry*, 151: 145–151.

Lindstrom, E. (1996) The hidden cost of schizophrenia. *Journal of Drug Development and Clinical Practice*, 7: 281–288.

Linehan, M. M. (1993) *Cognitive behavioural treatment of borderline personality disorder*. New York: Guilford.

Link, B. G., Struening, E. L., Neese-Todd, S., Asmussen, S. and Phelan, J. C. (2001) Stigma as a barrier to recovery. *Psychiatric Services*, 52: 1621–1625.

Littlewood, R. (1991) Against pathology: The new psychiatry and its critics. *British Journal of Psychiatry*, 159: 696–702.

London, N. J. (1980) Schizophrenia: Selected papers. Psychological issues, Monograph 38. *Journal of American Psychoanalysis*, 28: 199–210.

Lothian, J. and Read, J. (2002) Asking about abuse during mental health assessments: Clients' views and experiences. *New Zealand Journal of Psychology*, 31: 98–103.

Lysaker, P. H. and Lysaker, J. T. (2004) Dialogical transformation in the psychotherapy of schizophrenia. In Hermans, H. J. M. and Dimaggio, C. (eds) *The dialogical self in psychotherapy*. New York: Brunner-Routledge.

McGill, C., Falloon, I., Boyd, J. and Wood-Siverio, C. (1983) Family educational intervention in the treatment of schizophrenia. *Hospital and Community Psychiatry*, 34: 934–938.

McGlashan, T. H. (1987) Recovery style from mental illness and long-term outcome. *Journal of Mental and Nervous Disease*, 11: 681–685.

McGlashan, T. H. and Carpenter, W. T. (1981) Does attitude toward psychosis relate to outcome? *American Journal of Psychiatry*, 138: 797–810.

McGlashan, T. H. and Hoffman, R. E. (1995) Schizophrenia: Psychodynamic to neurodynamic theories. In Kaplan, H. I. and Saddock, B. J. (eds) *Comprehensive textbook of psychiatry*, 6th edn. Baltimore, MD: Williams and Wilkins.

McGlashan, T. H., Levy, S. T. and Carpenter, W. T. (1975) Integration and sealing over. *Archives of General Psychiatry*, 32: 1269–1272.

McGlashan, T. H., Docherty, J. P. and Siris, S. (1976) Integrative and sealing over recoveries from schizophrenia: Distinguishing case studies. *Psychiatry*, 39: 325–338.

McGorry, P. D. (1994) The influence of illness duration on syndrome clarity and stability in functional psychoses: Does diagnosis emerge and stabilise with time? *Australia and New Zealand Journal of Psychiatry*, 28: 607–619.

McGorry, P. D. (1995) A treatment-relevant classification of psychotic disorders. *Australia and New Zealand Journal of Psychiatry*, 29: 555–558.

McGorry, P. D., Bell, R. C., Dudgeon, P. L. and Jackson, H. F. (1998) The dimensional structure of first episode psychosis: An explanatory factor analysis. *Psychological Medicine*, 28: 935–947.

McKnight, C. (2003) Medicine as an essentially contested concept. *Journal of Medical Ethics*, 29: 261–262.

MacLeod, J., Oakes, R., Copello, A., Crome, L., Egger, M., Hickman, M., Oppenkowski, T., Stokes-Lampard, H. and Smith, G. D. (2004) Psychological and social sequelae of cannabis and other illicit drug use by young people: A systematic review of longitudinal, general population studies. *The Lancet*, 363: 1579–1588.

Mair, M. (1977) The community of self. In Bannister, D. (ed.) *New perspectives in personal construct theory*. London: Academic Press.

Mair, M. (1988) Psychology as storytelling. *International Journal of Personal Construct Psychology*, 1: 125–138.

Malo, V. (2000) *Pacific people in New Zealand talk about their experiences with mental illness*. Wellington, NZ: Mental Health Commission.

Mancuso, J. C. (1996) Constructionism, personal construct psychology and narrative psychology. *Theory and Psychology*, 6: 47–70.

Masson, J. M. (1984) *Freud: The assualt on truth. Freud's suppression of the seduction theory.* London: Faber and Faber.

May, R. (2002) *You could say I'm a mad psychologist.* Available online: www.brad.ac.uk/acad/health/research/cccmh/articles.php (accessed 3 July 2008).

May, R. (2003) *Understanding psychotic experience and working towards recovery.* Available online: www.brad.ac.uk/acad/health/research/cccmh/articles.php (accessed 3 July 2008).

Mayer-Gross, W. (1920) Uber die stellungnahme zur abgelaufenen akuten psychose. *Zeitschrifte für die gesamte Neurologie und Psychiatrie*, 60: 160–212.

Mechanic, D. (1972) Social psychological factors affecting the presentation of bodily complaints. *New England Journal of Medicine*, 21: 1132–1139.

Meehl, P. (1962) Schizotaxia, schizotypia, schizophrenia. *American Psychologist*, 17: 827–838.

Mehta, S. and Farina, A. (1997) Is being 'sick' really better? Effect of disease view of mental disorder on stigma. *Journal of Social and Clinical Psychology*, 16(4): 405–419.

Miller, G. A. (2003) The cognitive revolution: A historical perspective. *Trends in Cognitive Sciences*, 7: 141–144.

Molvaer, J., Hantzi, A. and Papadatos, Y. (1992) Psychotic patients' attributions for mental illness. *British Journal of Clinical Psychology*, 31: 210–212.

Morrison, A., Frame, L. and Larkin, W. (2003) Relationships between trauma and psychosis: A review and integration. *British Journal of Psychiatry*, 42: 331–353.

Morrison, J. K., Bushell, J. D., Hanson, G. D., Fentiman, J. R. and Holdridge-Crane, S. (1977) Relationship between psychiatric patients' attitudes toward mental illness and attitudes of dependence. *Psychological Reports*, 41: 1194.

Morse, J. M. (ed.) (1992) *Qualitative health research.* Newbury Park, CA: Sage.

Mosher, L. R. (2001) Treating madness without hospitals: Soteria and its successors. In Schneider, K. J., Bugental, J. F. T. and Pierson, J. F. (eds) *Handbook of humanistic psychology.* Thousand Oaks, CA: Sage.

Mosher, L. R. (2004) Non-hospital, non-drug intervention with first-episode psychosis. In Read, J., Mosher, L. R. and Bentall, R. P. (eds) *Models of madness: Psychological, social and biological approaches to schizophrenia.* Hove, UK: Brunner-Routledge.

Mosher, L. R., Gosden, R. and Beder, S. (2004) Drug companies and schizophrenia: Unbridled capitalism meets madness. In Read, J., Mosher, L. R. and Bentall, R. P. (eds) *Models of madness: Psychological, social and biological approaches to madness.* Hove, UK: Brunner-Routledge.

Mosher, L. R., Hendrix, V. and Ford, D. (2005) *Soteria: Through madness to deliverance.* Philadelphia, PA: Xlibris.

Mueser, K. T. and Berenbaum, H. (1990) Psychodynamic treatment of schizophrenia: Is there a future? *Psychological Medicine*, 20: 253–262.

Newnes, C. (2002) Brainwashed: Mental illnesses are caused by chemical imbalances in the brain, right? Wrong, says Craig Newnes. *Guardian.* Available online: www.guardian.co.uk/health/story/0,3605,630152,00.html (accessed 12 July 2008).

Nietzsche, F. (1966) *Beyond good and evil.* New York: Random House.

Nosé, M., Barbui, C. and Tansella, M. (2003) How often do patients with psychosis fail to adhere to treatment programmes? A systematic review. *Psychological Medicine*, 33: 1149–1160.

Nuechterlein, K. H. and Dawson, M. E. (1984) A heuristic vulnerability/stress model of schizophrenic episodes. *Schizophrenia Bulletin*, 10: 300–312.

O'Hagan, M. (1992) On being 'Not Quite Human'. In Patten, D. (ed.) *Public attitudes to mental illness*. Wellington, NZ: Department of Health.

O'Hagan, M. (1994) *Stopovers on my way home from Mars: A journey into the psychiatric survivor movement in the USA, Britain and the Netherlands*. London: Survivors Speak Out.

O'Hagan, M. (ed.) (2000a) *Four families of people with mental illness talk about their experiences*. Wellington, NZ: Mental Health Commission.

O'Hagan, M. (ed.) (2000b) *Three forensic service users and their families talk about recovery*. Wellington, NZ: Mental Health Commission.

O'Hagan, M. (2001) *Recovery competencies for New Zealand mental health workers*. Wellington, NZ: Mental Health Commission.

Olson, L. S. (ed.) (1994) *He was still my Daddy: Coming to terms with mental illness*. Portland, OR: Ogden House.

Pantelis, C., Yücel, M., Wood, S. J., McGorry, P. D. and Velakoulis, D. (2003) Early and late neurodevelopmental disturbances in schizophrenia and their functional consequences. *Australian and New Zealand Journal of Psychiatry*, 37: 399–406.

Pell, T. J. (1999) Contested concepts and racial preferences. Paper presented at Hamilton College, Clinton, NY, 5 April 1999. Available online: www.cir-usa.org/articles/71.html (accessed 3 July 2008).

Percival, J. (1840) *A narrative of the treatment experienced by a gentleman, during a state of derangment; designed to explain the causes and the nature of insanity, and to expose the injudicious conduct pursued towards many unfortunate sufferers under that calamity*. London: Effingham Wilson.

Persons, J. B. (1986) The advantages of studying psychological phenomena rather than psychiatric diagnoses. *American Psychologist*, 41: 1252–1260.

Pidgeon, N. and Henwood, K. (1997) Using grounded theory in psychological research. In Hayes, N. (ed.) *Doing qualitative analysis in psychology*. Hove, UK: Psychology Press.

Pistrang, N. and Barker, C. (1992) Clients' beliefs about psychological problems. *Counselling Psychology Quarterly*, 5: 325–335.

Plath, S. (1965) *Ariel*. London: Faber and Faber.

Poulton, R., Caspi, A., Moffitt, T. E., Cannon, M., Murray, R. and Harrington, H. (2000) Children's self-reported psychotic symptoms and adult schizophreniform disorder: A 15-year longitudinal study. *Archives of General Psychiatry*, 57: 1053–1058.

Power, P. and McGorry, P. D. (1999) Initial assessment in first-episode psychosis. In McGorry, P. D. and Jackson, H. J. (eds) *The recognition and management of early psychosis: A preventative approach*. Cambridge: Cambridge University Press.

Rabinow, P. and Sullivan, W. M. (1987) The interpretive turn. In Rabinow, P. and Sulllivan, W. M. (eds) *The interpretive turn*. Berkeley, CA: University of California Press.

Randal, P. and Argyle, N. (2005) 'Spiritual emergency': A useful explanatory model? A literature review and discussion paper. Spirituality and Psychiatry Special Interest Group of the Royal College of Psychiatrists: Publications Archive. Available online: www.rcpsych.ac.uk/PDF/DrPRandalDrArgyleEmergency.pdf.

Read, J. (1997) Child abuse and psychosis: A literature review and implications for professional practice. *Professional Psychology, Research and Practice*, 28: 448–456.

Read, J. (1998) Child abuse and severity of disturbance among adult psychiatric inpatients. *Child Abuse and Neglect*, 22: 359–368.

Read, J. (2004a) The invention of 'schizophrenia'. In Read, J., Mosher, L. R. and Bentall, R. P. (eds) *Models of madness: Psychological, social and biological approaches to schizophrenia*. Hove, UK: Brunner-Routledge.

Read, J. (2004b) Biological psychiatry's lost cause. In Read, J., Mosher, L. R. and Bentall, R. P. (eds) *Models of madness: Psychological, social and biological approaches to schizophrenia*. Hove, UK: Brunner-Routledge.

Read, J. (2007) Why promulgating biological ideology increases prejudice against people labelled 'schizophrenic'. *Australian Psychologist*, 42: 118–128.

Read, J. (2008) Schizophrenia, drug companies and the internet. *Social Science and Medicine*, 66: 99–109.

Read, J. and Harre, N. (2001) The role of biological and genetic causal beliefs in the stigmatisation of 'mental patients'. *Journal of Mental Health*, 10: 223–235.

Read, J. and Haslam, N. (2004) Public opinion: Bad things happen and can drive you crazy. In Read, J., Mosher, L. R. and Bentall, R. P. (eds) *Models of madness: Psychological, social and biological approaches to schizophrenia*. Hove, UK: Brunner-Routledge.

Read, J. and Law, A. (1999) The relationship of causal beliefs and contact with users of mental health services to attitudes to the 'mentally ill'. *International Journal of Social Psychiatry*, 45: 216–229.

Read, J., Perry, B. D., Moskowitz, A. and Connolly, J. (2001) The contribution of early traumatic events to schizophrenia in some patients: A traumagenic neurodevelopmental model. *Psychiatry*, 64: 319–345.

Read, J., Agar, K., Argyle, N. and Aderhold, V. (2003) Sexual and physical abuse during childhood and adulthood as predictors of hallucinations, delusions and thought disorder. *Psychology and Psychotherapy: Theory, Research and Practice*, 76: 1–22.

Read, J., Goodman, L., Morrison, A. P., Ross, C. A. and Aderhold, V. (2004) Childhood trauma, loss and stress. In Read, J., Mosher, L. R. and Bentall, R. P. (eds) *Models of madness: Psychological, social and biological approaches to schizophrenia*. Hove, UK: Brunner-Routledge.

Read, J., van Os, J. and Morrison, A. P. (2005) Childhood trauma, psychosis and schizophrenia: A literature review with theoretical and clinical implications. *Acta Psychiatrica Scandanavica*, 112: 330–350.

Read, J., Haslam, N., Sayce, L. and Davies, E. (2006) Prejudice and schizophrenia: A review of the 'mental illness is an illness like any other' approach. *Acta Psychiatrica Scandinavica*, 114: 303–318.

Read, J., Fink, P., Rudegeair, T., Filetti, V. and Whitfield, C. (2008) Child maltreatment and psychosis: A return to a genuinely integrated bio-psychosocial model. *Clinical Schizophrenia and Related Psychoses*, 2: 235–254.

Rhodes, J. E. and Jakes, S. (2004) The contribution of metaphor and metonymy to delusions. *Psychology and Psychotherapy*, 77: 1–17.

Ridgway, P. (2001) Restorying psychiatric disability: Learning from first person recovery narratives. *Psychiatric Rehabilitation Journal*, 24: 335–343.

Riedel-Heller, S., Matschinger, H. and Angermeyer, M. (2005) Mental disorders: Who and what might help? Help-seeking and treatment preferences of the lay public. *Social Psychiatry and Psychiatric Epidemiology*, 40: 167–174.

Ritsher, J. B. and Phelan, J. C. (2004) Internalized stigma predicts erosion of morale among psychiatric outpatients. *Psychiatry Research*, 129: 257–265.

Robbins, M. (1993) *Experiences of schizophrenia: An integration of the personal, scientific and therapeutic*. New York: Guilford.

Roberts, G. (1999a) Introduction: A story of stories. In Roberts, G. and Holmes, J. (eds) *Healing stories: Narrative in psychiatry and psychotherapy*. Oxford: Oxford University Press.

Roberts, G. (1999b) The rehabilitation of rehabilitation: A narrative approach to psychosis. In Roberts, G. and Holmes, J. (eds) *Healing stories: Narrative in psychiatry and psychotherapy*. Oxford: Oxford University Press.

Roberts, G. and Wolfson, P. (2004) The discovery of recovery: Open to all. *Advances in Psychiatric Treatment*, 10: 37–49.

Rodriguez, M. G., Cabeza, I. G., Diaz, E. and de Chavez, M. G. (2000) Depressive experiences in schizophrenia. *Archivos de Psiquiatria*, 1: 81–91.

Roe, D. and Ben-Yashai, A. (1999) Exploring the relationship between the person and the disorder among individuals hospitalized for psychosis. *Psychiatry*, 62: 370–380.

Roe, D. and Davidson, L. (2005) Self and narrative in schizophrenia: Time to author a new story. *Medical Humanities*, 31: 89–94.

Romme, M. and Escher, A. (1989) Hearing voices. *Schizophrenia Bulletin*, 15: 209–216.

Romme, M. and Escher, A. (eds) (1993) *Accepting voices*. London: MIND.

Romme, M. and Escher, A. (1996) Empowering people who hear voices. In Haddock, G. and Slade, P. D. (eds) *Cognitive behavioural interventions with psychotic disorders*. London: Routledge.

Rook, D. and Geekie, J. (2004) A storytelling group. Paper presented at NZ ISPS Making Sense of Psychosis conference, Auckland, New Zealand, October 2004.

Rook, D. and Geekie, J. (2006) The importance of being author: Story-telling groups for clients of a first episode psychosis service. Paper presented at Fifteenth ISPS International Conference, Madrid, Spain, June 2006.

Rorty, R. (1980) *Philosophy and the mirror of nature*. Oxford: Blackwell.

Rosenhan, D. (1973) On being sane in insane places. *Science*, 179: 250–258.

Ross, C. A. (2006) Dissociation and psychosis: The need for integration of theory and practice. In Johannessen, J. O., Martindale, B. V. and Cullberg, J. (eds) *Evolving psychosis: Different stages, different treatments*. London: Routledge.

Ross, C. A. and Read, J. (2004) Antipsychotic medication: Myths and facts. In Read, J. and Mosher, L. R. (eds) *Models of madness: Psychological, social and biological approaches to schizophrenia*. Hove, UK: Brunner-Routledge.

Rudegeair, T. and Farelly, S. (2003) Is all psychosis disocciative? Paper presented at the Annual Conference of the International Society for the Study of Dissociation, Chicago, IL, November 2003.

Russo, J. (2001) Reclaiming madness. In Read, J. (ed.) *Something inside so strong: Strategies for surviving mental distress*. London: Mental Health Foundation.

Santayana, G. (1948) *Dialogues in limbo*. New York: Charles Scribner's Sons.

Sartorius, N., Jablensky, A., Korten, G., Ernberg, G., Anker, M., Cooper, J. E. and

Day, R. (1986) Early manifestations and first-contact incidence of schizophrenia in different cultures. *Psychological Medicine*, 35: 130–131.

Sass, L. A. (1992) Heidegger, schizophrenia and the ontological difference. *American Psychologist*, 5: 109–132.

Sass, L. A. (2004) 'Negative symptoms', commonsense, and cultural disembedding in the modern age. In Jenkins, J. H. and Barrett, R. J. (eds) *Schizophrenia, culture, and subjectivity: The edge of experience*. Cambridge: Cambridge University Press.

Sass, L. A. and Parnas, J. (2003) Schizophrenia, consciousness and the self. *Schizophrenia Bulletin*, 29: 427–444.

Saunders, A., Duan, J., Levinson, D., Shi, J., He, D., Hou, C., Burrell, G. and Rice, J. (2008) No significant association of 14 candidate genes with schizophrenia in a large European ancestry sample: Implications for psychiatric geriatrics. *American Journal of Psychiatry*, 4: 497–506.

Sayce, L. (2000) *From psychiatric patient to citizen*. New York: St Martin's Press.

Scheff, T. J. (1984) *Being mentally ill: A sociological theory*. New York: Aldine.

Searles, H. F. (1961) Anxiety concerning change as seen in the psychotherapy of schizophrenic patients – with particular reference to the sense of personal identity. *International Journal of Psychoanalysis*, 42: 74–85.

Seikkula, J., Aaltonen, J., Alakare, B., Haarankangas, H., Keränen, J. and Lehtinen, K. (2006) Five-year experience of first-episode nonaffective psychosis in open-dialogue approach: Treatment principles, follow-up outcomes, and two case studies. *Psychotherapy Research*, 16: 214–228.

Selton, J. P., van der Bosch, R. J. and Sijben, A. E. S. (1998) The subjective experience of negative symptoms. In Amador, X. F. and David, A. S. (eds) *Insight and Psychiatry*. Oxford: Oxford University Press.

Shapiro, S. (1991) Affect integration in psychoanalysis: A clinical approach to self-destructive behaviour. *Bulletin of the Menninger Clinic*, 55: 363–374.

Sharfstein, S. S. (2005) Big Pharma and American psychiatry: The good, the bad, and the ugly. *Psychiatric News*, 40: 3.

Shotter, J. (1981) Vico, moral worlds, accountability and personhood. In Hellas, P. and Lock, A. (eds) *Indigenous psychologies: The anthropology of the self*. London: Academic Press.

Shotter, J. (1993) *Conversational realities: Constructing life through language*. London: Sage.

Siegler, M. and Osmond, H. (1966) Models of madness. *British Journal of Psychiatry*, 112: 1193–1203.

Siirala, M. (1961) *Die Schizophrenie des Einzelnen und der Allgemeinheit*. Göttingen: Vandenhoeck and Ruprecht.

Silver, A.-L., Koehler, B. and Karon, B. (2004) Psychodynamic psychotherapy of schizophrenia: Its history and development. In Read, J., Mosher, L. R. and Bentall, R. P. (eds) *Models of madness: Psychological, social and biological approaches to schizophrenia*. New York: Brunner-Routledge.

Sims, A. (1988) *Symptoms in the mind*. London: Baillière Tindall.

Sims, A. (1994) 'Psyche': Spirit as well as mind? *British Journal of Psychiatry*, 165: 441–446.

Slater, L. (2004) *Opening Skinner's box: Great psychological experiments of the 20th century*. New York: Norton.

Sloane, T. O. (ed.) (2001) *Encyclopedia of rhetoric*. New York: Oxford University Press.

Sommer, R. and Osmond, H. (1960) Autobiographies of former mental patients. *Journal of Mental Science*, 106: 648–662.

Sommer, R. and Osmond, H. (1961) Autobiographies of former mental patients: Addendum. *Journal of Mental Science*, 107: 1030–1032.

Sommer, R. and Osmond, H. (1983) A bibliography of mental patients' autobiographies 1960–1982. *American Journal of Psychiatry*, 140: 1051–1054.

Sommer, R., Clifford, J. S. and Norcross, J. C. (1998) A biography of mental patients' autobiographies: An update and classification system. *American Journal of Psychiatry*, 155: 1261–4.

Spataro, J., Mullen, P. E., Burgess, P. M, Wells, D. L. and Moss, S. A. (2004) Impact of child sexual abuse on mental health: Prospective study in males and females. *British Journal of Psychiatry*, 184: 416–421.

Srinivasan, T. N. and Thara, R. (2001) Beliefs about causation of schizophrenia: Do Indian families believe in supernatural causes? *Social Psychiatry and Psychiatric Epidemiology*, 36: 134–140.

Strauss, A. and Corbin, J. (1990) *Basics of qualitative research: Grounded theory procedures and techniques*. Newbury Park, CA: Sage.

Strauss, J. S. (1969) Hallucinations and delusions as points on continua function. *Archives of General Psychiatry*, 21: 581–586.

Sullivan, H. S. (1956) *Clinical studies in psychiatry*. New York: Norton.

Sullivan, H. S. (1962) *Schizophrenia as a human process*. New York: Norton.

Sundquist, K., Frank, G. and Sundquist, J. (2004) Urbanisation and incidence of psychosis and depression: Follow up study of 4.4 million women and men in Sweden. *British Journal of Psychiatry*, 184: 293–298.

Symington, N. (2006) Sanity and madness. *International Journal of Psychoanalysis*, 87: 1059–1068.

Szasz, T. S. (1961) *The myth of mental illness*. New York: Harper and Row.

Szasz, T. S. (1991) Diagnoses are not diseases. *Lancet*, 338: 1574–1576.

Tait, L., Birchwood, M. and Trower, P. (2004) Adapting to the challenge of psychosis: Personal reslience and the use of sealing-over (avoidant) coping strategies. *British Journal of Psychiatry*, 185: 410–415.

Taitimu, M. (2007) Ngā Whakawhitinga: Standing at the crossroads. Māori ways of understanding extra-ordinary experiences and schizophrenia. Unpublished PhD thesis, University of Auckland.

Tarrier, N. (2002) The use of coping strategies and self-regulation in the treatment of psychosis. In Morrison, A. P. (ed.) *A casebook of cognitive therapy for psychosis*. Hove, UK: Brunner-Routledge.

Taylor, D. (1996) *The healing power of stories: Creating yourself through the stories of your life*. Dublin: Gill and MacMillan.

Theuma, M., Read, J., Moskowitz, A. and Stewart, A. (2007) Evaluation of a New Zealand early intervention service for psychosis. *New Zealand Journal of Psychology*, 36: 119–128.

Thirthalli, J. and Benegal, V. (2006) Psychosis among substance users. *Current Opinion in Psychiatry*, 19: 239–245.

Tien, A. Y. (1991) Distributions of hallucinations in the population. *Social Psychiatry and Psychiatric Epidemiology*, 26: 287–292.

Tomecek, O. (1990) A personal commentary on 'Schizophrenia as a brain disease'. *American Psychologist*, 45: 550–551.

Toomey, R., Faraone, S. V., Simpson, J. C. and Tsuang, M. T. (1998) Negative, positive and disorganized symptom dimension in schizophrenia, major depression and bipolar disorder. *Journal of Nervous and Mental Disease*, 186: 470–476.

Turkington, D., Kingdon, D. and Weiden, P. J. (2006) Cognitive behaviour therapy for schizophrenia. *American Journal of Psychiatry*, 163: 365–373.

Turner, B. S. (1987) *Medical power and social knowledge*. London: Sage

Van Os, J. (2004) Does the urban environment cause psychosis? *British Journal of Psychiatry*, 184: 287–288.

Van Os, J., Hanssen, M., Bijl, R. V. and Ravelli, A. (2000) Strauss (1969) revisited: A psychosis continuum in the normal population? *Schizophrenia Research*, 45: 11–20.

Van Putten, T., Crumpton, E. and Yale, C. (1976) Drug refusal in schizophrenia and the wish to be crazy. *Archives of General Psychiatry*, 33: 1443–1446.

Vaughn, C. E. and Leff, J. (1976) The influence of family and social factors on the course of psychiatric illness: A comparison of schizophrenic and depressed neurotic patients. *British Journal of Psychiatry*, 129: 125–137.

Vellenga, B. A. and Christenson, J. (1994) Persistant and severly mentally ill clients' perceptions of their mental illness. *Issues in Mental Health Nursing*, 15: 359–371.

Wagner, L. C. and King, M. (2005) Existential needs of people with psychotic disorders in Porto Alegre, Brazil. *British Journal of Psychiatry*, 186: 141–145.

Walker, I. and Read, J. (2002) The differential effectiveness of psychosocial and biogenetic causal explanations in reducing negative attitudes toward 'mental illness'. *Psychiatry: Interpersonal and Biological Processes*, 65: 313–325.

Walton, J. A. (1995) Schizophrenia: A way of being in the world. Unpublished PhD thesis, Massey University, Auckland.

Warner, R. (1994) *Recovery from schizophrenia*. New York: Routledge.

Waxler, N. E. (1979) Is outcome for schizophrenia better in nonindustrial societies? *Journal of Nervous and Mental Disease*, 167: 144–158.

Whitaker, R. (2002) *Mad in America: Bad science, bad medicine, and the enduring mistreatment of the mentally ill*. Cambridge, MA: Perseus.

White, M. (1991) Deconstruction and therapy. *Dulwich Centre Newsletter*, 3: 21–39.

White, M. and Epston, D. (1990) *Narrative means to therapeutic ends*. New York: Norton.

Whitehorn, J. C. and Betz, B. J. (1960) Further studies of the doctor as a crucial variable in the outcome of treatment with schizophrenic patients. *American Journal of Psychiatry*, 117: 215–223.

Wiles, N. J., Zammit, S., Bebbington, P., Singleton, N., Meltzer, H. and Lewis, G. (2006) Self-reported psychotic symptoms in the general population. *British Journal of Psychiatry*, 188: 519–526.

Wittgenstein, L. (1922) *Tractatus logico-philosophicus*. London: Routledge and Kegan Paul.

Wittgenstein, L. (1953) *Philosophical investigations*. Oxford: Basil Blackwell.

Wundt, W. (1897) *Outlines of psychology*. Leipzig, Germany: Wilhelm Englemann.

Wynne, L. and Singer, M. (1963) Thought disorder and family relations of schizophrenics. *Archives of General Psychiatry*, 9: 191–212.

Zachar, P. and Kendler, K. S. (2007) Psychiatric disorders: A conceptual taxonomy. *American Journal of Psychiatry*, 164: 557–565.

Zubin, J. and Spring, B. (1977) Vulnerability: A new view of schizophrenia. *Journal of Abnormal Psychology*, 86: 103–126.

Index